CULTURAL HERITAGE ETHICS

Cultural Heritage Ethics

Between Theory and Practice

Edited by
Constantine Sandis

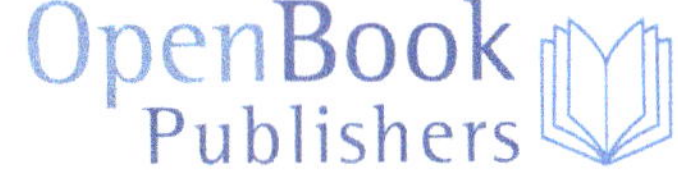

http://www.openbookpublishers.com

© 2014 Constantine Sandis. Copyright of individual chapters is maintained by the chapter's author(s).

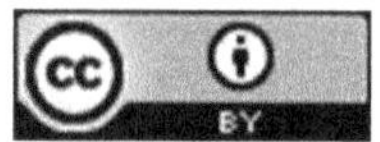

Digital material and resources associated with this volume are available at http://www.openbookpublishers.com/isbn/9781783740673#resources

ISBN Paperback: 978-1-78374-067-3
ISBN Hardback: 978-1-78374-068-0
ISBN Digital (PDF): 978-1-78374-069-7
ISBN Digital ebook (epub): 978-1-78374-070-3
ISBN Digital ebook (mobi): 978-1-78374-071-0
DOI: 10.11647/OBP.0047

Cover image: *Paint Pot Angel* by Banksy, Bristol City Museum and Art Gallery. Photograph © Diane Potter. Creative Commons License, Attribution-NoDerivs CC BY-ND.

All paper used by Open Book Publishers is SFI (Sustainable Forestry Initiative), and PEFC (Programme for the Endorsement of Forest Certification Schemes) Certified.

Printed in the United Kingdom and United States by Lightning Source for Open Book Publishers

For Eleni Cubitt

Κι οι ποταμοί φουσκώναν μες στη λάσπη το αίμα
για ένα λινό κυμάτισμα για μια νεφέλη
μιας πεταλούδας τίναγμα το πούπουλο ενός κύκνου
για ένα πουκάμισο αδειανό, για μιαν Ελένη.

Γιώργος Σεφέρης

Contents

Notes on Contributors

Geoffrey Belcher was formerly Coordinator for the UNESCO Maritime Greenwich World Heritage Site. He is a member of the RTPI and a RIBA Awarded Conservation Architect.

Sir John Boardman is Professor Emeritus of Classical Art and Archaeology at Oxford. He has excavated in Turkey, Greece and Libya, and published books on Greek art, classical gems and the Greeks in Asia. These include *The Greeks Overseas* (1964; 4th ed. 1999), *Excavations at Emporio, Chios* (1964), *Archaic Greek Gems* (1968), *Greek Burial Customs* (1971), *Greek Gems and Finger Rings* (1970, new ed. 2001), *Persia and the West* (2000), *The History of Greek Vases* (2001), *The Archaeology of Nostalgia* (2002), *Greece and the Hellenistic World* (2002), *The World of Ancient Art* (2006), *The Marlborough Gems* (2009), and *The Relief Plaques of Central Asia and China* (2010).

Michael F. Brown is President of the School for Advanced Research, Santa Fe, New Mexico, USA, and Professor Emeritus of Anthropology, Williams College, Williamstown, Massachusetts, USA. His books include *Who Owns Native Culture?* (2003), and *Upriver: The Turbulent Life and Times of an Amazonian People* (2014).

Marie Cornu is Research Director at the National Centre for Scientific Research (CNRS) and director of the CECOJI (Research Centre on the International Legal Cooperation). Her research interests focus on cultural property law and art law. In cooperation with Prof. Jérôme Fromageau, she co-leads an international research group that recently published a comparative dictionary on cultural property law.

Tom Flynn is founder of The Sculpture Agency and a visiting lecturer at Kingston University. He has written for *The Art Newspaper, Art & Auction, Art Review, Apollo, Art News, Museums Journal, The Spectator*, and many others. His books include *The Body in Sculpture* (1998), *Colonialism and the Object: Empire, Material Culture and the Museum* (1998, co-edited with T. Barringer), *The Paintings of Clive Head* (2000), *Jedd Novatt* (2008), *Sean Henry* (2009), *Skate's Art Investment Handbook*, (2nd ed. 2010), and *The Sculpture of Terence Coventry* (2012).

James Fox is a Research Fellow in Art History at Gonville and Caius College, Cambridge. He has previously held research positions at Harvard, Churchill College, Cambridge, and the Yale Center for British Art. He is currently preparing a monograph on British art during the First World War.

Sudeshna Guha is Associate Researcher at the Faculty of Asian and Middle Eastern Studies (FAMES), and the Centre of South Asian Studies, Cambridge, UK. She researches the history of archaeology and South Asia and has recently submitted for publication her first monograph, *Artefacts of History: Archaeology, Historiography and Indian Pasts*.

Sir Mark Jones is currently Master of St Cross College, Oxford. He was a curator in the British Museum for seventeen years before becoming Director of the National Museums of Scotland and then of the Victoria and Albert Museum.

Benjamin Ramm is a writer and broadcaster, and Research Fellow at Gladstone's Library, Wales. He is the former editor of *The Liberal* magazine, and author of *Citizens: A Manifesto*.

Constantine Sandis is Professor of Philosophy at Oxford Brookes University and a Fellow of the Royal Society of Arts. He is the author of *The Things We Do and Why We Do Them* (2012) and has edited numerous books on the philosophy of action and human nature.

Geoffrey Scarre is Professor of Philosophy at Durham University, UK and founder and director of the Durham University Centre for the Ethics of Cultural Heritage. His books include *Death* (2007), *Mill's 'On Liberty': A Reader's Guide* (2007) and *On Courage* (2010); he has also edited (with Chris Scarre) *The Ethics of Archaeology* (2006) and (with Robin Coningham) *Appropriating the Past* (2013).

William St Clair is a Fellow of the British Academy and Senior Research Fellow at the Institute of English Studies, School of Advanced Study, University of London. His books include *Lord Elgin and the Marbles* (1967; 3rd rev. ed. 1998), *That Greece Might Still Be Free* (1972, 2nd rev. ed. 2008), *Trelawny, the Incurable Romancer* (1977), *The Godwins and the Shelleys* (1989), *The Reading Nation in the Romantic Period* (2004), and *The Grand Slave Emporium* (2006).

Nira Wickramasinghe is Professor of Modern South Asian Studies at Leiden University and the author and editor of numerous books including *Dressing the Colonised Body: Politics, Clothing and Ethnic Politics in Colonial Sri Lanka 1927-1947* (1995), *Civil Society in Sri Lanka. New Circles of Power* (2001), *History Writing: New Trends and Methodologies* (2001), *Identity in Colonial Sri Lanka* (2003), *Sri Lanka in the Modern Age – A History of Contested Identities* (2006), and *Metallic Modern – Everyday Machines in Colonial Sri Lanka* (2014).

List of Illustrations

Preface and Acknowledgments

This is neither a textbook nor a manifesto for any particular approach to heritage ethics. I invited the contributors to speak about issues they deeply care about, using the volume as a platform from which to argue for their own points of view. Their focus is sometimes general, and at other times takes the form of case studies. Our collective aim was not to present an overview of the field, but to showcase the value of promoting awareness of difficult questions through debate which bridges the gap between theory and practice. For ease of reference the Appendix to the volume contains links to selected international charters and conventions on cultural heritage mentioned in the essays.

It would be ungracious to not mention here three obvious predecessors to this volume. One is Elazar Barkan and Ronald Bush's *Claiming the Stones/Naming the Bones: Cultural Property and the Negotiation of National and Ethnic Identity* (Getty Research Institute, 2002). This excellent volume contains fourteen essays addressing a variety of controversies from across numerous academic and vocational perspectives including anthropology, archaeology, ethnobiology, law, and literary studies. Another, which shares two contributors with this volume, is John Henry Merryman's more specialised volume, *Imperialism, Art and Restitution* (Cambridge University Press, 2006). Finally, there is Astrid Swenson and Peter Mandler's recent book *From Plunder to Preservation: Britain and the Heritage of Empire, c.1800-1940* (Oxford University Press, 2013).

One of the issues surrounding cultural heritage is that of access and it has been hugely important to me that everyone has free unrestricted access to the essays in this book. I am extremely grateful to William St Clair for proposing Open Book Publishers as a possibility, to Alessandra Tosi for all her work, help, and advice from submission to production, and to Bianca Gualandi for her invaluable assistance with the inclusion of images. Fellow philosopher Jonathan Webber came up with the suggestion of Banksy's *Paint Pot Angel* for the cover of this volume. I'm very grateful to Diane Potter for permission to reuse her photograph of it.

I also wish to thank the anonymous referees for their incredibly astute comments and constructive suggestions and, of course, all of the contributors for their stellar work. A generous Visiting Fellowship at the Helsinki Collegium of Advanced Studies has given me the time to put the final version of the manuscript together in the most pleasant of academic environments.

Over a decade ago Eleni Cubitt sparked my interest in cultural heritage ethics and this volume was her idea. Like her namesake of Troy, Eleni has launched a thousand ships in her time. But it is equally fitting that she was named after St Helena, mother of Constantine and patron saint of archaeologists. Though she will not necessarily agree with all the ideas within this volume, I trust that she will find them thoroughly engaging. I dedicate the book to her, with much love.

Constantine Sandis
Helsinki, May 2014

Introduction

Constantine Sandis

Theory without practice is empty, practice without theory is blind, to adapt a phrase from Immanuel Kant. Cultural heritage ethics has certainly suffered from such a dichotomy. This book seeks to bridge the gap between theory and practice through conversations which promote the awareness and debate of difficult questions, collectively pointing to a just medium between academic and vocational approaches.

The intra-disciplinary essays that follow have been written by academics, consultants, journalists, lawyers, and museum practitioners. I have divided them into four sections: (i) meaning and memory; (ii) history and archaeology; (iii) ownership and restitution; and (iv) management and protection. The book thus guides the reader from the abstract to the concrete, and back again. What follows is a brief overview of the essays in each section.

Part I: Meaning and Memory

In 'Culture, Heritage, and Ethics', I introduce a number of themes taken up in more detail by the other contributors. Given the range of questions and complexities surrounding heritage, I am sceptical about the possibility of a unified account of it. Heritage, cultural or otherwise, is not always good. It may be preserved in fundamentally different, indeed contradictory, ways. *Pari passu*, the range of rights relating to it is not a straightforward one. My essay has been written in the faith that 'a repertoire might be more useful than a conviction', sketching out a very partial and rudimentary conceptual

    http://dx.doi.org/10.11647/OBP.0047.14

cartography of the area of cultural heritage ethics. In so doing, I hope to have marked some of the numerous pitfalls which face the bolder theorist.

James Fox's 'Poppy Politics: Remembrance of Things Present' takes as its starting point the scandal ignited in November 2011, when FIFA (the international football governing body) refused to allow the English football team to wear remembrance poppies on their shirts during a match against Spain. FIFA had long enforced a universal ban on the wearing of political symbols during its games, but under intense pressure from both the government and the Royal Family it finally relented. British lobbyists had argued that the poppy was a 'universal symbol of remembrance', and had no political, religious or commercial connotations. Fox's essay explores the origins and development of Britain's rituals of remembrance, arguing that the poppy is far less neutral than its supporters claim: Fox demonstrates that in fact the poppy has deeply political associations which legitimise the conflict that it ostensibly seems to condemn. His insights on the politics of remembrance suggest that heritage in this case refers to the past rather than to the present.

The first section concludes with Benjamin Ramm's essay 'The Meaning of the Public in an Age of Privatisation'. Ramm takes on the New Right's characterisation of the private realm as the abode of meaning, investigating how this attack on the value of shared culture has impoverished citizens by robbing them of a vocabulary with which to make sense of the world. The neoliberal concept of 'private persons, public consumers', he concludes, has little time for public memory – a context in which heritage takes on radical new meaning.

Part II. History and Archaeology

In 'History as Heritage: Producing the Present in Post-War Sri Lanka', Nira Wickramasinghe explores the consolidation by a patriotic post-conflict state of a notion of history reinvented as national heritage. The distinction between history as an analysis of the past and heritage had rarely been made explicit in the public discourse. After the war ended the distinction disappeared almost entirely from the national discourse, with the exception of a few voices in history departments. In Wickramasinghe's view, heritage as we understand it, is created, shaped and managed by, and in response to, the demands of the present. It is, to follow David Lowenthal, not history at all, but a special pleading. Wickramasinghe draws from an array of sources and practices relating to post-war Sri Lanka to assess the feasibility of devising alternative strategies in the production of historical knowledge. Williams St Clair's 'Looking at the Acropolis of Athens from Modern Times to Antiquity' does just what it says on the tin. St Clair guides the reader through the history of ways of looking at the Acropolis – how and when different perspectives emerged and how they were mediated. St Clair takes this analysis even further, using the Acropolis as a case study to prove that the meaning of cultural sites and artefacts is at least partly determined by the viewer. St Clair argues that the wish to offer viewers a means of understanding the relationship between the then present, the then past, and the then future, was among the explicitly stated aims of those who built the classical Acropolis, as well as by others in later times. By relocating the site where meanings are made to the minds of viewers and by admitting them as active participants in a complex dynamic system, we become able to take into account factors that are not given sufficient attention in current conventions.

In her essay 'South Asian Heritage and Archaeological Practices', Sudeshna Guha demonstrates how archaeological practices have been consistently deployed within South Asia for over two hundred years in order to establish truths about the origins and legacy of that civilisation. Guha focuses on histories of civilisational traditions that have been unearthed in colonial and post-colonial India through seemingly disparate archaeological practices, but which have historiographic crossings and mutations. With reference to the nineteenth-century creation of a Buddhist Banaras, as well as to recent interpretations regarding the cultural legacies of the Indus Civilisation, Guha aims to sow seeds of caution towards all forms of valorisation of civilisational ethos within disciplinary archaeology. In so doing, she situates the importance of critiquing such constructs in an academic milieu that shows an increasing concern towards archaeological productions of tangible 'heritage-industries'.

Geoffrey Scarre's 'The Ethics of Digging' asks how archaeologists should select their research material, and whether they make their choices on the basis of academic considerations alone. Whose interests should archaeological research be serving: those of the profession, of local ethnic or indigenous groups, of the general public, or the good of mankind? And how should these be prioritised? What permissions (and whose) do archaeologists need to obtain if their digging is to be ethical? Is excavation which permanently damages or changes a site ethically acceptable? Should archaeologists, in a Lockean vein, take care to leave 'as much and as good' material for later researchers, and avoid depleting archaeological resources? What duties do archaeologists have following excavation in regard to recording, publication, dissemination and display? Is archaeological digging ethically consistent with the principle of stewardship to which most archaeologists pay lip-service? Would stewardship, strictly construed, imply a 'hands-off' approach to the archaeological resource, and permit excavation only in the case of endangered sites? What special ethical responsibilities do archaeological researchers have in regard to human remains and grave-sites? These are the key questions which Scarre posits and begins to answer.

Part III: Ownership and Restitution

John Boardman's '"National" Heritage and Scholarship' considers the fifty-year old debate over the handling and publication of ancient artefacts acquired through channels other than official excavation. Boardman reminds us that while the UNESCO declaration has effectively increased the value of objects known before 1970, it has done nothing to halt the acquisition and marketing of 'recovered' objects. It is still not uncommon to hear the term 'national heritage' being used and this can easily lead to a more casual approach to some aspects of the problem. Better by far, claims Boardman, to speak of 'global heritage', the 'heritage of man' or even just 'heritage'. There are very few relevant countries whose modern population has any serious genetic or cultural links with their distant past. Jealousy seems a very strong motive in many cases, often abetted by extreme views about what 'copyright' entails.

Moving from jealousy to 'Fear of Cultural Objects', Tom Flynn reads some of the recent and current disputes over global cultural heritage through the metaphor of fear. The essay opens with an analysis of the little-known early German expressionist feature film *Fear*, the narrative of which centres upon the illicit removal of a cultural object from a distant sacred site and its subsequent re-location to a European private collection. The subsequent 'haunting' of the collector, triggered by the illicit act of removal, provokes our ethical reflections on heritage by suggesting that many of today's cultural heritage disputes are fuelled by different types of fear. Western 'universal' museums fear losing their collections, which symbolise their identity and power, to repatriation. This can be contrasted with the fear felt by many in the formerly subaltern nations of the developing world who interpret these mainly European and North American encyclopaedic institutions as tyrannical symbols of imperial greed. Flynn explores the roots of this mutual fear, asking how it can be assuaged in an increasingly globalised world of contested cultural objects.

Further worries about 'Restitution' are investigated by Mark Jones who considers the arguments for the return of cultural property and tests them against some well-known contested objections. While recognising the difficulty of reaching an agreement, Jones combines case studies with sharp critical insights to suggest ways in which contested objects instead of being divisive might on the contrary become catalysts for international partnerships. Inaction in this case may be a better way of serving the public interest.

Part IV: Management and Protection

The fourth and final section of the volume opens with Michael F. Brown's exploration of 'The Possibilities and Perils of Heritage Management'. Although the right of communities to practice their culture and defend it from unwanted appropriation is widely regarded as a human right, the precise means by which this right can be defended and administered remains uncertain. Brown argues that the very notion of 'managing' a society's multiple forms of collective expression entails a degree of objectification that poses a potential threat to culture's inherent (and necessary) fluidity. His essay considers the challenge of finding an appropriate balance between ethical considerations and the law of unintended consequences in the vexed arena of heritage protection. Using brief case studies, Brown highlights the tendency of heritage protection strategies to gravitate to top-down, 'patrimonial' models of control that treat culture as a commodity. He concludes by making the ethical case for more informal and flexible approaches to heritage protection.

Geoffrey Belcher begins his essay 'Values in World Heritage Sites' by considering the variety of World Heritage sites, from the symbolic value of Auschwitz and Hiroshima to the beauty of the Taj Mahal and the Great Barrier Reef. All these sites are selected by the Conservation Committee at UNESCO. Even though the management of the sites is formally undertaken by the national state party (DCMS in the case of the United Kingdom), in practice it falls to local organisations. Belcher argues that the chain of responsibility from international to local levels creates various tensions, the concept of World Heritage being informed by the ten UNESCO criteria at the universal level, and by national and local aspirations at the area level. In order to rationalise this, statements of 'outstanding universal values' are produced for each site, identifying the special qualities and also their 'authenticity' and 'integrity'. But without a precise system of rules at the international level, local agencies have to rely on national and local systems such as town-planning legislation for protection. At present this legislation in the UK does not fully encompass the listing and management of World Heritage Sites. The result is that the simple, popular concept of World Heritage is being *de facto* challenged in its application and administration. Belcher's essay fleshes out some of the problematic areas and identifies opportunities for creating clearer guidelines in the future.

Having begun with a series of conceptual questions, the volume ends on the legalistic note of Marie Cornu's essay 'Safeguarding Heritage: From Legal Rights over Objects to Legal Rights for Individuals and Communities?' There are numerous ways of regulating the connection between memory, history and heritage and, in this respect, diversity rules. Cornu discusses the second wave of laws on heritage protection, which have taken on board wider concerns about development and integration. Cornu outlines the process by which other fields of the law (environmental but also economic law) are now part of cultural heritage law, a field originally created as an autonomous and distinct body of legislation. Whilst positive outcomes are likely to result from the intersection of different legal fields, there is also a risk that the level of protection of cultural heritage sites may decrease.

The thirteen essays collectively cover questions relating to access (essays 1-2, 4-5, 7-11); acquisition (3, 8-10); antiquities (5-6, 9-10); apartheid (1); archaeological practice (6-7); barbarism and plunder (3, 10-13); capitalism (1, 3); celebration (1-3, 6, 10-12); citizenship (3-5, 11); colonialism and post-colonialism (1, 3-6, 9-10); curatorship (3, 9-10); education (3-5, 8, 12); enlightenment (3, 5, 7, 9); ethnology (3-4, 9, 11, 13); fear (2,7,9-10); hegemony (3-4); historiography (1, 4-6); history (1, 3-4, 6-7, 9-13); human remains (7, 10-11, 13); integrity (7-8, 12, 13); intellectual property (11); jealousy (8-9); legislation (4, 8, 13, 10); management (3-5, 7, 8-13); memory (1-5, 13); myth (4, 6-7); nationalism (2, 4-6, 8, 10-11); nostalgia (1, 4, 12); ownership (1, 5-6, 8-11); policy (1-2, 4-5, 10-11); prejudice (3, 10); preservation (1, 4, 5, 7-8, 10-11, 13); pride (1, 3, 5-7); protection (1, 5, 7, 10-13); public interest (2-3, 7, 10-13); privatisation (3, 9-10); relics (3-4); religion (1-2, 4-6, 9); respect (4, 6-7,

9-10, 12-13); responsibility (1, 4-5, 7-8, 12-13); restitution and repatriation (5-11, 13); restoration (4, 6-7, 10); revolution and dissent (3-5, 9); rights (1, 5, 11-13); scholarship (6, 8); shame (1, 5, 10); slavery (1); stewardship (5, 7, 19); technology (1, 3-5, 6-7); tourism (1, 3-5, 7-8,10-12); trusteeship (4, 10); understanding (3-4, 6-7, 9-10, 12); UNESCO (4-5, 7, 10-13); and world heritage sites and conventions (8, 11-13). Of telling but unplanned significance is the fact that all thirteen essays mention war.

It would have been impossible to cover all the relevant examples of cultural heritage, but the range of examples included across the volume is sufficiently geographically diverse to include references to Afghanistan (2), Australia (2, 7, 11-12), Bangladesh (6, 13), Belgium (12), Bolivia (1, 11-12), Brazil (2, 11), Canada (2, 10-11), Chile (11-12), China (6, 10-11), the Czech Republic (1), Cuba (1, 11), Denmark (1, 5, 10), Ecuador (11), Egypt (1, 3, 5-6, 8-10, 12-13), England (1, 2, 5, 10), Estonia (11), Ethiopia (10), Finland (1), France (2, 6, 10, 13), Greece (1, 5, 8, 10, 13), India (1, 3-6, 9--12), Ireland (2, 10, 12), Israel (1, 6), Italy (1, 8-9, 10, 13), Japan (12-13), Kenya (11), Korea (10-11, 13), Madagascar (1), Mali (4, 7, 11), Mexico (11-12), New Zealand (2, 7), Nigeria (10), Norway (1, 10), Pakistan (6), Peru (11), Poland (1, 12), Russia (1), Scotland (5, 10, 12), Senegal (12), South Africa (1, 4-6, 10-11), Spain (2, 12-13), Sri Lanka (4), Sweden (1, 6), Switzerland (1), Tunisia (13), Turkey (11), the United States (2, 4-5, 7,10-13), and Wales (12).

The subject is far from exhausted however, and there remains much ground to be covered. I would like to have been able to showcase contributions from across even more disciplines, to have covered wider geographical ground, and to have been able to include essays on additional topics such as those of the digital humanities (from online collections to 3D printing of souvenirs and archaeological artefacts), the heritage of morally tainted gifts, pollution as the counterpart of sacralisation, and the distinction between the ethics of returning artefacts for preservation vis-à-vis those of returning human remains often for destruction. But if we have learned one thing from the ethics of cultural heritage it is not to let greed infect our aspirations.

I

MEANING AND MEMORY

1. Culture, Heritage, and Ethics

Constantine Sandis[1]

1. Introduction

Heritage is that which has been or may be inherited, regardless of its value. Unfortunately, the term 'heritage' (the thirteenth-century English word is derived from the Latin *haeres*, meaning heir or heiress) is nowadays frequently used for purposes best described as touristic, to sell everything from beer and tomatoes to cars, gardens, and hotels. It is possible to think of some of this heritage as non-cultural, or perhaps even anti-cultural. An even more plausible contender for this last set would be hooliganism, yet this is unlikely to feature in British magazines about heritage such as *Heritage, Discover Britain*, or *British Heritage Magazine*. And yet such anti-cultural behaviour may be as much a part of Britain's culture as Big Ben, the Monarchy, Stilton cheese, the National Health Service, and Top of the Pops — the sort of things celebrated in Danny Boyle's 2012 Olympic Ceremony Opening.

Heritage magazines may choose to focus on castles, lakes, and gardens (and do so for ostensibly sound commercial and aesthetic reasons), but it would be wrong to think of these paradigm cases as being definitive. On the contrary, we should be questioning whether they are even as common

---

1   This essay greatly benefited from discussions with Geoffrey Belcher, Eleni Cubitt, Max de Gaynesford, Alon Lischinsky, and Erasmus Mayr. It was presented in near-final form at the Ethics, Museums and Archaeology workshop, Ashmolean Museum (Oxford), 3-4 April 2014, after which I made some improvements thanks to feedback from Anna Bergqvist, Ivan Gaskell, Erin Kavanagh, and Andreas Pantazatos. Finally, thanks to Candida Lord for careful proofreading which saved me from several embarrassments.

          http://dx.doi.org/10.11647/OBP.0047.01

as contemporary popular opinion portrays them to be. To this conceptual mix we might wish to add the spurious distinction between so-called 'high' and 'low' culture. It is a mistake to think that cultural heritage is reserved for the former, that it privileges opera over football, Shakespeare over EastEnders, though we may of course choose to use terms like 'culture' in a more technical, narrower, sense.

2. Achievement and Atrocity

In distinguishing heritage from history, David Lowenthal has influentially argued that the former is a 'celebration' of the past.[2] But one need only think of the heritage of slavery to note that we should not assume that one's cultural heritage is always, or even usually, celebrated. Even when it is, it doesn't follow that the celebration in question is of the past, as opposed to a continuity that remains present. Nor need it be the case that the celebration is a justified one.

French Law explicitly allows for the production of *foie gras* as part of the country's 'cultural and gastronomic heritage'. By contrast, in July 2012 the state of California banned the production of *foie gras*, implementing a $1000 per-day penalty for serving it. Production has already been banned in the Czech Republic, Denmark, Finland, Germany, Italy, Norway, Poland, Israel, Switzerland, Sweden, and the United Kingdom. The city of Chicago banned its sale in 2006, only to have it overturned by then mayor Richard M. Daley. More surprisingly, perhaps, Germany's Nazi Government had banned *foie gras* production in 1933, as part of a wider animal protection law signed by Hitler which began with the statement that 'it is forbidden to unnecessarily torment or roughly mishandle an animal'. I do not intend to voice my own views on the ethics of food production here, but only to note that this much-bandied phrase 'cultural heritage' can include past, present, and future practices that are arguably immoral, from the exploits of Alexander the Great to fox-hunting and page three of *The Sun*.[3] This is so

---

2   D. Lowenthal, *The Heritage Crusade and the Spoils of History* (Cambridge: Cambridge University Press, 1998), p. x.

3   S. Peck, 'Why does a Tory MP think that getting your tits out is a "National Institution"?', *The Telegraph*, 10 December 2013, http://www.telegraph.co.uk/women/sex/10508530/Boobs-on-Page-3-Why-does-a-Tory-MP-think-that-getting-your-tits-out-is-a-national-institution.html (unless otherwise specified, all links cited in this volume were active on 23 June 2014).

even when the heritage in question is celebrated (I shall later look at cases of heritage that is perceived as being tainted).

Though it may not be everybody's cup of tea, Jennie Bristow is right to claim that 'page Three is as much a part of British culture as a cup of tea'.[4] The positive judgment implied is, however, questionable. *Pace* Bristow, being part of one's culture does not magically bestow a thing with positive value; it does not make it worthy of preservation. In the case in point, I believe we should regret that The Sun (let alone its third page) is part of our culture at all and take appropriate measures to change this state of affairs. But whatever one makes of this specific case, the point I wish to emphasise in this context is that even if anti-page-three campaigns were to prove successful, the page would remain part of British cultural heritage.

Heritage matters, but removing something from one's culture does not eliminate it from one's heritage. The acknowledgment of heritage forms part of the ethics of remembering, and it is important to remember both the good and the bad, atrocities as well as achievements. But at times we also have a duty to forget such things, for example when this is the best way of forging new relationships that avoid the perils of nostalgia. Lowenthal quotes a native American complaining that 'white people don't know what to remember and what to forget, what to let go of and what to preserve'.[5] Arguably, there is a corresponding right to be forgotten which in some countries allows for criminal records to be erased once convictions are spent. The European Court of Justice has recently appealed to such a right (convincing or otherwise) in relation to online privacy.[6]

The duty to remember something is a duty to preserve it in memory, be it individual or collective (such duties are frequently non-teleological in that they need not be driven by the prospect of some future good). This obligation must not be conflated with a duty to preserve its actual existence in the world. English Heritage's Sites of Memory, for example, mark the story of both the Atlantic slave trade and its abolition, including controversial benefactors such as Edward Colston (see Figures 1.1 and 1.2).

---

4   J. Bristow, 'Page three girls and porn-again feminists', 22 November 2010, http://www.spiked-online.com/newsite/article/9922

5   Lowenthal, 1998, p. 29.

6   'The European Court of Justice forces Google to remove links to some personal information', *The Economist*, 17 May 2014, http://www.economist.com/news/business/2160 2239-european-court-justice-forces-google-remove-links-some-personal-information-cut

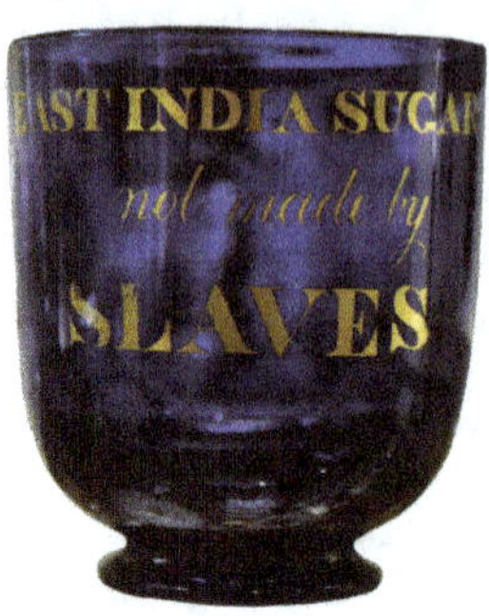

Fig. 1.1 Blue glass sugar bowl inscribed in gilt 'EAST INDIA SUGAR *not made by* SLAVES', Bristol, 1820-30. British Museum..

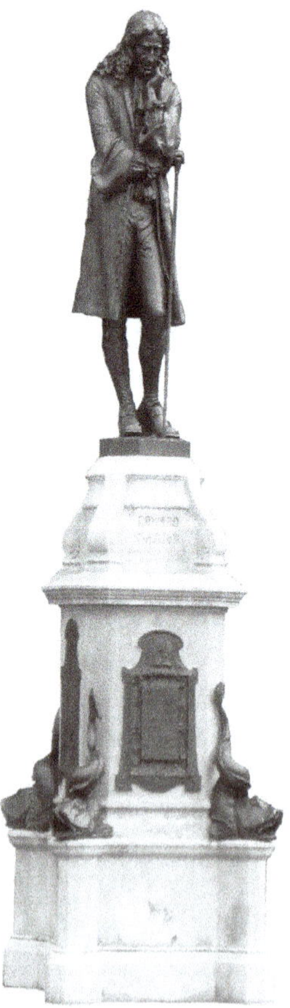

Fig. 1.2 Statue of Edward Colston by John Cassidy, erected in 1895 on Colston Avenue, Bristol.

We must not forget the legacies of those who accumulated vast wealth from the trade any more than we must forget the human beings who were traded and the anti-slavery campaigners. Each has left their own mark on history, for better or worse.[7]

The distinction between what should be preserved and what is best gone (but not forgotten) rests on the reasons why we ought to remember. When Margaret Thatcher unveiled the English Heritage blue plaque for Nancy Astor in 1987 (Figure 1.3), this was intended to honour Astor for being the first woman to take a seat in Parliament. The plaque scheme itself was introduced in 1866 by the (now Royal) Society of Arts with the ambiguously-worded aim of increasing 'the public estimation for places which have been the abodes of men [sic] who have made England what it is'. Strictly speaking, one may think that Astor's home should be remembered in this way without believing that she personally deserves any honour.

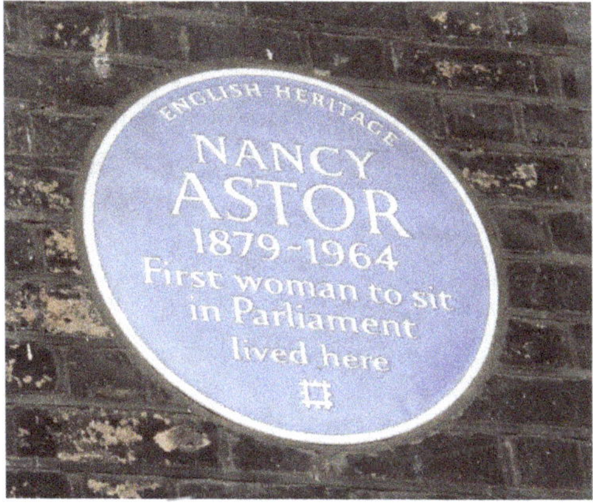

Fig. 1.3 English Heritage blue plaque for Nancy Astor.

It is impossible to codify the precise correct relation between past atrocities and present duties. There are sound reasons for wishing to preserve the Roman Colosseum, but not the practices related to it. These reasons are largely aesthetic and historical, but are not primarily to do with remembrance. Our duty to preserve Auschwitz, by contrast, has nothing to do with any architectural merit. The line of taste, in matters that we might term 'atrocity heritage', is easily crossed however. For example, while we should be doing much more to commemorate victims of rape, Jerzy

---

7   http://www.english-heritage.org.uk/discover/people-and-places the-slave-trade-and-abolition/sites-of-memory

Bohdan Szumczyk's life-sized sculpture Komm, Frau ('Come, woman') – depicting a Russian soldier raping a heavily pregnant woman – is an extremely inappropriate way of doing so, even if its creator did intend it as a political statement condemning rape.[8] Again, it is important to get right the reasons why it is inappropriate. It is one thing to agree with the Polish journalist Marek Gorlikowski that 'this type of monument is far from the way to commemorate the victims of rape' and quite another to agree with the Russian ambassador to Poland Alexander Alexeyev, when he denounces the monument as having 'defiled the memory of 600,000 Soviet servicemen who gave their lives in the fight for the freedom and the independence of Poland'.[9] This may seem obvious, but it did not stop the Huffington post from claiming that Gorlikowski's sentiments 'echoed' those of Alexeyev.[10] There are no hard and fast rules about what counts as appropriate commemoration any more than there are about what counts as good art. But the fact that there is not one right way of commemorating atrocities does not mean that all attempts are of equal merit.

Some years ago, the white South African philosopher Samantha Vice caused a stir by claiming that she was ashamed of being white.[11] Summarising her initial article, Vice writes that she 'explored the moral burden that whiteness places on us and was met by a similar outbreak of self-righteous outrage', suggesting that 'white people should cultivate humility and silence, given their morally compromised position in the continuing racial and economic injustices of this country'. She continues:

> [I]t is appropriate for whites to feel shame at their white identity, given its destructive legacy and the way it continues to shape us. Of course, we did not choose to be born white but that does not stop us benefiting from it still – in ways that are far subtler than merely social and economic. We move easily about a world made in our own image, validating our own values and beliefs and sustaining our own comfort, unimpeded by the kinds of structural and systemic challenges black people face daily. That is something to feel ashamed about.

---

8   A photograph of the statue taken by the artist is available at http://www.openbook publishers.com/isbn/9781783740673#resources

9   http://www.rusemb.pl/index.php?option=com_content&view=article&id=729%3Ao-in cydencie-w-gdasku&catid=1%3Aaktualnoci&Itemid=5&lang=ru

10 'Polish rape sculpture draws international backlash', 18 October 2013, http://www. huffingtonpost.com/2013/10/18/jerzy-bohdan-szumczyk_n_4123355.html

11 S. Vice, 'Why my opinions on whiteness touched a nerve', 2 September 2011, http:// mg.co.za/article/2011-09-02-why-my-opinions-on-whiteness-touched-a-nerve

Vice has been accused of being stupid, neurotic, self-hating, attention-seeking, and blinded by 'womanly political views'. But her point was that we must sometimes move beyond what we might call the heritage ethics of memory. She writes:

> We forget the vast background of institutions, state support and opportunities that made our success possible; we forget that we do not develop in a vacuum or create ourselves *ex nihilo*. Apartheid's dubious gift to whites was the chance to live comfortably, securely and with opportunities for creative development and worldly success. Apartheid cushioned whites at the expense of making life very hard for others – and the effects of this injustice are still present … So, however attached whites are to this country – and part of my point is that, whether we admit it or not, we are fundamentally attached to its sad history and legacy – and however much we care for its success, we shouldn't feel completely comfortable. The refusal to acknowledge one's luck is a manifestation of the careless complacence and arrogance that make whites feel entitled to these advantages – and convinced that their own efforts alone made their success possible.

Sometimes the sins of our parents should be inherited not only via preservation in memory, but through shame and activism.

3. Heritage Rights from Feta to Burka

In the opening chapter of his classic 1961 study *What Is History?*, E.H. Carr rightly noted that not all facts and events are historical. Pope John Paul II's 1997 visit to Cuba is a historical fact, but my own visit in 2006, alas, is not. We might similarly ask why an object or event forms part of some heritage, be it the world's, a specific nation's, or that of some other specified set of people. As with historical facts, such matters are not fixed across time. There was a moment in time when it seemed to some that Oasis might become as central a part of British popular culture as The Beatles, but that moment is long gone (Lowenthal is right in his assertion that we cannot simply equate heritage with history).

Even when we are confident in perceiving something as 'cultural heritage', how are we to decide to whom this belongs to? The question seems to imply that some people may have special (though typically not exclusive) ownership rights to it over others. There is an obvious (albeit trivial) sense in which 'British Heritage' belongs to the British, but what does this actually translate to pragmatically? Do the British have some kind of special right to eat pork pies and photograph Westminster Abbey? It is one thing to reserve the name 'Champagne' for products of a certain geographical region and 'Feta' for those of another,[12] but do the French have a special right to champagne and the Eiffel Tower, the Greeks to Feta and the Parthenon? And what about coffee, which we associate more with Italy than the American and African countries which actually grow the beans?

Such questions are comic, in part because all heritage is universal in the sense that we should all be free to access it if possible, if not always for free. It is not always viable for everyone to access everything, or to do so easily and at little or no cost: nobody thinks that the people of Greece have a right to free Feta cheese; by contrast it takes a libertarian like the Nestlé Chairman Peter Brabeck-Letmathe to deny that there is a universal right to free clean water.[13] So this kind of rights-speech is really a misleading way of talking about access priorities. The criteria here are a mix of the practical and ideological: if only X amount of people can visit a monument a year, should priority not be given to the local community? In some countries locals pay a lower (or no) fare for entrance to sites than other visitors do. These others, or 'other others', used to be called tourists, viz. they who tour around. But the word has become pejorative and sites are increasingly opting for the gentler – less discriminatory – term 'visitors'. But the policy of giving preferential rates to local residents is not always limited to 'visitor sites'. In Egypt, for example, this policy extends to commodities like hotel rooms. And everywhere we have import taxes. In the case of transportable physical objects the key access issue is that of location, location, location. Unfortunately, questions about access priorities are typically overshadowed by legal and ethical concerns about ownership, as in the case of the Parthenon sculptures.

Cultural heritage rights – be they moral and/or legal – are rarely human rights, but there are exceptions. So, while it is absurd to view the right to have free or affordable access to French cinema as a human right, if there is a right to wear a burka (be it for religious or cultural reasons), this will be a human right. The issue is certainly not one of limited availability. Unlike

---

12 See, for example: 'Greece wins exclusive rights to market Feta in Canada', 18 October 2013, http://www.ekathimerini.com/4dcgi/_w_articles_wsite2_1_18/10/2013_523829

13 Nestlé have since changed their official position, though it is difficult not to adopt a cynical stance towards such revisionary 'clarifications': http://www.nestle.com/aboutus/ask-nestle/answers/nestle-chairman-peter-brabeck-letmathe-believes-water-is-a-human-right

some moral rights, all human rights ought to be legal rights. Cultural heritage rights, then, do not necessarily deserve legislative support. This will largely depend on their importance. We may wish to give certain groups of people near-absolute legal rights to burkas, and priority access to the pyramids, but no special right whatsoever to, say, caviar.

Where there are rights there are also duties, such as those of preservation, in memory or actuality. These too will be constrained by resources such as space, money, manpower, time, and so on. Mistakes of judgment, here as elsewhere, are inevitable. A salient example is that of the BBC prior to the *Heritage Collection* initiative. The *Heritage Collection* gathers radio and television productions, artwork, props, and paraphernalia. These have been largely compiled from personal collections, bequests by former staff, and the BBC *Archive Treasure Hunt* (a public appeal to recover pre-1980s productions that had been lost) as until then the BBC had a questionable policy of wiping old videotapes for re-use, with no apparent realisation of their historical significance.

Unfortunately, practical issues frequently end up bringing heritage concerns too close for comfort to those of the tourist industry. Tristan Platt has expressed this worry well:

> ... the funding of Bolivian Worlds by Lufthansa, and of Madagascar, Island of the Ancestors by Air Madagascar (both airlines clearly interested in boosting their tourist bookings to each country), ... reminded me of the uncomfortable continuum between ethnography and the travel-brochure ... Could I persuade myself that these artefacts were in fact to be perceived as 'ambassadors' of their peoples to the English capital of Britain?

This passage serves as a stark reminder of the multiple national and commercial interests which lie behind claims to heritage. Separating these from ethical concerns has become as difficult to manage in practice as it is easy to do in theory. But some degrees of compromise are more acceptable than others. When people like Brabeck-Letmathe make statements such as 'access to water is not a public right'[14] and shorelines become increasingly open to commercial development, we should consider carefully the increasingly close connection between commerce and heritage. As the heritage industry grows, there is a serious danger that it will purchase anything of value and sell access to it at rates that only the privileged few can afford.

---

14 See note 13 above.

4. Outro

Given the range of questions and complexities surrounding heritage, I am sceptical about the possibility of a unified account of it.[15] Heritage, cultural or otherwise, is not always good. It may be preserved in fundamentally different, indeed contradictory, ways. The range of rights relating to it is by no means a straightforward one. This elucidatory essay has been written with the faith that 'a repertoire might be more useful than a conviction'.[16] This is not to say that we do not even know what cultural heritage ethics is, but only that exploring these concepts is an integral part of it. I have barely sketched what even a partial conceptual cartography of the area might look like. Nonetheless, I hope to have marked some of the numerous pitfalls which face the bolder theorist.

---

15 Cf. L. Smith, *The Uses of Heritage* (London: Routledge, 2006), ch. 1.

16 Adam Phillips, *On Kissing, Tickling and Being Bored* (London: Faber and Faber, 1993), p. xvi.

2. Poppy Politics: Remembrance of Things Present

James Fox

In October 2011 the English football association requested permission from FIFA (the International Football Federation) for its national team to wear poppies on their shirts when they played Spain the following month. Poppies had been worn across Britain every November for the best part of a century, having been an integral part of the nation's remembrance of its war dead since 1921. FIFA, however, was unmoved by such traditions, and immediately rejected the request. In an official statement the organisation asserted that in line with its existing regulations, players' equipment could not 'carry any political, religious or commercial messages' for fear that they would 'jeopardise the neutrality of football'.[1]

The decision triggered an outcry. The British press published a series of enraged editorials, and before long politicians took up the cause as well. On Tuesday 8 November the government's sports minister Hugh Robertson told FIFA that the poppy was 'not religious or political in any way'. Later that day Prime Minister David Cameron declared that it was 'absurd' to think that 'wearing a poppy to remember those who have given their lives for our freedom is a political act'. And only hours after that, Prince William wrote directly to FIFA, stating that the poppy was a 'universal symbol of remembrance' with 'no political, religious or commercial connotations'.[2]

---

1 FIFA, 'Regulation 54.1', Equipment Regulations, 1 April 2010, http://www.fifa.com/aboutfifa/officialdocuments/doclists/laws.html

2 'Prince William demands Fifa u-turn on poppy ban', *BBC News*, 9 November 2011, http://www.bbc.co.uk/sport/0/football/15643295

  http://dx.doi.org/10.11647/OBP.0047.02

Under ever increasing pressure, FIFA – whose reputation had barely recovered from a recent corruption scandal – quickly capitulated. On Wednesday 9 November it gave permission for poppies to be worn, with the proviso that they were attached to black armbands rather than embroidered directly onto players' shirts.[3] Yet when the match was played three days later, poppies were not just restricted to armbands: a poppy wreath was placed on the pitch before kick-off; players wore poppy-embroidered training tops and poppy-embossed anthem jackets; poppies were attached to scoreboards and advertising hoardings; and poppy-sellers were positioned in conspicuous locations around the stadium.[4]

The debacle is a highly revealing case study in cultural heritage for two reasons. First, it showed that in less than a century, Remembrance had established itself as such a powerful cultural force that any challenge to it – however trivial it may have seemed – had the potential to cause a national furore. Second, the incident indicated that most Britons considered Remembrance to be a resolutely apolitical practice – little more than an ethical duty to the dead. This chapter, however, will take issue with these sentiments. By exploring the origins, development and current heritage rhetoric surrounding the remembrance poppy, I will demonstrate that the poppy has always been, and continues to be, a profoundly political symbol.

***

Most accounts of the remembrance poppy begin in the spring of 1915. The first winter of the Great War was just winding to a close, and the battlefields of the Western front were wastelands. Pastures had been turned to mud, wildlife had all but been obliterated, and underneath the agitated earth lay the bodies of countless dead servicemen. Nevertheless, as the weather improved through April and May of that year, something unexpected happened: red corn poppies began to bloom in huge numbers across the fields. It is believed, somewhat ironically, that the season's unusually abundant crop had been germinated by the very bombardments that had wreaked so much natural damage elsewhere.

Poppies, of course, had long possessed symbolic properties. Since antiquity they had been associated with sleep, death and resurrection. So

---

3   FIFA, 'Statement on England shirts and the use of the poppy', 5 November 2011, http://www.fifa.com/aboutfifa/organisation/media/news/newsid=1537881/index.html

4   'FA Statement: Remembrance Day', 9 November 2011, http://englandfans.thefa.com/ef/pages/news.aspx?id=207e49d4-327a-4d92-b4d3-47bbf126d54c

when one amateur poet saw the flower blossoming across Flanders, he set about reconfiguring its ancient connotations for the new wartime context. Lieutenant Colonel John McCrae was a Canadian medical officer serving in Ypres. He first noticed the region's poppies in May 1915 while burying a friend who had been killed in action. Shortly afterwards, McCrae composed a poem, which he called *In Flanders Fields*.[5] The poem appeared later that year in *Punch* magazine, and before long was widely known and admired. Inspired by the funeral he had just attended, McCrae started the poem by juxtaposing the death of men with the birth of the poppies:

> In Flanders fields the poppies blow
> Between the crosses, row on row,
> That mark out place; and in the sky
> The larks, still bravely singing, fly
> Scarce heard amid the guns below.

McCrae's intention was clear. Like many poets before him, he was invoking pastoral imagery as an antithesis to the war. It is in fact tempting to read his poppies as pacifistic symbols: of nature defeating man, peace defeating war, and life defeating death. This interpretation, however, is dramatically disproved by reading on. In the second verse, McCrae establishes the poem as the voice of the dead, and then, in the third and final verse, he recounts the message they wish to communicate to the living:

> Take up our quarrel with the foe;
> To you from failing hands we throw
> The torch; be yours to hold it high,
> If ye break faith with us who die
> We shall not sleep, though poppies grow
> In Flanders fields.

It is, by any reasoning, an abrupt shift in tone, for it is here that an initially elegiac text is transformed into something altogether more belligerent. McCrae's interred soldiers are, after all, calling on the living to avenge their deaths. For this reason, his poem does not condemn war but legitimises it; does not demand the conflict to end but demands that

---

5   For the full and often disputed story behind the poem, see John F. Prescott, *In Flanders Fields: The Story of John McCrae* (Erin, ON: Boston Mills Press, 1985).

it continues; and though McCrae mourns the loss of life, he calls for yet more sacrifice to come.

John McCrae's *In Flanders Fields* is responsible for first establishing the cultural connection between poppies and the Great War. However, its author deployed the former as a smokescreen behind which he could legitimise the latter. Written early in the war when hopes were still high, volunteers were still needed, and the outcome of the conflict was far from decided, his poem was little more than a propagandistic recruitment call.[6] It is therefore hardly surprising that his words – and his poppy imagery – were soon enlisted in North America and Great Britain to sell war bonds and recruit volunteers. The poppy's wartime origins were nowhere near as peaceful as we often like to think.

If anyone was responsible for converting McCrae's propagandistic poppy into today's remembrance poppy, it was the American academic and humanitarian Moina Michael. Michael had read *In Flanders Fields* as the allies were finalising their victory in November 1918, and she was convinced that the conflict's outcome had vindicated its author's rallying cry. She even went so far as to draft a poem in response to McCrae's interred soldiers, writing that the victors had 'caught the torch' that they had thrown and 'kept the faith' when others had lost it. So while her poem may well be a heartfelt salute to the dead, it is also a defence of their sacrifice: Michael, in short, was implying that the war's many casualties were justified because they had been in the service of victory. And that is why her poem, though now called *We Shall Keep the Faith*, was referred to by contemporaries as *The Victory Emblem*.[7]

Shortly after composing *The Victory Emblem*, Michael purchased twenty-five silk poppies at a New York department store and distributed them in honour of the dead. Her memorial flowers soon caught on around the world: from the United States in November 1918, they arrived in France in October 1920, and Canada, Australia, New Zealand and Great Britain in 1921. Tellingly, all of these countries were victors. The poppy never found its way into the cultural practices of the war's defeated nations, and that may be because the only men whose sacrifice was believed to deserve such a symbol were those who had fought on the 'right' side. Poppies, in other

---

6   An example of this interpretation is found in Paul Fussell, *The Great War and Modern Memory* (Oxford: Oxford University Press, 1975), pp. 248-50.

7   See Moina Michael, *The Miracle Flower: The Story of the Flanders Field Memorial Poppy* (Philadelphia, PA: Dorrance and Co., 1941).

words, had been converted into victory medals. And if doubts still linger over the partisan politics of the memorial poppy, one only need name the person who introduced it to Britain: Field Marshall Douglas Haig – a man who had a vested interest in justifying the conflict to whose victory he had so controversially contributed.

The first part of this chapter has proved that it is far from easy to claim that the remembrance poppy was born out of a universal and apolitical heritage moment. It was conceived when the war was still young and when volunteers still had to be recruited; it was deployed during the following three years to mobilise, raise morale, and legitimise the increasingly unpopular conflict; and in the war's aftermath it was reformulated as a symbol that commemorated the Allied dead precisely as it celebrated the Allied victory. And thus, for all of its pacifistic associations today, the poppy was a thoroughly bellicose symbol from the start: a medal of honour as well as a bleeding wound. But these associations did not expire with the conflict. In the decades after the end of the Great War, the poppy acquired yet more political significance, and yet more public prominence.

One way to demonstrate the poppy's growing popularity through the decades is to examine the statistics for the Royal British Legion's annual poppy appeal. They reveal that its campaign has raised ever-increasing sums across the century of its existence, from £106,000 in 1921 to a staggering £40 million in 2011. These figures suggest that despite receding ever further into the past, the rituals of remembrance that originated with the First World War are more relevant than ever. The question that remains is why? Why, after so much else has happened, after so many other seminal events have come and gone, do the British people remain so fixated on the Flanders poppy? The answer, I think, lies less in the wars of the past than it does in the wars of the present.

The British Legion's statistics show that its poppy appeals have nearly always been more successful when they have taken place during ongoing conflicts. The pattern began with the Second World War. Through the 1920s and most of the 1930s, the British Legion's campaign income had grown only modestly. In the war years, however, that figure almost doubled, from £578,188 in 1938 to over £1 million in 1945. A comparable leap, of almost twenty percent, was recorded between 1981 and 1982, during the Falklands War; and there was another substantial increase between 1989 (£11.9 million) and 1991 (£13.1 million), the years that spanned the first Gulf War. More recently, figures have followed the same trend. At the very beginning of the millennium, poppy appeal income remained relatively static at between £20 million and £21 million each year; in the second half of the decade, when major wars were being fought in both Afghanistan and Iraq, that number virtually doubled, to £40 million.[8]

The Royal British Legion's figures should not be surprising. After all, its poppy appeal commemorates those who have died in all modern and ongoing conflicts, and its funds support active servicemen and living veterans. Moreover, in order to boost its public relevance and thus its financial success, the organisation makes frequent and explicit connections between the remembrance of past wars and the honouring of present ones. In one official statement, it claimed the following:

> We remember those who fought for our freedom during the two World Wars. But we also mourn and honour those who have lost their lives in more recent conflicts. Today, with troops on duty in Afghanistan and other trouble spots around the world, Remembrance … [is] … as important as ever.[9]

The sentiment is doubtless honourable, and the British Legion's fund-raising figures confirm that it has also been highly effective. Nevertheless, at the same time the passage suggests that the poppy has become a problematic nexus in which past and present, poetry and policy, are uneasily intertwined.

In recent years, the poppy's linkage between past wars and present wars has proved particularly controversial. With the outbreak of unpopular conflicts like those in Afghanistan and Iraq, many Britons came to question the political role that the poppy appeared to be playing. Some claimed that by connecting the 'justifiable' world wars of the past to the 'unjustifiable' anti-terrorist wars of the present, the poppy enabled the former to legitimise the latter. In November 2010 a group of six veterans, who had between them served in Northern Ireland, Dhofar, the Falklands, Macedonia, Afghanistan and Iraq, went so far as to write a letter to the British press:

> The poppy appeal is once again subverting Armistice Day. A day that should be about peace and remembrance is turned into a month-long drum roll of support for current wars … The public are being urged to wear a poppy in support of 'our Heroes' … There is nothing heroic about fighting in an unnecessary conflict.[10]

---

8   These figures were given to me by the Royal British Legion.

9   The Royal British Legion, 'The Nation Remembers', http://www.britishlegion.org.uk/remembrance/the-nation-remembers/

10   'Poppies and "Heroes"', *The Guardian*, 5 November 2010, http://www.guardian.co.uk/uk/2010/nov/05/poppies-and-heroes-remembrance-day

This view became so widespread that in the following November the influential 'Stop the War Coalition' re-introduced white poppies as an alternative to red poppies. While the red poppy marked only British military casualties, the white poppy – with its traditionally pacifistic connotations – commemorated all humans who had died as a result of all conflicts, as an anti-war symbol.[11]

The anti-war criticisms of the poppy are not always entirely accurate. The assertion that remembrance was initially about peace and was only recently 'subverted' is contradicted by the poppy's bellicose origins; similarly, the claim that British politicians 'hijacked' the symbol to justify their own wars remains difficult to prove.[12] After all, the British Legion – which administers the poppy appeal – remains steadfastly independent of government. Nevertheless, the very fact that these debates have occurred is proof that the poppy has acquired a raft of controversial political associations. They also reflect the fact that, whether by design or not, the poppy has indeed emboldened the warmongers' cause: for how can one honour the men and women who have died in war and not end up endorsing the conflicts in which they have fought?

The poppy is now such a pregnant symbol of heritage that its ideological reverberations have spread far beyond debates about the legitimacy of individual conflicts; they have come to invade and influence the many fault-lines elsewhere in British society. Immigrant groups, particularly Muslims, have started to reject the poppy as a symbol of western imperialism. At one demonstration in November 2010, the group 'Muslims against Crusades' even went to the lengths of burning a large model poppy as the rest of the nation entered its annual two-minute silence.[13] At the same time, right-wing groups like the British National Party and the English Defence League have appropriated the poppy as a symbol of militant nationalism. Indeed, following FIFA's refusal to permit English footballers to wear poppies in 2011, two members of the English Defence League climbed on to the roof of

---

11 'Stop the War bids to reclaim 11.11.11 Remembrance Day for peace', 6 November 2011, http://web.archive.org/web/20120312083217/http://stopwar.org.uk/index.php/united-kingdom/920-reclaiming-111111-remembrance-day-for-peace-not-war

12 These arguments were made by the Master of the Queen's Music, Sir Peter Maxwell Davies. 'Remembrance Sunday: Queen's composer says he will boycott poppies', *The Telegraph*, 14 November 2010, http://www.telegraph.co.uk/news/uknews/8132185/Remembrance-Sunday-Queens-composer-says-he-will-boycott-poppies.html

13 A. Bloxham, 'Muslims clash with police after burning poppy in anti-Armistice protest', *The Telegraph*, 11 November 2010, http://www.telegraph.co.uk/news/uknews/law-and-order/8126357/Muslims-clash-with-police-after-burning-poppy-in-anti-Armistice-Day-protest.html

FIFA's headquarters in Zurich and brandished a banner that read: 'English Defence League: How dare FIFA disrespect our war dead and wounded'.[14]

The poppy is surely most controversial in Northern Ireland. Here, the British Army has been a divisive institution for decades, having played an often violent role in policing clashes between Unionists and Nationalists since 1969. For this reason, the high-profile commemoration of British servicemen has only intensified the rancour between the two groups. Most Nationalists consider the poppy to be deeply offensive because, as Revd Tomas Walsh has claimed, many of the soldiers it honours had 'colluded with loyalist murder squads ... and killed hundreds of innocent Irish people'.[15] In fact, Remembrance has been such an inflammatory symbol of British power in Ireland that in 1987 the Irish Republican Army targeted it specifically, detonating a bomb at the Enniskillen war memorial on Remembrance Sunday and killing twelve people. Yet in Northern Ireland the poppy means much more than simply an attitude to the British army; it has become a powerful marker of identity in a region where identity is so fiercely contested: Unionists embrace it as an emblem of Britishness, Protestantism and Monarchism, while Nationalists reject it as an assertion of their Irishness, Catholicism and Republicanism.

Poppies do not only mediate identity at the political extremes; they are custodians of national heritage and identity in the mainstream as well. The paper flower may well remind British people of the nation's darkest moments, but it also reminds them of the nation's finest moments: the hard-won victories of the First World War; the Battle of Britain; the D-Day landings – all of which have become integral components of British national identity. This is surely why, when politicians defended the poppy following FIFA's initial ruling, their phrases were soaked in such patriotism. Immediately after claiming that the poppy was not political 'in any way', the government's sport minister Hugh Robertson declared that it was nonetheless 'a display of national pride, just like wearing your country's football shirt'.[16] His argument was as perplexing as it was revealing, not least

---

14 'Poppy row: English Defence League climb onto roof of FIFA HQ', *The Mirror*, 9 November 2011, http://www.mirror.co.uk/news/uk-news/poppy-row-english-defence-league-277327

15 Revd Tomas Walsh, 'Lest we forget who they honour', *Irish Independent*, 14 November 2007, http://www.independent.ie/opinion/letters/lest-we-forget-who-they-honour-1218939.html

16 'Prince William demands Fifa u-turn on poppy ban', *BBC News*, 9 November 2011, http://www.bbc.co.uk/sport/0/football/15643295

because it is patently incorrect to think of 'national pride' as an apolitical sentiment. Moreover, by likening poppies to football shirts Robertson was implying that the former, like the latter, was the uniform of a patriotic and competitive team that its supporters cheered on at the expense of others. His words thus endorsed what they had intended to refute: that beneath a thin façade of universal grief and quiet humility, the poppy remained the red badge of a belligerent nationalism.

The FIFA scandal reveals one more political dimension of the poppy: that much-pilloried bugbear of political correctness. In recent years poppy-wearing has become an increasingly ubiquitous cultural practice. In Britain, television presenters rarely appear on camera without them in the month of November; politicians have started wearing them earlier and earlier every year (and have at times been humiliated by doing so before the official start of the British Legion's appeal); and as the FIFA row demonstrated, even sportsmen now seem unable to compete without them. The last development is particularly recent: indeed, when the English football team played Brazil at the same time in November two years earlier, the poppies that in 2011 seemed so essential were neither requested nor worn. It is, then, only in the last few years that poppies have fully tightened their grip on British cultural life. While this ubiquity is undeniably good news for the Royal British Legion, it does cast some doubt on the politics of Remembrance. It is not only that in such a climate individuals might wear poppies for performative rather than contemplative reasons; it is also that the increasingly obligatory nature of poppy-wearing sits uneasily with the 'freedom' for which the wars it commemorates were allegedly fought. Indeed, one disgruntled British journalist famously described the pressure to fall into line as nothing short of 'poppy fascism'.[17]

This brief essay has shown that in spite of the many claims to the contrary, the poppy is a potent political symbol. It was born out of a desire to promote, prolong and propagandise the Great War, and in the conflict's aftermath it was reconfigured as a medal of triumph that celebrated the Allied victory. As the First World War receded into the past, the poppy acquired affiliations with the agendas of succeeding governments, and in the new millennium it is believed to have helped legitimise unpopular

---

17 Paul Revoir, 'I won't surrender to "Poppy Fascism": C4 News host Jon Snow refuses to bow to viewer demand to wear the emblem', *Daily Mail*, 3 November 2010, http://www. dailymail.co.uk/news/article-1326063/Jon-Snow-poppy-fascism-row-C4-News-host-refuses-surrender.html

conflicts in Afghanistan and Iraq. Yet the poppy's political connotations have spread far beyond war. In an increasingly diverse Britain, it has been violently appropriated and violently rejected as fringe groups define themselves for and against mainstream British values. Conversely, in the mainstream itself the poppy has become a focus for patriotic sentiments that cannot easily be expressed in other ways. Finally, this essay has shown that in recent years, Remembrance has strengthened its grip on the nation's cultural practices. In the process, poppy-wearing has become as much about political correctness and public performance as it has been about the remembrance of the dead. The poppy's meanings have evidently changed since John McCrae saw it blossoming in the fields of Flanders, but that little red flower continues to feed off the carnage of a catastrophic century.

3. The Meaning of the Public in an Age of Privatisation

Benjamin Ramm

And we rebuild our cities, not dream of islands.

W.H. Auden, 'Paysage Moralisé'

In an interview with *The Sunday Times* in 1981, Margaret Thatcher declared her intention: 'Economics are the method; the object is to change the heart and soul'. The culture of competition that drove the New Right's revolution may not have altered our souls, but it did change how we perceive ourselves, at least in relation to our fellow citizens. This chapter will explore how aspects of civic culture have taken on radical meaning in the age of neoliberalism, and consider how we can rediscover the 'civic soul'.

To diagnose the crisis of the public, it is necessary to understand why, in recent decades, the private has become the dominant sphere of meaning. The radical ideas harnessed by the New Right were incubated during the social upheavals of the twentieth century, prompted by democracy and catalysed by technology. As trust in elites declined, the civic notions associated with Victorian society, such as duty and sacrifice, came to be regarded as (self-) deceptions: at best naïveté – the 'delusion' of altruism – at worst coercion, the reinforcing of existing social hierarchies. The notion of a 'public' consensus was rejected as an imposition of elite order, inculcated by an educational system based on deference. Instead of nurturing curiosity

          http://dx.doi.org/10.11647/OBP.0047.03

and critical thinking, schools were accused of narrowing and disciplining; of creating subjects – 'another brick in the wall' – rather than citizens.

Against this austere and conformist public culture, the 'private' represented a realm of sincerity and self-expression. Auden himself had pined for an Age of Intimacy: 'Private faces in public places / Are wiser and nicer / Than public faces in private places'. Moreover, it was becoming clear that bureaucracy – the promise of a rational public system, in Saint-Simon's words, 'replacing the government of persons by the administration of things' – had failed: state socialism and state capitalism alike had proved not to be a political *science*. Bureaucracy promised to liberate society from the unpredictability of politics and the drudgery of a mechanised economy, but its systems created their own unforeseen irrationalities, and a degree of alienation and monotony as extreme as that produced by the unregulated market. Against the 'hegemony of the public', embodied by an oppressive state architecture, the private became the domain of the human: individual and consensual.

The term 'revolution' is overused in the political context; rarely does it signify 'the world turned upside down'. Yet in relocating meaning away from the public realm, the New Right overthrew the central tenet of Enlightenment thought: that we find meaning in our interaction with, and commitment to, the civic. The historical development of the 'public', a sphere of free association and exchange, altered the perception of individual identity and emphasised the social aspect of liberation: far from being a solipsistic pursuit – the monastic cultivation of the soul for salvation – self-realisation demanded civic emancipation. At the core of this vision was a generational optimism, formulated by Hegel and celebrated by Trotsky:

> Man will become immeasurably stronger, wiser, and subtler; his body will become more harmonized, his movements more rhythmic, his voice more musical. The forms of life will become dynamically dramatic. The average human type will rise to the heights of an Aristotle, a Goethe, or a Marx. And above this ridge new peaks will rise.[1]

This renewed interest in the civic drew the theorists of the Enlightenment back to the classical models from which citizenship derived. For the ancient Greeks, declining to take part in public life was a mark of dishonour and

---

1   Leon Trotsky, *Literature and Revolution* (1924), ed. William Keach, trans. Rose Strunsky (Chicago, IL: Haymarket, 2005), p. 207.

a sign of immaturity. The word 'idiot' is derived from the Greek διώτης [idiōtēs], denoting 'a private citizen', one concerned primarily with his or her own affairs. (Pericles, the great leader of democratic Athens, famously castigated this self-centred attitude: 'We do not say that a man who takes no interest in politics minds his own business; we say that he has no business here at all'). The public is itself a vehicle of maturation: to go 'into society' is to mark a coming of age, in which we learn to negotiate our desires, to mediate our self in relation to other selves. As consumers, however, we behave privately *even in public*, seeking to satisfy our particular taste. The universality at the heart of the civic ideal does not appeal to the consumer, for whom individuality (or at least the perception thereof) is preferable to uniformity. The New Right succeeded in transforming this desire for individuality into an ethic of individualism. By conflating 'equality and regimentation', Thatcher was able to argue against the central tenet of the Enlightenment – universality – by employing the rallying cry of the Enlightenment: *liberation*. With the crisis of capitalism of the 1970s, both the New Right and the statist Left set up a dichotomy – the state against the individual – that elided the role of the civic:

> They're casting their problem on society. And, you know, there is no such thing as society. There are individual men and women, and there are families. And no government can do anything except through people, and people must look to themselves first. It's our duty to look after ourselves and then, also to look after our neighbour.[2]

Ultimately, Thatcher's radicalism was less about the privatisation of public amenities than the suppression of the civic imagination. In 2009, Editorial Intelligence – 'an intelligent knowledge networking business which runs an agenda-setting opinion former network' – launched an annual 'residential experiential' weekend event called 'Names Not Numbers'. This 'thought leader symposium' bills itself as 'a private ideas festival', the buzzword of which is 'individuality'. The notion of a 'private idea' would have disturbed the Enlightenment mind, with its commitment to what Kant called 'the public use of one's reason'. But for the organisers of this event, the general public – those counted only as 'Numbers' – are insufficiently bespoke: 'Names' are a discerning elite. (Sponsors of the festival include Jaguar and

---

2   Interview with Margaret Thatcher, 'Aids, education and the year 2000!', *Woman's Own*, 31 October 1987, http://www.margaretthatcher.org/document/106689

The Groucho Club). So it is with audacity, and seemingly without irony, that one strand at the 2013 festival was titled: 'How Can Politics Reconnect to People?'

***

the dark backward and abysm of time.

Shakespeare, *The Tempest*

Previous ages romanticised the old, whereas ours lusts after the new. Planned obsolescence and perceived obsolescence have accelerated our ever-increasing appetite for technology, and transformed our attitude towards production: that which is new is regarded – by the very nature of its newness – as superior, as if new culture, like the technology it produces, had incorporated all the wisdom of the old. In a culture in which knowledge is reduced to the status of information – data, to be sorted according to its utility – earlier civilisations are viewed as merely unplanned obsolescence, whose extinction is a mark of their irrelevance. If capitalism has, in Marx's words, 'accomplished wonders far surpassing Egyptian pyramids, Roman aqueducts, and Gothic cathedrals', it has also 'drowned the most heavenly ecstasies of religious fervour, of chivalrous enthusiasm, of philistine sentimentalism, in the icy water of egotistical calculation'.[3] The baggy, messy civilisations of the past are co-opted into the market of things, but fail to compete with modernism's zeal for creative destruction:

> Come on! set fire to the library shelves! Turn aside the canals to flood the museums!.. Oh, the joy of seeing the glorious old canvases bobbing adrift on those waters, discoloured and shredded![4]

The cultural violence of neoliberalism is not akin to the iconoclasm of Futurism, or the coercive brutishness of Stalinism. Instead, it is realised in the worlds it prevents from being born, in the monuments and artworks to which it pre-emptively shrugs 'What's the use of this?' Thatcher's Benthamite utilitarianism, with its governing triad of 'Economy, Efficiency, Effectiveness', reduces all behaviour to 'egotistical calculation', thereby

---

3   Karl Marx and Friedrich Engels, *The Communist Manifesto* (1848), ed. A.J.P. Taylor, trans. Samuel Moore (London: Penguin, 1967), pp. 82-83.

4   Filippo Tommaso Marinetti, 'The Founding and Manifesto of Futurism' (1909), in Mary Ann Caws, *Manifesto: A Century of Isms* (Lincoln, NE: University of Nebraska Press, 2001), p. 188.

failing to comprehend the nature of culture, which is a social life made possible by the fulfilment of basic needs ('Our basest beggars / Are in the poorest thing superfluous: / Allow not nature more than nature needs, / Man's life is cheap as beast's').[5] Civic culture is a challenge to utilitarian assumptions because it knows that *use* is not the same as *value*: indeed, culture has value in part because it comprehends a world *beyond* use, where truths are uneconomic and inefficient. That which has little utility may have great value: 'poetry makes nothing happen', wrote Auden, but it is 'a way of happening, a mouth'.

The term 'Capitalist Realism' has been coined to describe the triumph of TINA – 'There Is No Alternative' – and the capture of the civic and political imagination by consumer capitalism. In the 'knowledge economy', with its division of 'intelligent' [useful] and unintelligent [useless] knowledge, the non-capitalist world becomes a museum, and museums are regarded as relics, curiosities. Yet it is precisely this 'irrelevance' – the assertion of *non*-exchange value, outside the profit-motive – that transforms the museum into a potential locus of radicalism. At its best, the museum offers an imaginative alternative to the totalitarianism of 'Capitalist Realism', which dismisses other ways of organising and valuing the world. The museum is an epistemological affront to capitalism, as it validates the 'useless' and offers an encounter with objects that *cannot be bought*, that lie outside the realm of economic aspiration, that have taken on a value – incomprehensible to capitalist assumptions – beyond their rate of exchange. The museum rekindles a civic aspiration for acculturation rather than acquisition, against the New Right's appropriation of 'self-improvement' as solely material advancement. It provides a rare public space in which the individual behaves primarily as a citizen rather than a consumer, and in which s/he recognises citizenship as a shared identity. It is for this reason that entry charges ought to be resisted: museums contest the privatisation of value, and should seek to minimise the degree to which citizen relations are mediated by money. If, as Adorno argued, art imagines a totality that the fragmented world cannot – a utopian possibility in formal perfection – then the institutions of culture must offer a glimpse of a society unfractured by inequality.

The dissolution of a civic 'consensus' is a key aspect of the culture of postmodernity, and a primary cause of scepticism about curation. This is understandable: curators, as gatekeepers and educators, have been

---

5   William Shakespeare, *King Lear*, II.ii.453-56, ed. R.A. Foakes (London: Arden, 1997), p. 255.

responsible for telling a selective story of civilisation. But in an age of consumer democracy, curators can be invaluable: we need their *cura* ('care, heed, attention') in navigating the flood of knowledge from the digital world. Consumer democracy purports to offer 'choice' but its market parameters are often mandated by monopolistic corporations, which scupper diversity and accentuate simplicity. 'Choice' remains the clarion call of the New Right, whose populism conflates the notion of cultural elitism – 'the best which has been thought and said' – with *an* elite. (A different elite, of course, than the financial class created by the New Right's reforms). The corporate calculator assumes the lowest common denominator of Benthamism, which can only comprehend value in terms of instant gratification:

> The utility of all these arts and sciences — I speak both of those of amusement and curiosity — the value which they possess, is exactly in proportion to the pleasure they yield. Every other species of pre-eminence which may be attempted to be established among them is altogether fanciful. Prejudice apart, the game of push-pin is of equal value with the arts and sciences of music and poetry. If the game of push-pin furnish more pleasure, it is more valuable than either. Everybody can play at push-pin: poetry and music are relished only by a few.[6]

In contrast, museums affirm the virtues of enrichment: a slower, more arduous process, but one with the prospect of sweeter fruits. Yet museums often seem reticent about asserting their cultural importance, wary of making value judgments in a climate of relativism, and instead justify themselves in terms of social utility. As Peter Jenkinson, the founding director of Creative Partnerships, claimed: 'Suddenly we are able to think that museums and galleries are not sad, marginal locations of dust and decay and heritage gloom, but alive and connected and critical to the futures of communities the length and breadth of the United Kingdom'[7]. This self-justification shifts the focus away from the exhibited items onto the visitor, whose attention must be 'targeted'. But this corporate emphasis on personalisation does not allow room for the growth or discovery inherent in the idea of Enlightenment, because it aims to capture consumer preference at any particular point, and it makes individuals, with their unique appetites, seem further away from each other than they are. The

---

6   Jeremy Bentham, *The Rationale of Reward* (London: John & H.L. Hunt, 1825), p. 206.
7   Peter Jenkinson, 'Regeneration: Can Culture Carry the Can?', *RSA Journal*, 5494, 2000, pp. 32-39.

civic approach – universalist curation – adopts a 'veil of ignorance', which is not prejudiced by the perception of (constructed and malleable) tastes.

'Museum and mausoleum are connected by more than phonetic association', wrote Adorno, and for all the virtues of global museums, their acquisitions are intimately bound up with the history of conquest. How can these institutions offer an alternative vision to exploitation when they are born of the original sin of colonialism? How can they counter hegemony when they celebrate civilisations? For in the words of Walter Benjamin, 'There is no document of civilisation which is not at the same time a document of barbarism'.[8] How can these museums claim to be a refuge from 'getting and spending' when they direct us, at almost every opportunity, to the gift shop, and when major international exhibitions – already burdened by diplomatic and ethical challenges – are sponsored by the Bank of America? The corporate attempt to appropriate civic spaces for consumerism at least acknowledges what capitalist logic had dismissed: that citizens still value the 'un-profitable', and have an appetite for 'useless' knowledge. Perhaps a greater concern is the commodification of curation, in which objects are evacuated of their history and 'hollowed out'.[9] In her novel *The God of Small Things*, Arundhati Roy describes this transformation from 'History House' to 'Heritage Hotel'. History is vital and contested – a story of conflict, coercion, rebellion, failure and martyrdom – whereas Heritage is a rarefied, sterilised ornamentation. Heritage offers gift shop trinkets as tourist *souvenirs* – 'remembrances' in the French – but their remembrance is also an act of forgetting, an eliding of History. This 'reification' (the hypnotising effect of commodity fetishism) represses the memory of production: as Adorno wrote to Benjamin, 'every reification is a forgetting'[10].

All Enlightenment ideologies dedicated to liberation are confronted with the question of how to respond to their cultural inheritance. For Mao Zedong, it was necessary to destroy the Four Olds – Old Culture, Old Customs, Old Habits and Old Ideas – for the New to be born. The spectre of civilisation could not be allowed to haunt the socialist imagination: the Cultural Revolution would 'Sweep Away All Monsters'. (Capitalism,

---

8   Walter Benjamin, 'Theses on the Philosophy of History' (1940), in *Illuminations: Essays and Reflections*, ed. Hannah Arendt, trans. Harry Zorn (London: Pimlico, 1999), p. 248.

9   Letter to Walter Benjamin, quoted in Eli Friedlander, *Water Benjamin: A Philosophical Portrait* (Cambridge, MA: Harvard University Press, 2012), p. 156.

10 Quoted in Martin Jay, *Marxism and Totality* (Berkeley, CA: University of California Press, 1984), p. 229.

Mao confidently asserted, would 'soon be relegated to the museum'). For Trotsky, by contrast, workers must 'master all the culture of the past', so that it can be incorporated and transcended:

> The art of past centuries has made man more complex and flexible, raising his psyche to a higher level and enriching his mind in many ways. This enrichment is an invaluable conquest of culture. Mastery of the old art is therefore a necessary prerequisite not only for the creation of a new art, but for the construction of a new society, because for communism, people are needed with a highly developed psyche. Is the old art capable, however, of enriching us with the artistic cognition of the world? Yes, it is. And it is precisely for this reason that it is capable of nourishing our feelings and cultivating them. If we were to indiscriminately renounce the old art, then immediately we would become poorer in spirit.[11]

The curation of 'civilisation' compels us to reassess our understanding of the relationship between power and culture. ('Art never lies', declared Waldemar Januszczak in his BBC Four series *The Dark Ages*, but we can deceive ourselves with it, often in ingenious ways). Intelligent curation is able to reveal a hidden history of civilisation:

> Who built the seven gates of Thebes?
> In the books you will find the names of kings.
> Was it kings who hauled the craggy blocks of stone? …
> Young Alexander conquered India.
> He alone?[12]

Curation can broaden as well as narrow; it can frame Alexander as a leader among men, at once inspired and fallible, while at the same time acknowledging the loss for civilisation of the library in the city that bears his name. The Dark Ages that followed its destruction may not have been an abysm – indeed, they may have been 'the darkness of the womb' – but we are incalculably poorer for the loss of Alexandria's treasures, even if sealed with the names of kings.

In the permanent collection of the British Museum there is an Aztec mirror of pure black obsidian – in composition it recalls the iconic monolith in Kubrick's *2001: A Space Odyssey*. The mirror is wondrous in its obscurity: it purports to reflect, but shows us nothing of ourselves. What excites the

---

11 Leon Trotsky, *Culture and Socialism* (1927), trans. Brian Pearce (London: New Park Publications, 1962), p. 12.

12 Bertolt Brecht, 'A Worker Reads History' (1935), in *Selected Poems*, trans. H.R. Hays (New York: Grove Press, 1959), p. 108.

viewer is its otherworldliness, its indifference to our narcissism. Perhaps understandably, in an age vigilant of racism, we have become wary of the concept of 'strangeness', and the awe and awkwardness that comes with the encounter is regarded as the product of ignorance or parochialism. In addition, globalisation has proved to be a force for cultural homogeneity, creating an alphabet of shared (corporate) symbols and a political economy that restricts civic experimentation. We have become a civilisation in love with its own reflection, always demanding to know the 'relevance' of that which it does not recognise. But museums must be careful about being too familiar – they live by curiosity, and should seek to nurture it by being suggestive, imaginative, challenging, humbling, inspiring. Against consumer capitalism's assault on memory, a museum offers evidence of alternative ways of organising society, and in so doing plays a crucial role in 'the struggle of memory against forgetting'. Ultimately, it is the duty of public institutions to challenge the complacency and introspection of the private. Private domains and networks can limit our room for growth, as they tend to reinforce habit and opinion: by encountering other individuals and ideas – by participating in the public – we can evolve the 'heart and soul'.

***

Engines bear them through the sky: they're free
And isolated like the very rich

Auden, 'In Time of War'

The island paradise is the dream vision of neoliberalism: the idyll of the private, a haven from taxation and the burdens of society. Where 'hell is other people', heaven is a luxurious retreat, a perpetual indulgence of the self. It's an uninspiring vision, largely because it doesn't re-imagine our social world, and denies our interdependence – that each of us is 'a piece of the continent, a part of the main'[13]. Unmoored from one another, we have become privatised in temperament and habit, but the perspective of the distance allows us to rediscover the radical promise of the civic. What salvation for the lonely rower, lost in the sea of his desire? We must be saved, from ourselves, by each other.

---

13 John Donne, 'Meditation XVII', *Devotions Upon Emergent Occasions* (1624), http://www. luminarium.org/sevenlit/donne/meditation17.php

II
HISTORY AND ARCHAEOLOGY

4. History as Heritage: Producing the Present in Post-War Sri Lanka

Nira Wickramasinghe[1]

The state — actually a shifting complex of peoples and roles ...[2]

Introduction

Walter Benjamin warned against the 'appreciation of heritage', describing it as a greater 'catastrophe' than indifference or disregard.[3] Indeed, heritage can be considered an essentially cultural practice centred in the present, and an instrument of cultural power. Cultural heritage is as much a construction of the present as it is an interpretation of the past.

The changing fortunes and popularity of historical sites indicate that no specific place is inherently valuable as heritage. There is therefore no heritage per se and all heritage, as Laurajane Smith argues, is ultimately intangible.[4] What make sites valuable are the contemporary cultural

---

1   I thank Marina Carter, Anup Grewal, Sanayi Marcelline, Nilu Abeyratne and Sasanka Perera for their thoughtful reading of the original draft of this essay which enabled me to sharpen many of the arguments made here. A much longer version has been published as 'Producing the Present: History as Heritage in Post-War Patriotic Sri Lanka', *Economic and Political Weekly*, 48(43), 2013, pp. 91-100

2   M. Herzfeld, *Cultural Intimacy: Social Poetics in the Nation State* (London: Routledge, 1997), p. 5.

3   S. Mathur, *India by Design: Colonial History and Cultural Display* (Berkeley, CA: University of California Press, 2007), p. 168.

4   L. Smith, *The Uses of Heritage* (London: Routledge, 2006), p. 3.

     http://dx.doi.org/10.11647/OBP.0047.04

interpretations and activities that are undertaken around them. It is through the practice of cultural appropriation that artefacts and places acquire meaning and value. In this chapter we will investigate an example of hegemonic discourse on heritage 'which acts to constitute the way we think, talk and write about heritage'[5] by exploring the situation in post-civil war Sri Lanka, a country where political ideals, contemporary cultural and social values, debates and aspirations directly translate into a partisan interpretation of selected heritage sites.[6]

Return to Heritage

After the decimation of the Tamil Tigers in 2009 brought Sri Lanka's long civil war to an end, President Rajapaksa promised there would no longer be minorities, in spite of the fact that the idea of a multicultural society was endorsed in the Thirteenth Amendment to the 1987 Constitution. In the new 'civic nation' fleshed out in the President's speech, citizen-patriots would be ethnically undifferentiated, although at the same time all religions and ethnic identities would supposedly be respected. However, the President's vision of a nation at one with the state is based on patriotic feelings stemming from a particular reading of the history and foundation myth of the Sinhala people. In this context all other groups – those formally known as minorities – are relegated to a secondary role with no room in the country's common political culture. At the same time there has been, in the last few years, a singular but clearly identifiable phenomenon in the public sphere which I would describe as a 'return to heritage'.

Economic Development and Heritage

Since the 1930s – when a measure of self-government was granted to the crown colony under the Donoughmore constitution – Sri-Lankan society has experienced an underlying nostalgia for a bygone age when the peasantry was proud, prosperous, and embodied the moral values destroyed in modern times. As a consequence the post-colonial state invested heavily in restoring ancient irrigation tanks in the north-central

---

5 Ibid, p. 11.
6 Ibid.

province areas, constructing new dams in the south-east (Gal oya and Welawe ganga), and finally, from 1968, undertaking the large-scale project of developing the area around the Mahaweli river and its affluent. The purpose of the latter project was not purely economic. Developmental goals were intertwined with nationalist underpinnings centred on the Sinhala peasant, represented in popular ideology as a 'sublime object'. In the state ideology of the United National Party (UNP) government, which introduced a new economic policy based on economic liberalisation and an export-led economy, development through irrigated agriculture achieved a prominent place and was presented as a reincarnation of the ancient, indigenous and Buddhist culture of Sri Lanka's golden age. The Minister of Mahaweli Development in the UNP regime, Gamini Dissanayake, declared quite candidly in 1983 that 'the soul of the new Mahaweli society will be cherished values of the ancient society, which were inspired and nourished by the Tank, the Temple and the Paddy Field'.[7]

The link between economic policy and state ideology has been demonstrated by Hennayake who has shown the involvement of the agro-technology and insurance sectors in the process of connecting development to the concept of an ideal past. She cites the text from the advertisement of a fertiliser company from the post-1977 period:

> Agriculture is a part of Sri Lankan heritage, its culture and tradition. Our ancient kings were inspired agriculturists. Our people here, from the time immemorial, combined an affinity for the earth with a talent for innovative technology. Anglo-Fert and Anglo-Chem are two companies who share a corporate commitment to the growth of agriculture in this country.[8]

Another aspect of the appropriation of cultural heritage by the post-1977 liberalised state is testified by the government's policy of invoking the past and displaying its commitment to nurture the nation's heritage in order to push through its development agenda. The UNP government was responsible for requesting the United Nations Educational, Scientific and Cultural Organisation (UNESCO) to provide guidance and assistance in managing the archaeological sites in the regions containing the three ancient capitals of Anuradhapura, Polonnaruwa and Kandy in 1978. Two years later, the director general of UNESCO, when appealing

---

7 Cited in N.S.M. Tennekoon, 'Rituals of Development: The Accelerated Mahaväli Development Program of Sri Lanka', *American Ethnologist*, 15(2), 1988, p. 297.

8 N. Hennayake, *Culture, Politics and Development in Postcolonial Sri Lanka* (Lanham, MD: Lexington Books, 2006), p. 123.

internationally for the funds necessary to safeguard the Cultural Triangle, reminded his interlocutors that it 'must be preserved for the sake of the world at large because it forms an integral part of man's heritage'.[9] As these examples show, from the late 1970s the state's intention was to display its commitment to the deepest values of the nation. While the opening up of the economy was radically transforming other aspects of society, sometimes brutally bringing a peasant society into a modern world of consumption, the dominant discourse was more and more imbued with a sense of the pastoral care of the material past. Caring for the heritage of the nation would give the government the self-assigned right to radically alter the present. As Michael Herzfeld points out:

> The static image of an unspoiled and irrecoverable past often plays an important part in present actions. It legitimizes deeds of the moment by investing them with the moral authority of eternal truth and by representing the vagaries of circumstance as realization of a larger universe of system and balance.[10]

In the early twentieth century proponents of a nation that was modern yet unsullied by western influence defined their ancient past as heritage in order to create pride in the nation in the making, whereas the liberal state of the late 1970s, focusing on economic development, used heritage to strengthen their claim to moral authority to transform an agrarian society into a market-oriented export processing zone. The twenty-first-century government, however, uses heritage for purely political purposes. In the years since the end of the civil war in 2009, the concept of national heritage has been used to depoliticise citizens and to mute any possible dissent. A number of institutions, groups and personalities are involved in the construction of the present discourse around national heritage.

The Construction of the Present Hegemonic Discourse

Local and international bodies, governmental and non-governmental organisations and individuals all play a role in the creation of a specific understanding of 'heritage' that has gradually merged with what is generally known as history. This new interpretation of national heritage is

---

9   Cited in R. Silva, 'The Cultural Triangle of Sri Lanka', in Henry Cleere (ed.), *Archeological Heritage Management in the Modern World* (London: Routledge, 2005), p. 222.

10 Herzfeld, 1997, p. 206.

shaped in a number of ways: through acts and practices that define heritage, through legislation and policy decisions about specific heritage sites, through the allocation of state funding, and, finally, through conservation practices that transform heritage sites.

Education and Heritage

As Bourdieu has argued, educational structures aim to produce social agents worthy and capable of receiving the heritage of the group and adept at transmitting it in turn to a larger group.[11] Education in Sri Lanka is free at primary, secondary and tertiary levels. In 2010 there were 3,932,722 students enrolled in primary and secondary education.[12] A principal manner in which ideas about heritage are conveyed to a large public is through teaching in schools, universities and *Daham Pasala* (Buddhist Sunday schools), and through textbooks. Indeed, textbooks provide a fairly accurate reflection of the way history as critical assessment of the past has been superseded by a version of history that conveys a simplified account of the past.[13] This process is not a recent one, but it did gain momentum after the war against the secessionist movement in the north and east entered its last and bloodiest phase.

Issues pertaining to heritage are introduced in both history textbooks and Buddhism textbooks. History is now a compulsory subject in primary and secondary schools and a cursory look at the texts produced by the National Institute of Education reveals an emphasis on monumental histories associated with royal lineages. History as a subject that interprets the past, rather than glorifying it, is unrecognisable in these textbooks, which offer children a narrative of the glorious days before invaders from India and colonial powers shattered the equilibrium of Sri Lankan society by ushering in modernity.[14]

---

11 P. Bourdieu, 'Strategies de reproduction et modes de domination', *Actes de la recherche en science sociale*, 105, 1994, p. 6.

12 Data Management Branch, Ministry of Education, 2010, http://www.moe.gov.lk/web/images/stories/statistic/std_2010.pdf

13 R. Siriwardena, S. Bastian, K. Indrapala and S. Kottegoda, *School Textbooks and Communal Relations in Sri Lanka, Part I* (Colombo: Council for Communal Harmony through the Media, 1980); N. Wickramasinghe and S. Perera, 'Assessment of Ethno-Cultural and Religious Bias in Social Studies and History Texts of Years 7, 8, 10 and 11' (Colombo: World Bank, 1999).

14 In 2005 I was Consultant to the Ministry of Education on curriculum revision for schools (chairperson of the History syllabus committee).

Alongside grade-school history books, the syllabi and texts used for teaching Buddhism in *Daham Pasala* should be looked at as one of the main vehicles for transmission of ideas about heritage to a younger and often more naïve generation. Even a quick examination of the present *Daham Pasala* texts that contain sections on Sri Lankan history reveals certain trends. Just as in school histories, the history of Buddhism appears as one peppered with glorious deeds and exceptional individuals (*shresta minissu*). It is a history full of omissions and chosen emphases, one which resembles the heritage/mythic mode of recounting the past rather than modern historiography. If heritage is about the meanings placed upon artefacts or other traces and the interpretations that are created from them, what is dispensed in *Daham Pasala* is a 'heritagised' version of history in which interpretations are presented as evidence that cannot be contested or questioned.

Institutions

At the University of Colombo, where I taught for nearly 20 years, student Buddhist monks often chose to study history expecting to be taught a national culture set in stone, able to provide certainties in a world in constant flux. They were, of course, disappointed to find that the courses we offered did not deal with history as heritage but rather questioned their received ideas about monastic history conveyed by the Chronicles. History, as we taught it, was conceived as precisely the opposite of heritage studies. But this is not always the case in those fields of study where notions of the past are being fashioned – departments of history, archaeology, heritage studies, Pali and Buddhist studies.

Outside academia there are a number of ministries and government departments directly involved in the definition, production and preservation of heritage: the Ministries of Buddha Sasana and Religious Affairs, of Culture and the Arts, of National Heritage; the Archaeological Department, and those of the National Archives, National Museum, Buddhist Affairs, Christian Affairs, Hindu Religious and Cultural Affairs, Muslim Religious and Cultural Affairs, and Cultural Affairs and Educational Publications. These institutions earn their power and credibility by making themselves visible before the public eye, in particular through print and audio-visual media.

In addition to government ministries, a number of statutory bodies and non-governmental organisations are concerned with particular aspects of heritage, either through teaching, research or funding conservation. These include the Central Cultural Fund (CCF), the Galle Heritage Foundation (GHF), the National Art Council (also covering non-tangible heritage), the National Crafts Council (NCC), the National Performing Art Centre, and the UNESCO National Commission. These institutions earn power and credibility in various ways as they target different audiences through a variety of projects. Many experts sit on a number of these commissions, thus creating a message on heritage that consolidates its own foundations rather than questioning them.

Finally, non-governmental organisations play a considerable role in generating interest in heritage issues, among them the Royal Asiatic Society of Sri Lanka (RASSL), The National Heritage Trust, The Dutch Burgher Union (DBU), The Archaeologists Association, local branches of the International Commission on Museums (ICOM), and the local section of the International Commission on Monuments and Sites (ICOMOS).

Vying for Popular Appeal: Merging History and Heritage in Popular Culture

The realm of popular culture has always been filled with accounts of Sri Lankan history drawn from the Chronicles, myths, and Jataka tales which portray heroes and gods as the agents of history. Social forces or class conflict have no place in these accounts. The gap between histories written in English by professional academics and popular histories in the vernacular is not new, but widened with the opening up of the economy in the late 1970s, when a cosmopolitan class chose to consume western modernity with a vengeance after a decade of austerity. They consciously detached themselves from a past that was linked to myths and legends. The vernacular domain of culture was, however, recently re-energised under the influence of an entertainment industry that pandered to many people's need for reassurance at a moment when the nation was threatened by secessionist anti-systemic groups. The trend became especially pronounced in 2008, when the state began its full-scale patriotic war to overthrow the Tamil rebels in the north and east of the country.

This patriotic war had a direct impact on the film industry. In August 2008 the historical movie *Aba* was released in 38 cinemas across Sri Lanka. *Aba* was produced by EAP Edirisinghe, a group of companies that owned a popular TV channel called Swarnavahini. The film, directed by Jackson

Anthony, a well-known film actor and TV personality, depicted the life of King Pandukabhaya. Pandukabhaya was the first king of Anuradhapura who, according to the Chronicles, ruled for 70 years some 2,400 years ago. Cinema-goers watching the movie reached the impressive figure of 2,105,000, about 10 percent of the total population of the island.

This and other contemporary works revolve around common tropes, such as the hydraulic civilisation and the aesthetic of the gargantuesque. What is portrayed is not the past but Sri Lanka's fame, which is related to its past ability, for instance, to build *stupas*[15] deemed exceptional for being the largest brick structures known to the pre-modern world. Monumentality is a central value in the production of heritage by the state, businesses, journalists and consultants in Sri Lanka. The connection between the exceptional architectural prowess of the past and the present is implicit. Today's patriotic state needs the 'signatures of the visible' to construct a national imagination.[16] Creative works, monuments and archaeology thus create a heritage able to consolidate national identity and to strengthen the public profile of political figures.

Fictionalised versions of the past consumed by adults and children are also vehicles for a heritage discourse that naturalises certain narratives as well as cultural forms and social experiences that are often linked to ideas of nation and nationhood. Historical novels, for instance, are in great vogue. A case in point is Jayantha Chandrasiri's novel – soon to be made into a film – *The Great Dutugemunu* (*Maha Dutugemunu*), which relates the glories of a third century BC Sinhala hero who slayed the Tamil King Elara and recaptured the kingdom of Anuradhapura.

Today, it is clear that the public idea of what constitutes the past is fashioned in a vibrant commercial environment. Publishers, authors, film and teledrama makers use print media as well as visual technologies and the internet to reproduce a monumental, often exclusive, personality-oriented vision of the past as heritage, a vision that the state apparatus is also conveying through educational institutions. This vision is, however, contested on occasion by dissenting views, as well as by members of communities that are excluded from the official discourse.

---

15 A stupa is a hemispherical structure containing Buddhist relics, typically the ashes of Buddhist monks, used by Buddhists as a place of meditation.
16 A. Appadurai, 'The Globalization of Archaeology and Heritage: A Discussion with Arjun Appadurai', *Journal of Social Archaeology*, 35(1), 2001, p. 44

Heritage in Practice: Disputes and Dissent

The transformation of history into heritage must also be understood as a transformation from a selective and individualistic practice performed by professional historians into a public performance. Heritage practice involves visiting, interpreting and especially managing and conserving.

One initiative in this direction is the Ramayana Trail, which takes people to 52 sites related to the great Hindu epic of the same name, including the garden where the abducted Sita, wife of Prince Rama, was imprisoned by Ravana, king of Lanka. The National Tourism Development Authority (SLTDA)[17] started this initiative in 2007 with the aim of attracting Indian tourists in search of an authentic historical experience. In 2009, after the civil war ended, 4,000 Indian tourists arrived and numbers have been growing since.

The Royal Asiatic Society of Sri Lanka (RASSL), especially its director, Susantha Goonetilleke, were vehemently opposed to what they saw as the resurrection of a fictional trail based on no historical evidence and for purely commercial reasons. Historians, including those of a nationalist leaning, criticised the creation of an historical site that was not supported by 'proper scientific knowledge'. The Ramayana Trail controversy shows how in Sri Lanka promoters of the patriotic nation state select myths useful for propaganda purposes and to neutralise historical interpretations that do not conform to the dominant ideology.

Disputes over Sites

Heritage can be used by official cultural institutions and social elites as a tool to promote a version of history which tones down cultural and social tensions in the present time. It can also, however, be used by marginalised groups in a progressive way, to rethink the past and express social identities excluded by the official discourse.[18] Historical sites are a particularly powerful form of heritage as they are visual and material – and memory requires a display, an articulation via objects or representation to give it meaning. Moreover materiality makes these locations appear neutral as mere traces of history rather than political and social constructs, whilst in fact sites and landscapes are the terrain where conflicting claims

---

17 Formerly the Tourist Board of Sri Lanka.
18 Smith, 2006, p. 4.

over heritage clash. Post-conflict Sri Lanka is a case in point of cultural appropriation of national heritage by a state determined to present a glorified notion of the nation's history.

A recent example is provided by Kandarodai in the Jaffna Peninsula, where a collection of circular structures on a megalithic site possibly dating from the early part of the second millennium was discovered in the early twentieth century. After the end of the civil war pilgrims began to visit the place again and its name was subsequently Sinhalised as Kandurugoda, while the structures were refashioned as stupas. This connection with the Buddhist past of the country's north was meant to counter the entire Tamil nationalist historical narrative. Today, this interpretation of the site could fuel tension between communities as they battle over the cultural meaning of the place. Unlike the case of the Ramayana Trail, the stupas appear to offer concrete evidence of a Buddhist past, further strengthened by an inscription naming the place Kandurugoda. This serves Sinhalese claims that Buddhism encompassed the entire island, the stupas being dated to the ninth century AD, a period which bears similarities to Borobudur in Indonesia.[19] Tamil scholars have acknowledged the Buddhist remains in Jaffna, described as 'burial monuments of monks, a buddhicised version of megalithicism', as proof of the existence of Tamil Buddhists in ancient times.[20] Sinhalese nationalist Ven. Ellawalla Medhananda is championing the renovation of all Buddhist sites in areas 'desecrated' by decades of civil war.[21] In the post-conflict period Tamils felt the state was investing too much in renovating traces of Buddhist heritage in the north and east as well as building new temples, while their Hindu heritage was being neglected:

> Buddha statues have been found in places like Kandarodai, and this shows that Tamils have followed Buddhism and that Tamil Buddhism was practiced in Eelam, in a lesser extent, but the Sinhalese show these as Buddhist antiques and claim parts of the Tamil motherland as Sinhala areas.[22]

---

19 D.G.B. de Silva, 'Kantarodai Buddhist remains: A Sri Lankan Boro-budur lost for ever?', *The Island*, 14 August 2002, http://www.island.lk/2002/08/14/midwee01.html

20 N. Parameswara, *Early Tamils of Lanka* (Ilankai: KL Malaysia, 1999), pp. 123-24.

21 V.E. Medhananda, *Sinhala Bauddha Urumaya* (Sinhala Buddhist Heritage), 4th edition, (Colombo: Dayawansa Jayakodi and Company, 2008) describes sites in Anuradhapura, Vavuniya and Mullaitivu districts.

22 Navraj Parthiban, 'Hindu temples of Vanni and the lands of the Tamils are in danger', *Global Tamil News*, 29 September 2011, http://www.globaltamilnews.net/MobileArticle/tabid/81/language/enUS/Default.aspx?pn=articles&aid=53410

Tamils are countering with similarly grandiose claims of a 'Great Stone Age' in Kandarodai, using new media to disseminate their ideas.[23]

Monuments and sites are thus being invested with new meanings, a phenomenon that existed in the past but that has been infused with a new urgency in a post-conflict situation where power relations between communities are being redefined. Each group is trying to test the limits of toleration of the others under the watchful eye of the patriotic state.

The Conflict over the Nature of Restoration

Protecting built heritage and restoring it according to certain agreed criteria is an idea that was born in Europe in the nineteenth century and travelled to Sri Lanka with antiquarianism and colonial archaeology under H.C.P. Bell. In the post-colonial period, these principles were enshrined in a number of international treaties, among which the Venice Charter of 1964 is the most influential. The preamble of this seminal document indicates the underlying ideas about the past that prevailed in the 1960s:

> People are becoming more and more conscious of the unity of human values and regard ancient monuments as a common heritage. The common responsibility to safeguard them for future generations is recognized. It is our duty to hand them on in the full richness of their authenticity.[24]

It is on this crucial issue of 'authenticity' and the need to respect this principle when restoring monuments and sites that differences in interpretation arise between international organisations upholding these values and other parties who feel they have trusteeship of a monument.

The Temple of the Tooth (*Dalada Maligawa*) in Kandy is believed by the Buddhist community to house the Buddha's Tooth relic. The temple was constructed by King Wimaladharmasuriya (1593-1603) and is today under the control of two chief monks of the Malwatta and Asgiriya temples and a lay custodian (*diyavadana nilame*). The restoration of the Temple of the Tooth after part of it was destroyed by a Tamil Tigers bomb in 1998 offers a telling example of the local understanding of restoration as making anew. New tiles were laid, new sandakadapahana (moonstone) and new carvings

---

23 'People of the Great Stone Age Civilization had lived in Kandarodai', *Global Tamil News*, 24 June 2011, http://www.globaltamilnews.net/GTMNEditorial/tabid/71/article Type/ArticleView/articleId/63096/language/en-US/People-of-the-Great-Stone-Age-Civilization-had-Lived-in-Kandarodai.aspx

24 See http://www.international.icomos.org/charters/venice_e.pdf

were added, totally in contravention of the Venice Charter.[25] The clash is here between an historical temple as a living heritage where people come to practice their rituals, and the World Heritage view of historical places as unalterable entities fixed in time. The vision of the bhikkhus, as far as stupas and other Buddhist sites are concerned, is that heritage is a living thing that can be modified. Hence the restoration of the Dalada Maligawa to look exactly as it looked before, even if this meant using present day materials, or the painting of ancient stupas in white, which is a common occurrence in Sri Lanka and serves to make them similar to all other modern stupas in the country.

Conclusion

In Sri Lanka, as in most states which are signatories of international conventions, 'heritage', in its multifarious guises, is endorsed simultaneously by UNESCO, an international bureaucratic organisation, by a global tourist industry and by the country's government.[26] UNESCO's rhetoric appears to be progressive in that it purports to protect world cultures by means of protocols, declarations and inventories. But world heritage projects belong to a world system and world economy which are in no way at odds with the way nation states exhibit and promote a populist interpretation of the past. In that sense international organisations such as UNESCO facilitate the marginalisation of certain histories and the dominance of ideological and cultural appropriation by centres of political and economic power.[27] The state uses the framework of World Heritage Sites for its own agenda of cultural hegemony. The contradictions between Sri Lanka's nation state ideology, morphed into what I have elsewhere qualified as 'new patriotism' in the post-conflict years, and the lofty goals of UNESCO are rarely acknowledged by local representatives of UNESCO or members of ICOMOS.[28] There are few voices left to dissent.

---

25 See Article 6 of the Venice Charter, http://www.international.icomos.org/charters/venice_e.pdf

26 M. Askew, 'The Magic List of Global Status: UNESCO, World Heritage and the Agendas of States', in S. Labadi and C. Long (eds.), *Heritage and Globalisation* (Abingdon: Routledge, 2010), p. 19.

27 Ibid, p. 22.

28 Nira Wickramasinghe, 'After the War: A New Patriotism in Sri Lanka', *Journal of Asian Studies*, 68(4), 2009, pp. 1945-54.

At a time when Western thinkers have lost their legitimacy among the people of Sri Lanka, it might be strategic to re-introduce them to the thought of Rabindranath Tagore. Indeed, Tagore advocates that when a country is seen as morally transgressing, it forfeits its claim to the loyalty of its citizens. His contemporary, Leo Tolstoy, made the same point when he stated that one could be a critic while at the same time being a patriot. What both thinkers discredited was an extreme patriotism that entailed a belief in the superiority of one's country and an exclusive concern for one's country.[29]

Tagore's low-key nationalism is certainly at odds with the type of state patriotism promoted by the Sri Lankan government during the final phase of the civil war and the eventual victory over the Tamil Tigers. I have argued elsewhere that if the Rajapaksa regime takes patriotism seriously and expects non-Sinhalese communities to identify with a national identity that transcends their attachment to a specific group, it will need to avoid expressions of 'banal nationalism' that can easily alienate cultural minorities. Continuing to flag Sinhala-Buddhist traditions as the basis of the nation's patriotism, a practice that started in the mid-1950s, is certainly not a way to win over the hearts of members of racial and religious minorities.

---

29 Leo Tolstoy, 'On Patriotism' (1894) and 'Patriotism or Peace' (1896), in *Writings on Civil Disobedience and Non-Violence* (New York: New American Library 1968).

5. Looking at the Acropolis of Athens from Modern Times to Antiquity

William St Clair[1]

The Acropolis of Athens is one of the most famous places on earth, visited by over a million people every year, and instantly recognisable by millions more who know it only from pictures. With posters and postcards displayed in every street kiosk and hotel lobby in Athens, and countless images encountered in books, films, television, brochures, advertising, and social media in countries round the world, it must now be impossible for any visitor, whether a Greek child on a first educational visit or a stranger from a distant land, to look at the Acropolis without feeling that, in some sense, they have already seen it. Nor is the sense of immediate familiarity a recent or an incidental result of the rapid spread of modern information technology. Already by the end of the eighteenth century, the number of people who knew the Acropolis from pictures was greater than the number, whether local people or visitors, who saw it with their own eyes, and the gap continued to widen.

Partly as a result, thoughtful visitors have long been worried about loss of independence. Colonel J.P. Barry, a medical man, for example, visiting

---

1   Versions of this essay were given as the Runciman lecture, King's College, London, 2012, the Gaisford lecture, University of Oxford, 2012, the Duncan Sandys lecture, Europa Nostra UK, 2013, and at academic seminars at home and abroad. I am deeply grateful to the many friends and colleagues who have contributed to the development of the ideas. A book length study that sets out the full history is expected in 2015, but it seemed useful, at the risk of unbalancing the present essay, to offer the theoretical and methodological discussion as a contribution to the general debates in this volume.

http://dx.doi.org/10.11647/OBP.0047.05

the Acropolis from India in 1905, hoped to experience 'impressions not derived from reading', claiming that: 'The most valuable impressions for the traveller are those he makes his own not those made for him'.[2] Joseph Pennell, an artist from the United States, who in 1913 wanted to experience Greece without preconceptions, declared that before his visit he avoided reading any classical author even in translation, and deliberately refused to take any interest in architecture or proportion.[3] They and many others before and since have understood that, whether they chose to submit, to resist, or to negotiate, and whether in the event they were confirmed or 'agreeably disappointed' in their expectations, the seeing agenda had already been set.[4]

In many of the issues that have arisen in the development of modern notions of cultural property, including law, legitimacy, identity, history versus heritage, stewardship and trusteeship, appropriation and restitution, the Acropolis of Athens and its buildings (including the parts of the buildings removed by Lord Elgin) have provided a framework for understanding the changing issues. Continuing in that tradition, and as a potential contribution to the wider aims of the volume, I offer in this essay a summary history of ways of looking at the Acropolis and how and when they were constituted, from which some of the contemporary ethical questions emerge. There can be no other monument in the world in which the potential long view is so long, the ways of seeing so different across time, the claims made so varied, and the evidence available for developing answers so complete.

Two general observations underpin everything that follows. First, without viewers, the Acropolis is a culturally inert accumulation of animal, vegetable, and mineral – and even these are categories invented and imputed by human observers. It is the man, woman, or child who looks at the Acropolis who confers the value and makes the meanings, not the Acropolis as such. And, secondly, the transformation in the mind from the physiological act of seeing to the psychological act of interpretation cannot occur unless the experience has been mediated. Any act of looking at the

---

2   Lieut-Col. J.P. Barry, A.B. M.B., *At the Gates of the East: A Book of Travel among Historic Wonderlands* (London: Longman, 1906), pp. vii and 17.

3   *Catalogue of an Exhibition of Lithographs and Etchings of Grecian Temples* by Joseph Pennell (New York: Frederick Keppell, 1913), Preface.

4   The phrase is from Murray's *A Handbook for travellers in the Ionian Islands, Greece, Turkey, Asia Minor, and Constantinople … with maxims and hints for travellers in the East* (London: Murray, 1840), p. 55.

Acropolis, I take as established, has required decisions on the part of the viewer, not normally consciously or explicitly taken, about the organising categories within which the seeing experience is to be understood.[5] The situation today, when all on-the-spot seeing has been prefigured, is only one example of a cognitive process that, we can be confident, has occurred at all times in the past, including during the centuries when there were no pictures and hardly any written words. Even those viewers about whom we know least, such as women and girls forcibly brought from distant alien cultures and immured in the Acropolis as slaves, brought their own interpretative categories, even if it may now be impossible to recover what they were. And, at the other end of the spectrum, I could give long lists of men and women whose sincere accounts of their experience of looking at the Acropolis conform so closely to the conventions of their cultural group that it is impossible to tell from their words alone whether they ever really saw what they describe.

Discussing the relationship of words with images, Socrates is reported by Plato to have remarked:

> Writings, Phaedrus, have a strange quality in which they resemble portraits. They stand before you like living things, but if you ask them a question, they preserve a solemn silence. And it is the same with written words. They seem to talk to you as if they had minds, but if you ask them about what they say, from a wish to understand them more fully, they go on telling you the same thing for ever.[6]

The Acropolis, our generation can readily agree, does not converse, but, with all respect to Socrates, we also know that it does not speak, let alone that it goes on telling the same story forever. The aspiration to 'let the mute stones speak', a proverbial phrase since ancient times, ignores the inescapable fact that no meanings exist in stones, nor indeed in any of the other material remains of the past, until they have been imputed by live human beings applying their own categories. The belief, associated with western romanticism, that great art can transcend its cultural circumstances and material conditions and offer timeless truths direct to the minds of viewers, is itself a mediating category, as historically contingent as the others. The eye, except possibly in newly born babies, is never innocent.

---

5   The general insight by Bloch and others is discussed with reference to the ancient Greek myths by Richard Buxton, *Imaginary Greece: The Contexts of Mythology* (Cambridge: Cambridge University Press, 1994), pp. 80 ff.

6   *Phaedrus*, 275, author's free translation.

Contemporary neuroscience discusses the operation of visual cognitive processes in terms of 'saccades', the eye movements that occur several times every second, and 'salience', the value that the mind attaches to the visual stimuli received, and the reward it hopes to receive by targeting its gaze. The assumption, mainstream until recently and still commonly held, that the act of viewing is a passive receiving of information, has been replaced by an understanding that viewing implies choice. Other assumptions about the ways in which the external world is understood, often categorised as 'natural', 'god-given', or otherwise essentialist or unchanging, that have in past epochs underpinned both the visual production and the consumption of the Acropolis no longer deserve our assent. For centuries, for example, it was generally believed, officially taught, and acted upon, that the human eye sends out light rays to touch the object of vision and returns, bearing the essence of that object. During the centuries of the iconoclasm controversies among competing Christian groupings in the Byzantine period, Athens and its acropolis were part of a society in which theories of anatomy, optics, the nature of light, and what happens to the mind in the act of looking, that have long since been proved to be fallacious, led to many violent deaths.[7] Or, to give a more modern example, when William Hugh Williams, a landscape artist who saw and drew the Acropolis in 1817, and who became known in his day as 'Grecian' Williams, wrote of the 'electrifying truths, which flash upon the mind in studying her ['Nature'] not only as she is, but as seen through the medium of works of genius', he was repeating a cliché of his time that few can now accept. Nor is his assumption that the natural world is designed and benevolent one that can now be accepted.[8]

Our generation can also bring to a history of looking at the Acropolis a modern appreciation of the difficulty of separating mental and bodily states. Emotions engaged by seeing experiences, it is now established, can lead to changes in and beyond the mind/brain, such as a sense of enhanced intensity, which may be mistaken for a confirmation of the validity of some opinion that the viewer already holds, whether of admiration or abhorrence. Dreams too have often been categorised as 'epiphanies' or 'prophecies', messages from supernatural beings or forces, that encourage the wakening dreamer to think and act in certain ways. Viewers of the

---

7   In the words of Liz James: 'Byzantium is the only major world power to have undergone political upheaval on a vast scale as a result of an argument about art'. Liz James (ed.), *Art and Text in Byzantine Culture* (Cambridge: Cambridge University Press, 2007), p. 1.

8   Hugh William Williams, *Travels in Italy, Greece, and the Ionian Islands* (Edinburgh: Constable, 1820), ii, p. 338. Among the predecessors whom he mentions are Poussin and Claude whose paintings he had gone to Italy to study.

Acropolis, acting on such beliefs, have in modern as well as in ancient times sometimes deliberately put themselves into a semi-conscious state in order to experience responses that they believed arrived from outside, and have frequently been encouraged to do so by those who have wished to influence them.

Memories, we can, I suggest, now accept as having been established by the work of Halbwachs and his successors, exist in relationship to a social group, situated in the mental and material spaces provided by, and often invented and maintained by, that group in order to enable them to be organised and conserved.[9] Besides functioning as a theatre of social memory, the Acropolis has itself been a technology of memory both for attempts to invent and control new memory by building and rebuilding, and for policies aimed at destroying and superseding the previously existing memory by knocking down, replacing, and what we may call monument cleansing. To those living in modern and in ancient times, but to a much lesser extent during the long millennium in between, the Acropolis has served as a store of cultural capital.[10]

When UNESCO, the organisation that was established in 1945 in the ruins of the world war, to promote peace 'on the basis of humanity's moral and intellectual solidarity', took the Parthenon as its symbol, it was picking up and reinforcing a tradition of regarding the building as more than an extraordinary survival from an ancient civilisation or as a fine work of architecture. Unlike, say the Pyramids of Egypt, the Acropolis of Athens has in recent centuries been presented, within the western political and artistic traditions, as an inspiration to the modern world, part of a precious identity shared with classical Hellas. And the imputations are themselves part of the history. As a material embodiment of immaterial values that many since the European Renaissance have wished to claim as their own, the Acropolis has provided a focal point for many of the intellectual – and occasionally of the physical – struggles from which the modern world has emerged. If there is a shared western identity, the Acropolis of Athens has participated in the debates and crises that have helped to shape it. Indeed, with its hold over the mental worlds of memory, myth, and fantasy, the

---

9   *Les Cadres Sociaux de la Mémoire* (1925) and *La Mémoire Collective* (1950). Discussed also by Eleni Bastéa, *The Creation of Modern Athens: Planning the Myth* (Cambridge: Cambridge University Press, 2000), pp. 2-6.

10   As far as ancient Athens is concerned, discussed by Bernd Steinbock, *Social Memory in Athenian Public Discourse: Uses and Meanings of the Past* (Ann Arbor, MI: University of Michigan Press, 2012).

Acropolis of the imagination has sometimes played as decisive a role in the course of events as the Acropolis of the stones.

A history of looking at the Acropolis that aims to address the implications of the two starting observations within a framework of established modern knowledge must therefore, I suggest, do more than add new information to the existing histories of the Acropolis as a monument, modifying the accounts and explanations as necessary, although it must try to do that. Nor can it be content with finding examples of people who saw the Acropolis at different times, and summarising what they are reported as saying or thinking or feeling, although it should build up this kind of historical data too. A history that pursues the implications of the two observations within a framework of established modern knowledge must, I suggest, also investigate the means by which the experiences of cultural constituencies were turned into categories, and how, by whom, and on whose authority, these processes of inscription, repetition, and ritualisation helped to establish and mediate ways of seeing, and how, when, and why changes occurred. Although seeing is individual and dynamic, the mediations that condition expectations, and the choices about salience, are social and often stable for long periods of time. And since the mediating, both the immaterial, such as cultural norms, and the material objects, such as the books and the pictures by which norms were constituted, could only have influenced those who already knew their languages, conventions, and genres, it follows too that questions about the nature and extent of the materiality of mediation, including the political economy of how they came into existence in the form that they did, who had access to them and when, and who assented to them or resisted, must also be part of the inquiry.

Until recently, the historic, as distinct from the implied, viewer has been largely absent from art history as practised, or has been conceived of as 'a passive reader or consumer of images'.[11] However, when we try to build a provisional model for conducting an inquiry into the history of the Acropolis as a dynamic cultural system – that is, as a series of transactions rather than as a changing text – we quickly find that the determining role of the mediations cannot simply be attached to the current conventions, leaving them otherwise unchanged. No historic viewer of the Acropolis, has, for example, ever followed the conventions that present the Acropolis as a chronological parade. A history arranged as a series of moments of first production is unable

---

11 The phrase used by Donald Preziosi, *Rethinking Art History: Meditations on a Coy Science* (New Haven, CT and London: Yale University Press, 1989), p. 46.

to accommodate the fact that the monuments of the Acropolis were designed and built so as to be seen into the future as it was then foreseeable, and that they often did continue to be looked at for centuries. It has become common, by those aware of the difficulties implicit in periodisation, to describe the continued existence of public monuments after the time when they were first built as their 'afterlife' from the German *nachleben*. But the word itself draws attention to its own lack of historicity. Except possibly (and to a limited extent) in the case, for example, of the first viewers personally present at the unveiling of a public monument, when the producers and the consumers were members of the same closely defined cultural group, we cannot assume that even broadly contemporaneous viewers categorised, interpreted, or responded in the same way. Since all monuments are attempts to influence viewing experiences beyond the moment when they were first made, their 'afterlife' begins the moment they are born, or in many cases even earlier. Nor have viewers of the Acropolis always, or even normally, privileged the immediately contemporary over the old, nor regarded the no-longer-new as being culturally no longer alive. Most visitors today look more closely at the Parthenon than at the ticket office.

What we can say with confidence is that the producers of the material Acropolis – walls, buildings, public and private dedications and inscriptions, sculptures, pictures, and symbols – have always wanted it to carry visual signs to live viewers, actual and potential, with the hope, intention, and expectation that meanings made by these viewers would be accepted, internalised, and acted upon. Indeed a wish to offer viewers a means of understanding the relationship between the then present, the then past, and the then future, was among the explicitly stated aims of those who built the classical Acropolis and by others later. And there has never been a time from the present back to classical times and earlier, when viewers did not see ruined as well as functioning buildings, and attempt to draw lessons from the experience. A study that faces the implications of the two observations is therefore, I suggest, certain to be different from a history (or an art history, or an archaeological history) of the stones, and cannot be derived solely from such histories. The theories and mediations, that coexisted and competed, form complex time patterns of their own that do not coincide with one another, let alone with the conventions of a chronological parade. When, however, we relocate the site where meanings are made to the minds of viewers, and admit them as active participants in a complex dynamic system, we may begin to undertake the more ambitious task of tracing the effects of cultural production through to cultural consumption, to the resultant construction of group mentalities, and on to real world consequences in at least some cases.

The fact that there are mismatches between current and past ways of seeing is, of course, well understood, as is the difficulty of the imaginative leap needed to emancipate even the recent past from modern assumptions. *The Past is a Foreign Country* was the title of one of David Lowenthal's pioneering studies of the notion of heritage published in 1985.[12] For more than a generation, scholars have rightly emphasised the need to recover and historicise past discursive practices, including ways of seeing, that were based on assumptions that have since been rendered untenable. My approach may meet the comment, associated with post-colonial theory, that I am imposing modern western European scientific and Enlightenment categories on societies whose world views were different and who valued different kinds of knowledge. In recent times, for example, some have re-conceptualised the notion of myth as 'meaningful history', an attempt to soften the distinction between a search for reliable knowledge of what actually happened in the past from a search for understandings of how the mediated past impinged on the minds of the people alive at any particular time.[13] However, although assessing the past within its own discursive terms may appear to protect the modern historian from the charge of condescension, it risks turning history into a mere collecting and chronicling of past stories that we now know to be untrue, an antiquarianism condemned to perpetual imprisonment within its own artificial conventions.

Preferable, I suggest, is to find a way that neither ignores the otherness of the past, nor adopts the reactionary fallacy that modern scientific and Enlightenment knowledge is just another passing discourse whose claims are no stronger than those of its many predecessors and modern competitors. Nor need such an approach accept a relativist position that all the pasts of the Acropolis are, or should be regarded as, of equal interest to the present day, what Werner Jaeger, the champion of the unique value of Hellenism, despairingly called 'a night in which all cats are grey'.[14] Rather, while accepting that my approach is inescapably a product of my time, as

---

12 'The past is a foreign country: they do things differently there', the opening lines of the novel, *The Go-Between*, by L.P. Hartley (1953), was made popular by the film of the same name.
13 Quoted by Steinbock, 2012, p. 8. Other terms he notes are 'usable past', 'imagined and remembered history', 'cultural memory', 'believed history', and 'intentional history'.
14 Werner Jaeger, Paideia, *The Ideals of Greek Culture*, trans. Gilbert Highet, 2nd edition, 3rd printing (New York: Oxford University Press, 1960), p. xxv.

well as an attempt to escape from it, I would say that recovering a critical understanding of the succession of pasts and how those who inhabited them understood their own pasts and possible futures, can both lessen the risks to our intellectual independence and improve our understanding of our present situation.

***

So how could such a history of looking best be attempted? How can we write a history of transactions rather than of texts, of minds as well as of things? History, in the sense of the past as it occurred, has proceeded chronologically, but historiography is inescapably counter-chronological, a looking back in time from a here and now. And, as was remarked by Karl Marx:

> Men make their own history, but they do not make it just as they please; they do not make it under circumstances chosen by themselves, but under circumstances directly encountered, given and transmitted from the past. The tradition of all the dead generations weighs like a mountain on the brain of the living.[15]

In the approach that I adopt, broadly counter-chronological with detours, I propose to excavate the conceptual and organising categories that were applied in various pasts, in the hope of discovering how they came into being, were circulated, modified, subsequently overlaid, and sometimes acted upon. In re-imagining the past, it may be safer to move in steps from one layer back to its immediate predecessor, thus developing an incremental understanding of how the imagined past has come down to us, than to risk making a single large leap from the here and now. Indeed the history of modern attempts to understand ancient Hellas is so replete with examples of cultural constituencies projecting back their own ideologies that it would be possible to read it as a set of reminders of the risks. Although concentrated on one specific object, this essay can therefore be taken as a response to Michel Foucault's call for an 'archaeology' or a 'genealogy' of knowledge, remembering that Foucault was not a theorist *qua* theorist, nor an ideologue, but a thinker whose ideas were founded upon his historical, critical, and Enlightenment-inspired attempt to understand the otherness of the past, including ancient Hellas.

For such a study, the Acropolis of Athens offers some unique advantages. Indeed it is probably only the presence of these unique advantages that makes a project with so many factors and feedbacks potentially feasible.

---

15 Translated from the opening paragraph of *The 18th Brumaire of Louis Bonaparte* (1852).

Firstly, the record is unusually full and long. From the time when the Homeric poems were composed and recited (eighth or ninth century BC), and probably long before that, there have been many people living far from Athens who knew enough about the Acropolis to recognise allusions in both epics. And there have been few times since then when some knowledge of the Acropolis has not been passed far from Athens across time and distance by word of mouth, by oral literature, by writings carried in manuscript and print, and by other media. And besides the direct reports of those who actually visited Athens, we also have many writings that were composed and promulgated in an attempt to influence ways of viewing. Admonitory writings, provided we read them as indications of recommended ways of seeing, stories that attempt to make the mute stones speak, rather than as examples of records of actual individual experiences, are a major resource, especially for the long periods of time when we have few others. Indeed for the task of recovering mainstream ways of seeing, the clichéd, the humdrum, the derivative, and even the fake, are particularly useful, and fortunately they are abundant.

Since the sources, although plentiful, are at all epochs heavily weighted towards those produced by males from the richer socio-economic groups, we are put on our methodological guard against arguing from the anecdotal to the general. Paradoxically, among the constituencies who have been largely lost from the record are the people who spent much of their lives within the Acropolis precincts, such as the men and women who looked after the buildings and serviced the rituals, the soldiers of the garrisons, and their women and slaves.

A second huge and specific advantage is that, as an object of study, the Acropolis constitutes its own visual and interpretative frame. Some of the locations in and around Athens from which viewers have chosen to look at the Acropolis, and from which artists have presented their pictures, the – using a term adopted by Adam Smith – 'viewing stations' were consistent for centuries, and we can be confident that it was to influence the seeing experience of viewers standing on these stations that the built Acropolis was designed during some epochs at least.[16] The Acropolis matches the classic definitions of landscape pioneered by J.B. Jackson and W.G. Hoskins as 'a portion of the earth's surface that can be comprehended at a glance', but also as a text that is open to be read, and as a dynamic cultural process by which, by selective emphasis and exaggeration, human identities are

---

16 Adam Smith, 'Of the Nature of that Imitation which takes place in what are called the Imitative Arts', in *Essays on Philosophical Subjects* (London, 1795), pp. 131-84.

constituted.[17] Like a literary text in a book, or a painting hung in a picture gallery, that is as an object of view already boundaried, the Acropolis can therefore be read, both historically, within past contexts, and critically in accordance with whatever modern criteria we may choose to apply.

A third specific advantage is that, throughout its long history, the Acropolis has always been an officially controlled site. The legal as well as *de facto* ownership of the Acropolis, recognised against the legal norms of each epoch, including right of conquest and treaty of surrender, can be traced back, through a succession of suzerainties, to ancient times more or less continuously from 10th of April 1833 – the day when it was handed over to the government of the recently established Greek nation state, and its modern history began. Apart from occasional catastrophes of earthquake, fire, sacking or bombardment, every substantial change – whether the first flattening of the summit, the clearance of caves or the vegetation, the building of temporary barriers and walls, the digging of pits, the design and the placement of fortifications, buildings, statues, and inscriptions, as well as their later removal – has required the approval of the authorities then in control, including those whose occupation was short-lived. Removals from the site, of which there have been many, have also required approval. In considering how changes to the appearance of the Acropolis came about, the study need not therefore be thrown back on, or restricted to, notions of cultural emergence or emanation, that equate the minds of viewers with those of artists as expressed in their production, and is liable to fall into circularity and romanticism. It is legitimate to discuss the whole history of the Acropolis, including the classical Acropolis, in terms of the aims, intentions, and hopes of the successive producers of its appearance, including the theories of cognition and of art and iconicity that influenced their decisions, without of course assuming that they were always successful in their aims. Because the sources are so rich we are also able to recover the political regulatory and the economic processes that brought about the material Acropolis in various forms at various epochs. In addition to the cultural agendas we can recover the formal administrative processes by which approvals were given and projects financed (including by slave or forced labour) and then executed and accepted.

Introducing the political economy component brings out the extent to which the determining decisions about the appearance of the Acropolis,

---

17 See the Introduction to I. Robertson and P. Richards (eds.), *Studying Cultural Landscapes* (London: Arnold, 2003) and W.J.T. Mitchell, *Landscape and Power* (Chicago: Chicago University Press, 1994).

and often also how it should be mediated in words and pictures, were taken not locally in Athens, but in ancient Rome, in Byzantine Nicaea and Constantinople, in Ottoman Istanbul, and in the capitals and other cities of modern western countries. Moreover decisions were often made or influenced by governments and international authorities and agencies, whose agendas did not necessarily coincide with the wishes of the local people of Athens, insofar as they are knowable. With the exception of the classical period, almost all the written and visual works on which we are reliant for a history of looking were not produced locally in Athens, and even in the classical period many of the most famous writers, such as Aristotle, came from elsewhere. The thought, still heard occasionally, that you have to be Athenian to understand the Acropolis, that implies an essentialism of nationalism, is especially out of place for a monument that has, for most of its history, been culturally constructed far from Athens, and that, even in the classical period, counted a wish to influence non-Athenians among its explicit aims.

Among the producers of the Acropolis, I therefore include the proposers and the instigators, the political and other institutions who voted the funds, the designers, engineers, architects, artists, skilled and other workers, whether forced or voluntary, both those who built and those who destroyed, replaced, adapted or altered. Among the producers I also include the intermediaries who composed, made accessible, and published visual representations, and those who attempted to regulate or influence the viewing experiences of others, such as political (including religious) leaders, authors and educators. Among the consumers, I include both those who saw the Acropolis directly with their own eyes and those who encountered it from a distance in images and words.

***

So let me begin the dig by offering a photograph of the Parthenon today, probably the most valued view of the Acropolis in recent times. Figure 5.1 shows a view of the Parthenon that at the time of writing opens up to the visitor arriving on the summit and following the tourist path. The pictures I show are mediations of mediations, and this offers advantages as well as potential losses. The once clear air of Athens, that was uniquely well captured by the technology of coloured aquatint, is now made even clearer when seen with the computer light behind in the online version. And we can use zooms to improve our appreciation of how visual technologies achieved their effects.

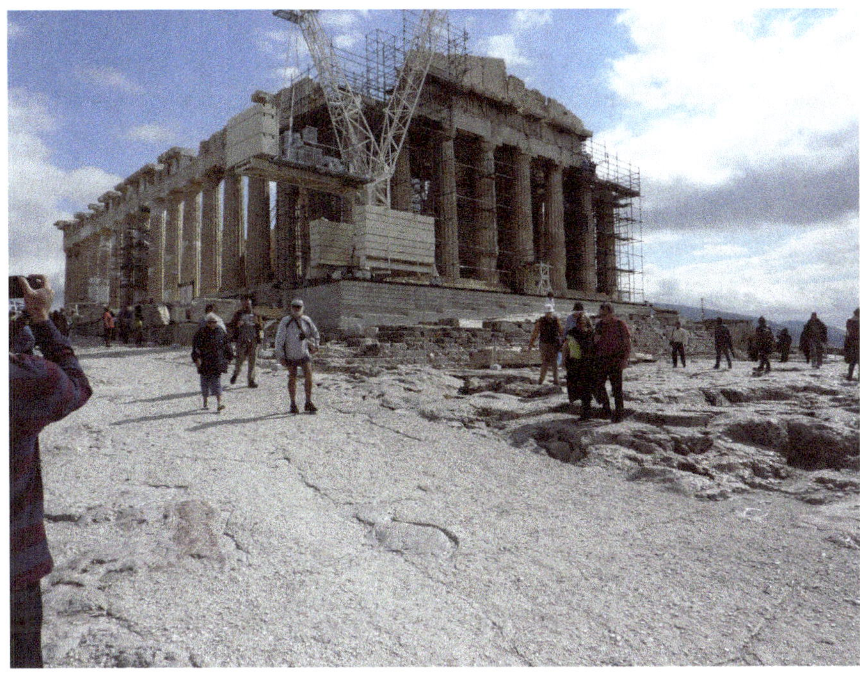

Fig. 5.1 The Parthenon from the north-west.

This is the temporary, constantly changing, Parthenon that visitors encounter and have encountered during the recent decades of conservation. It coexists with images of the timeless Parthenon, shown without scaffolding or people, that appears on the entrance tickets given to visitors, as shown in Figure 5.2.

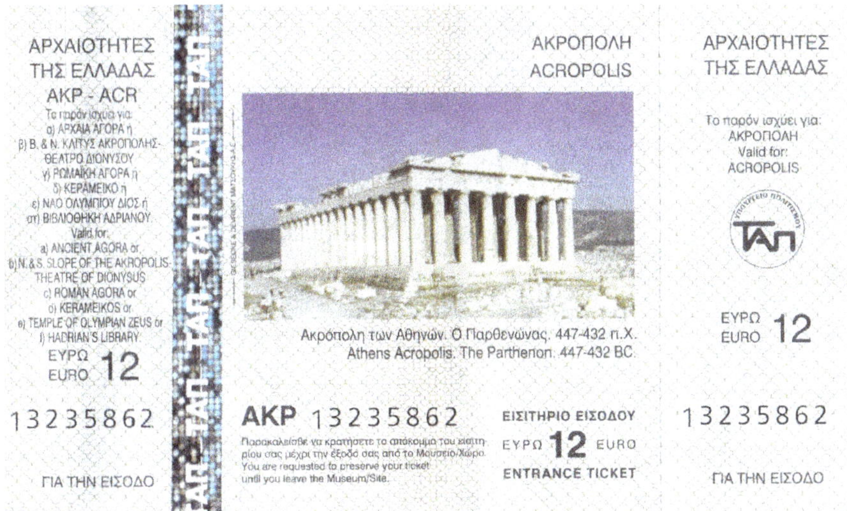

Fig. 5.2 The Parthenon from the north-west.

It is, almost without exception, the timeless Parthenon that is reproduced in the postcards, on the covers of guidebooks, and in the windows and frontages of the shops and kiosks that surround the Acropolis, and elsewhere. A periphery of iconicity, we can say, pre-sets the Acropolis viewing experience before visitors reach the site. And although there are occasional grumbles that the conservation works are taking too long, contemporary viewers appear to have no difficulty in cognitively negotiating both images simultaneously, eliding the scaffolds as easily as they elide the other apparently temporary, but in reality permanent, modern fixtures that they see on the Acropolis, such as the lamps for floodlighting. And just as the principles of the Venice Charter on the conservation of monuments, with which the recent Acropolis programme conforms, requires that viewers of the Acropolis buildings are able to distinguish the ancient marble from the new used in repairs, that is, to operate simultaneously in two temporalities, they also operate simultaneously at different levels of cognition, seeing the actual stones, imagining what has been lost, and often also according the experience some wider signification and meaning.[18] In Figures 5.3, 5.4, and 5.5, I trace the view back through the era of photography.

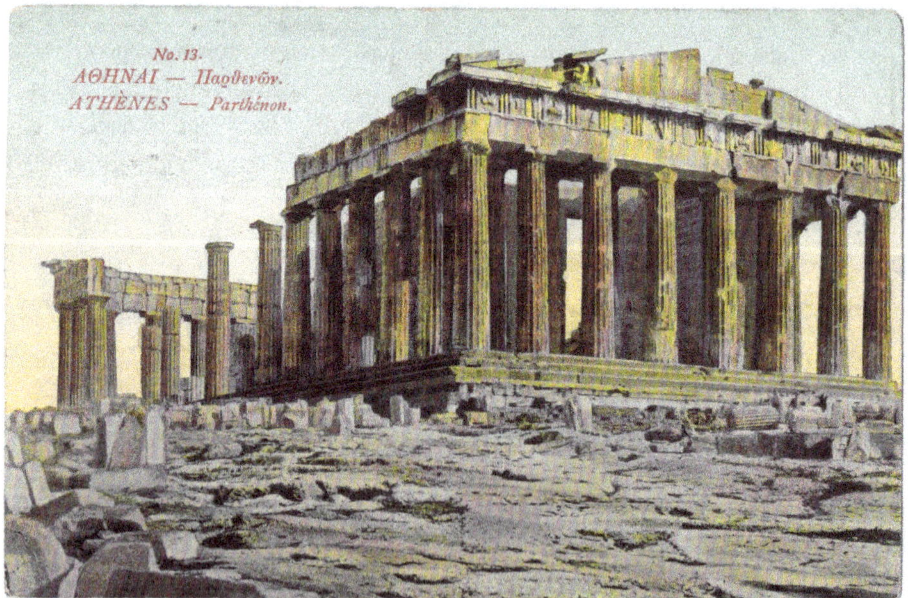

Fig. 5.3 The Parthenon from the north-west, c.1909 before the re-erection of the colonnade in the 1920s.

---

18 See http://www.international.icomos.org/charters/venice_e.pdf.

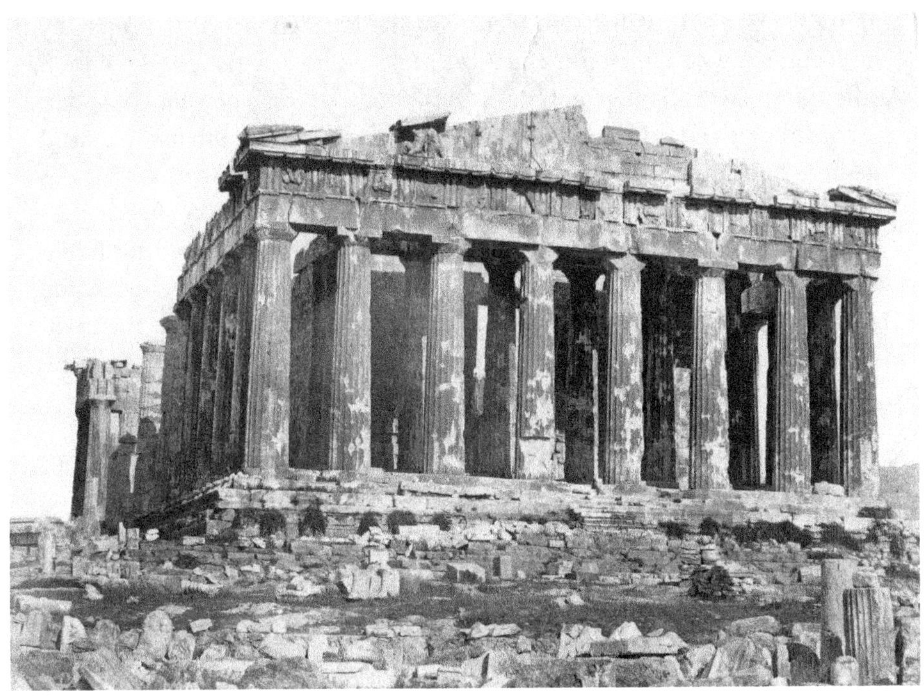

Fig. 5.4 The Parthenon from the north-west.

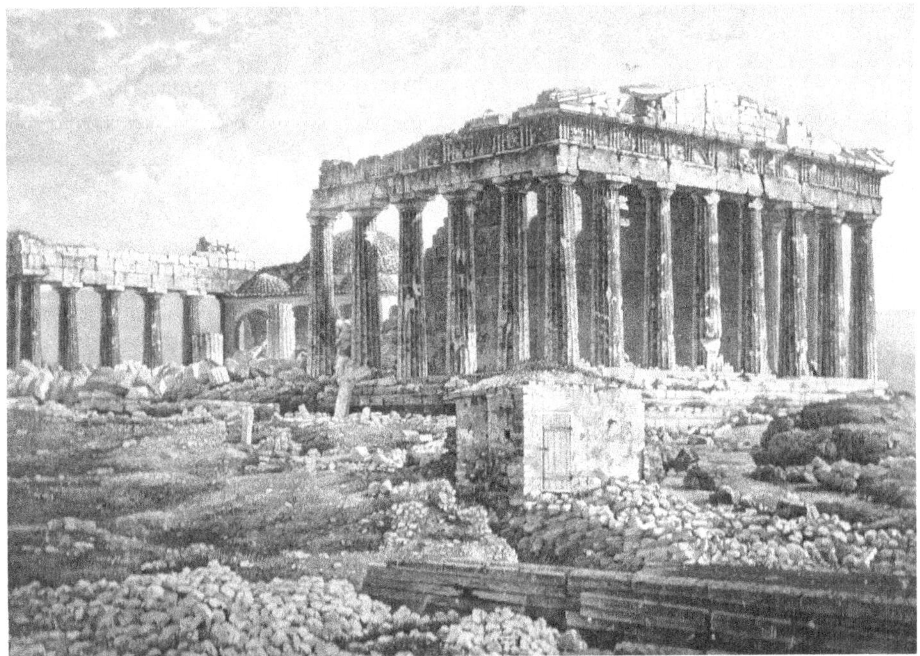

Fig. 5.5 The Parthenon from the north-west, autumn 1839.

Figure 5.5 reproduces the first picture of the Parthenon made directly by the technology of light on a chemical plate without artistic intervention, although since the daguerreotype camera produced only one copy it had to be copied by an engraver. It shows how the lens of the camera made central the little building that the salience of the selecting eye of a human viewer elided or ignored. The building was physically removed soon after.

The image reproduced as Figure 5.6, frequently re-engraved for half a century, accompanied *The Travels of the Younger Anacharsis in Greece*, the book on ancient Greece that was most often encountered in all the main languages across western Europe and elsewhere from 1788 until into the age of photography and beyond.

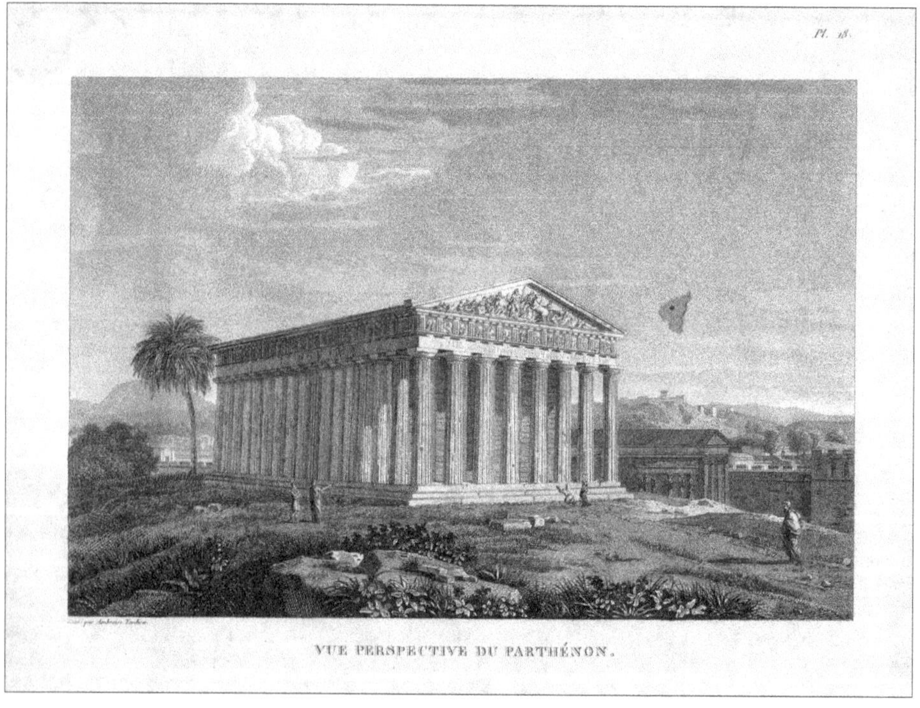

Fig. 5.6 The Parthenon as it appeared in antiquity, as imagined in 1788.

Since the 1830s, the actual Acropolis has gradually come to match the engravings of the eighteenth century whose artists imagined how the Parthenon appeared in antiquity. It derives from the explicitly stated aim of those who, in 1834, decided that the four principal ancient buildings should be visible from all sides.[19] They regarded the buildings primarily as

____

19 Costas Tsarouchas [publisher], 'Akropolis von Athen.' Facsimiles, with translations, and

free-standing works of architecture – rather than as a complex of stories in stone in which the official memory and values of the ancient *polis* had been visually presented and around which they had been ritually performed. And it was not only the Parthenon as a building that was iconised but an interpretative frame that excluded just as it included. We also see that the net effect of the successive conservation interventions till now has been, step by step, to make the real Parthenon resemble the Parthenon as imagined in the eighteenth century. The most recent interventions, such as the introduction, for conservation and tourist-management purposes, of the roped-off concrete path shown in Figure 5.1, have helped to entrench that way of seeing the monument even further.

Figure 5.7 reproduces a view of how the Acropolis summit looked when there was still a town on the summit, the Acropolis, taken from an imagined viewing station that was not available, except to birds.

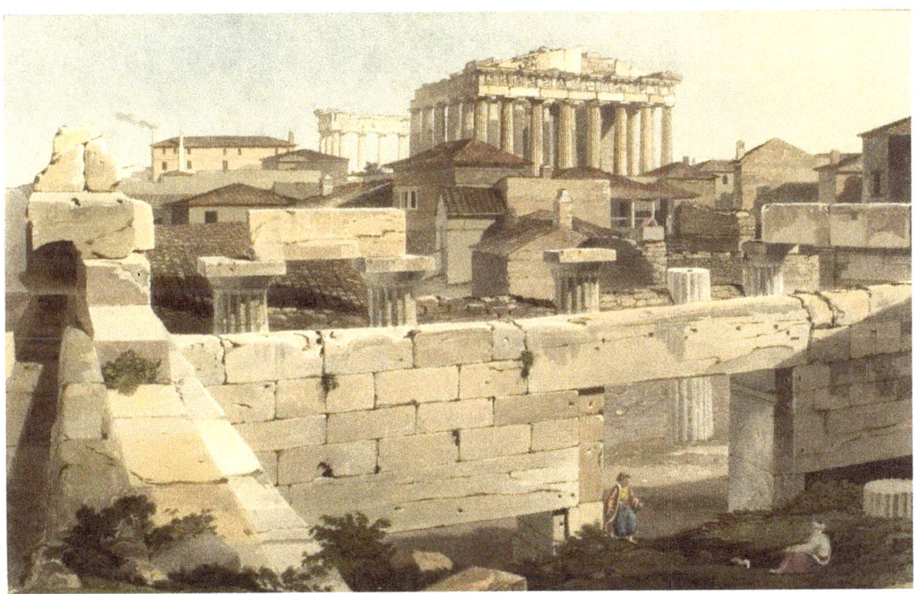

Fig. 5.7 The Parthenon from the north-west, c.1805.

The modern view of the Parthenon only became available when the town was removed in the nineteenth century. In this clearance the unsculpted marble, stones, and tiles, almost everything that could be recycled as

comments on, a selection of twenty documents from the official papers in a file of the Bavarian Regency Government, 1834 to 1842 (Athens: Alethea, 2012), p. 29, translated from the German. The decision was explicitly noted by Charles Lévèque, 'Les Etudes archéologiques en Grèce', *Revue des Deux Mondes*, August 1851, p. 646.

building materials, was sold and are now spread through modern Athens. Enormous quantities of earth, and the remains of eight thousand years of human and animal occupation, several metres deep, were dumped over the walls on three sides as shown in Figure 5.8.

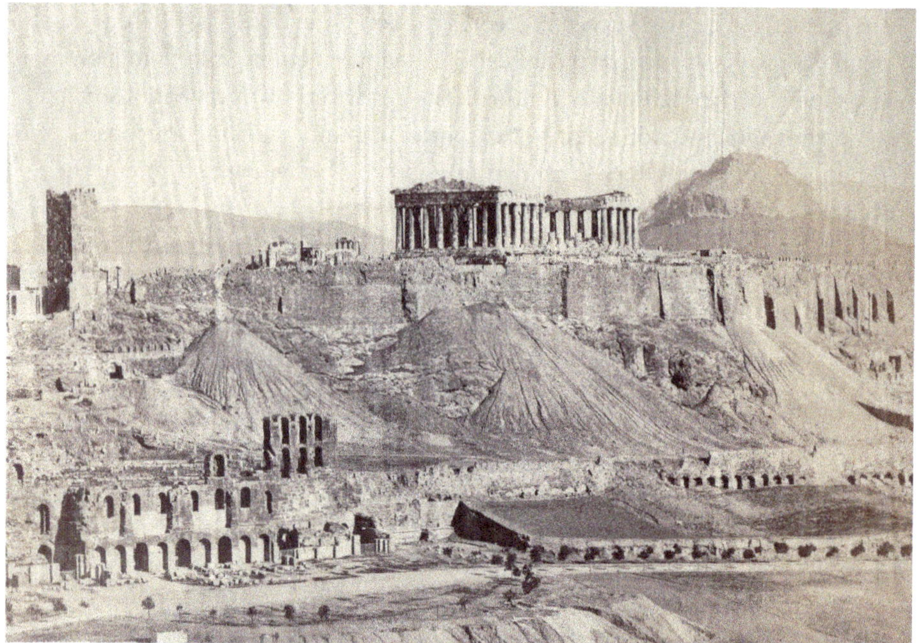

Fig 5.8 The Acropolis south slopes around 1858.

The present Acropolis summit, we can say, is a triumph of science and archaeology, but it is also the result of a quite narrow way of viewing that looks at ancient architecture, and even at ancient architectural sculpture, as discreet 'works of art', with insufficient regard to cityscape, context, or function.

One point about the recent conservation programme has, in my view, not been sufficiently appreciated. Without fanfare, the ancient path that circles the Acropolis on its slopes, long cordoned off with fences and barbed wire, has recently been reopened. Visitors can now visit more sites, both natural and man-made, look at more vistas, and experience more ways of seeing both directly and in their historical imagination, than have been possible for half a century or more. The old photograph reproduced in Figure 5.9, taken when the Acropolis vegetation had been temporarily scrubbed out, records a view of part of the ancient path that is no longer so clearly available.

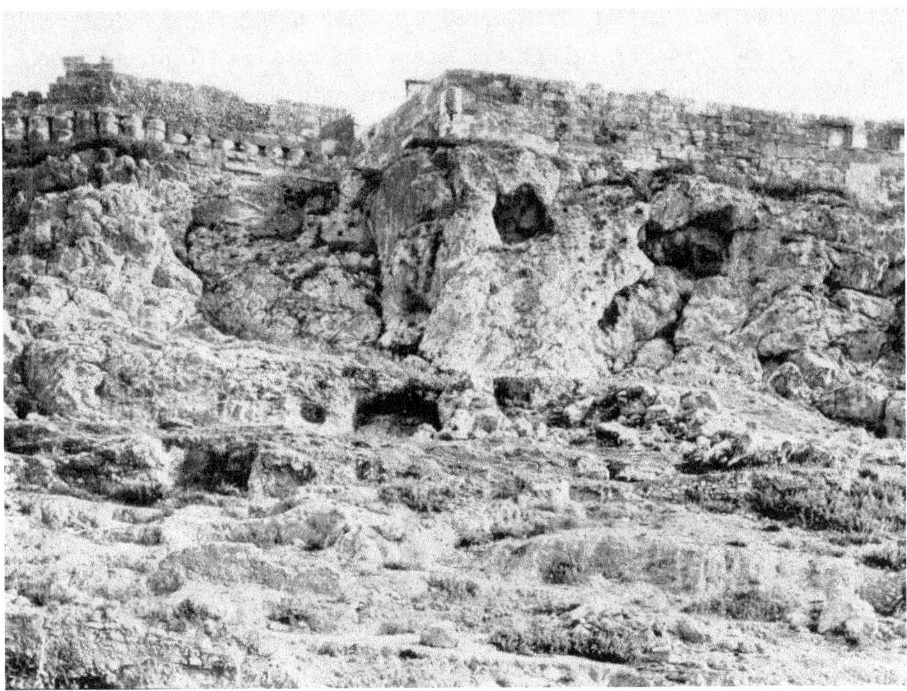

Fig. 5.9 The ancient path on the north side under the caves.

To the viewer looking up from the old town, as well as from distances far beyond to the north, the row of column drums built conspicuously into the defensive summit walls, still catches the attention. They are among the remains of the pre-classical buildings that were destroyed by the Persian invaders in 480 BC. The Athenians of the classical age and later looking up from the centre of town, the *agora* where much of the daily life occurred, encountered every day this permanent reminder of the foreign invasion that had once destroyed their material city, but not the real city, the people.[20] It was the remains of the older, destroyed, Parthenon that they mostly saw in their daily lives, not its classical replacement that lies outside the sightlines from the town on this side.

The path round the slopes was not an informal track beaten through the vegetation made by generations of trespassing feet, although there are

___

20 That the drums had been deliberately placed on the walls so as to be a visual reminder to the town below, suggested by Ludwig Ross in the 1830s and probably by others earlier, is discussed by Manolis Korres in 'A Conversation with Manolis Korres, Athena's Worship and the Semiology of the Monuments of the Acropolis', in M. Korres et al. (eds.), *Dialogues on the Acropolis. Scholars and Experts Talk on the History, Restoration and the Acropolis Museum* (Athens: Skai Books, 2010), p. 144.

some of these too. Cut into the rock the path was a designed and engineered feature of the Acropolis and of the cityscape that, we can be confident, must have been officially approved and financed by the city's authorities at some moment in the remote past. Visually, as was noted by Aelios Aristides in his panegyric of 155 AD, the road that circled the acropolis of a Hellenic city was like a jewelled necklace, that unified as well as adorned.[21] Inside, until the nineteenth century, many caves were brightly coloured and lit. The acropolis of Smyrna, a colony of Athens that followed many of its customs, was according to Aristides, laid out like an embroidered gown, another comparison that reminds us that women were included in the metaphors, as well as in much of the iconography, of the ancient city.

Also visible from the town, and now visitable, is the Cave of Pan. Figure 5.10 shows the present view looking out over the ancient agora, with the Hephaisteion in the distance.

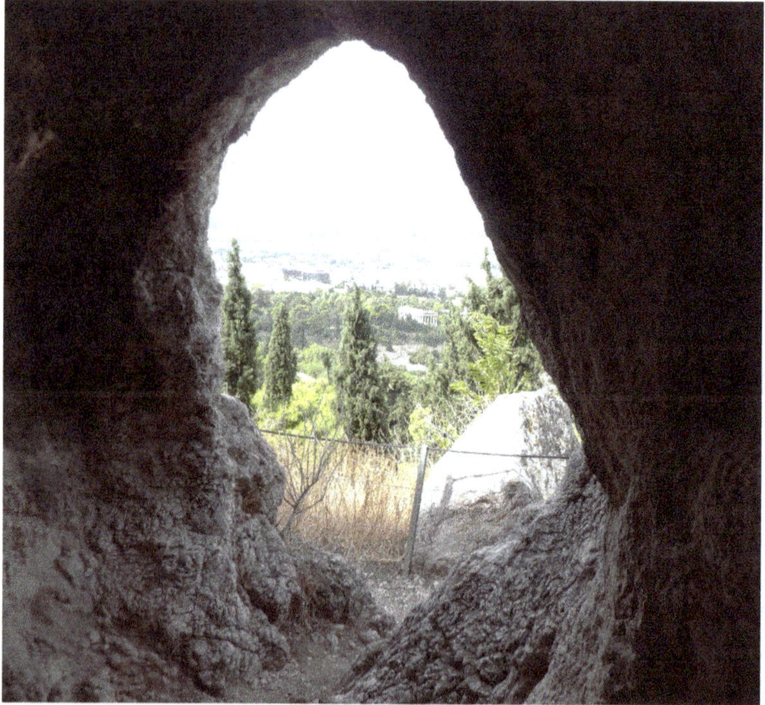

Fig. 5.10 The cave of Pan on the north slope, looking out.

---

21 P. Aelius Aristides, 'A Monody for Smyrna', in *The Complete Works, vol. II: Orationes XVII-LIII*, ed. and trans. Charles A. Behr (Leiden: Brill, 1986), p. 7. Aristides imagines a viewer looking down from above, but the metaphor works well looking from ground level.

It was here, as the story was retold by Euripides, that Creusa was raped by Apollo and to here that she secretly returned to give birth.[22] Pan was given the Cave by the Athenians as a reward for spreading 'panic' among the enemy at the battle of Marathon, but as we know from the satirist Lucian, he did not much like it. It was noisy and cramped as I can confirm. The Athenians occasionally killed a goat in his honour, inappropriate, Pan thought, for he was half goat himself. No wonder, as Lucian tells us, Pan hated paying the tax as a non-domiciled resident, a non-dom.[23]

On the ancient path, visitors can now stand on the exact spot where in classical Athens the young male Athenian citizens under military training took their oath to defend the city and what it held sacred, and to increase its power.[24] They can share the vistas across to the surrounding mountains and seas that visually enclose the territory within its natural amphitheatre, confident that most of the famous men of classical Athens, whether poets, playwrights, philosophers, historians, or politicians, once stood on this exact spot, regarding themselves at that moment as citizen-soldiers. Standing in ranks with the steep Acropolis crags at their backs, the young men were obliged by the steepness of the Acropolis slope to look forward and outward, and to hold their ranks without jostling, as they might soon have to stand in a real battle. Many rituals began on the slopes where the view was outward and unlimited to the horizon, before moving to the summit where the view is inward and confined. In ancient drama too, comedy as well as tragedy, the Acropolis slopes and the horizons of mountains and sea were always in sight, with many of the best known ancient stories, such as those surrounding the families of Orestes and Oedipus, firmly anchored to the visible landscape, both close up, and to the mountains and seas on the horizons.

The Acropolis summit, especially now, is a place of imposed order, a clean, bare, enclosed, controlled environment of straight lines, built by human hands, where the natural world is unwelcome – every sprouting plant is immediately weeded out. In ancient Athens, the paths and the caves of the slopes were also integral to the ceremonial, ritual, and formal life of the whole city, important to the cults favoured by non-citizens and slaves of both sexes as much as to those of citizens and their official wives and

---

22 In the *Ion*.

23 Lucian, *Double Indictment*, 9.

24 The words of the oath are quoted by Lycurgus, Against Leocrates, i, 77. The wording may have changed over the centuries but its essence remained unchanged and familiar, as was shown by P. Siewert, 'The Ephebic Oath in Fifth-Century Athens', *Journal of Hellenic Studies*, 97, 1977, pp. 102-11.

daughters.[25] The *peripatos* too, a word that brings out the role of the path as a place for peripatetics, performed social functions beyond its usefulness as a road along which to move from A to B. As an unsupervised meeting place, it allowed, for example, political conspirators and transgressing lovers to escape inquiring eyes. As Lucian reports, Pan used to say that he had a thing or two he could tell about what he saw from his cave after nightfall.[26] A modern psychologist might look on the Acropolis as a layer of conscious human rationality resting on an unconscious swirl of dreams, desires, and fears.

Today I think it is fair to say that the dominant way of looking at the Acropolis is as an archaeological and art-historical site. But it is also often invested with modern political messages. That the Acropolis celebrates ancient Athenian democracy is often presented as a fact — Athens as the birthplace, or the cradle, of democracy, the political ancestor of modern democratic nation states.[27] When we dig down through the layers, however, we find that this imputation is seldom made before the mid-nineteenth century.[28] From the epigraphic evidence of over forty cities it now appears that, in the classical period, Athens was not unique in having a democratic form of government, nor was Athens the first.[29] And although the Parthenon was commissioned during the century when classical Athens was governed by a democracy, albeit one confined to male citizens, there is little or nothing democratic in the iconography of the buildings, that, as throughout the Hellenic world, present traditional scenes from local and pan-Hellenic myths as was the convention long before the democracy began and continued after it had gone.

---

25 The numerous peri-acropolitan cults are discussed by, for example, Robert Parker, *Polytheism and Society at Athens* (Oxford: Oxford University Press, 2005), p. 52. For the sanctuaries and cults on the slopes, and some recent photographs, see the conversation with Constantinos Tsakos in Korres et al., 2010, pp. 166-87.

26 *Double Indictment*, 11.

27 For example 'The Athenian Democracy pervades all in the classical Acropolis', Korres et al., 2010, p. 7.

28 A moment of transition may be Edward Bulwer Lytton's *Athens: Its Rise and Fall, With Views of the Literature, Philosophy, and Social Life of the Athenian People*, first published in 1837 in which, as the full title indicates, the cultural achievement is brought into the political and moral history, although only as a supplement. The grand narrative histories of the eighteenth century, including Mitford and Ferguson, mostly favoured Sparta over Athens, and presented 'democracy' as a political system to be feared (summarised by Oswyn Murray in his introduction to the bicentenary edition). In 1873, the historian Edward A Freeman, in an essay 'The Athenian Democracy', *Historical Essays, Second Series* (London: Macmillan, 1873) suggested that 'the pre-eminence of Athens in literature, philosophy and art' was the result, not the cause, of its democracy.

29 Eric W. Robinson, *Democracy beyond Athens: Popular Government in the Greek Classical Age* (Cambridge: Cambridge University Press, 2011).

Another political way of looking at the Acropolis is to see it as a monument to the continuity of modern Greece back to ancient Hellas. In the recent book prepared by the experts who managed the Acropolis conservation programme, the point was put in the form of a question: 'Why is it that Greeks regard these monuments as being theirs, regardless of whether or not they visit them regularly or whether they really know them? Why do they regard them as their very own, their "home", the trademark of Greece through the ages and of the present day?'[30] This way of looking appears to be no longer much emphasised in Greece itself, being for example, largely absent from the official educational programmes for Greek children visiting the Acropolis.[31] One of the clearest statements can be found in the speech of Melina Mercouri of 12 June 1986, when as the Minister of Culture, speaking in English, she addressed the students of the Oxford Union in England: 'You must understand what the Parthenon Marbles mean to us. They are our pride. They are our sacrifices. They are our noblest symbol of excellence. They are a tribute to the democratic philosophy. They are our aspirations and our name. They are the essence of Greekness'.[32]

Like many nation states, in the nineteenth century Greece produced a series of long, often learned, and apparently authoritative, histories that, by mixing historical fact, myth, ideology, and some self-congratulation, gave a unified narrative to the imagined community of 'the nation' as a metaphysical entity continuing in its essentials unchanged across time and situation. The historian Constantinos Paparrigopoulos, for example, in his six volume work, first published between 1860 and 1877, commented on the long period between modern and ancient Hellas: 'The city of Athens still preserved its ancient traditions, its love of beauty and reverence for the masterpieces of art … These descendants of the Athenians of the age of Pericles had indeed forgotten how to cultivate literature and the arts, but they had preserved the nobility of their race, and although they had lost its intellectual force, they retained its reverence for all that stirred the enthusiasm of their ancestors'.[33] Despite much searching in recent decades, however, no-one has found any evidence for the local Christian Orthodox community before the Greek Revolution associating their own identity with the ancient ruins before

---

30 Blurb to Korres et al., 2010.

31 The current official education programmes are described by Cornelia Hatziaslani in Korres et al., 2010, pp. 426-43.

32 Available on the website of the Melina Mercouri Foundation: http://www.melina mercourifoundation.org.gr/index.php?option=com_content&view=article&id=73&Item id=49&lang=en

33 Quoted in translation by Demetrios Sicilianos, *Old and New Athens* (London: Putnam, 1960), pp. 20-21.

the 1790s, and that was under influences from expatriates.[34] Nor is this surprising as the last thing a theocracy wants is democracy, especially when it is associated – as it was in ancient Athens – with open intellectual debate. An example of the transplanting of philhellenism into Greece, where it has since become native, is shown as Figure 5.11.

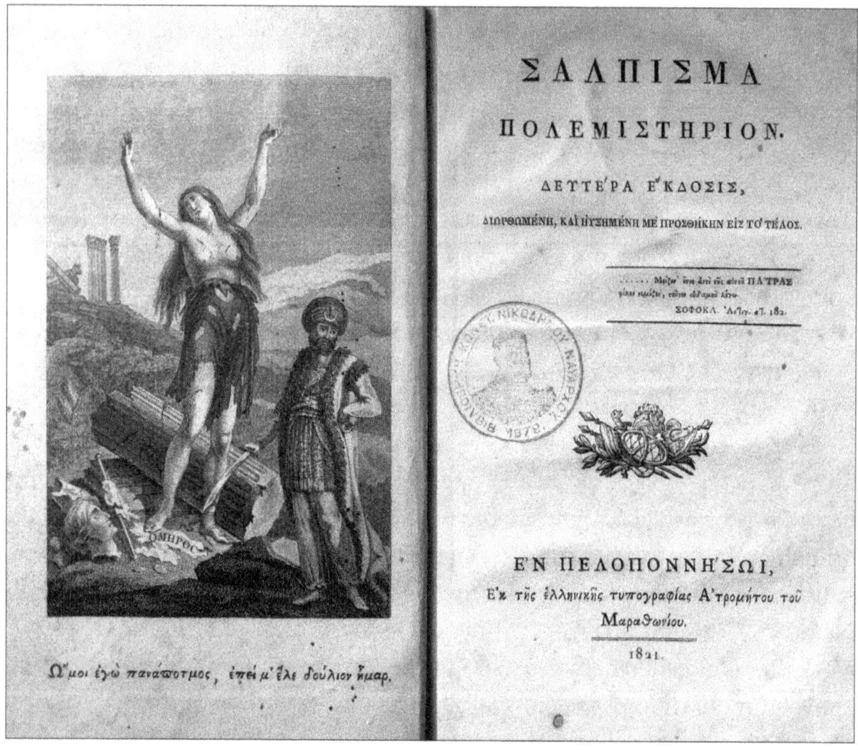

Fig. 5.11 Greece, invoking Homer and the ruins of ancient Hellas, calls on Europe for help, 1821.

Without implying that they are invalid just because they are historically contingent, we can note that all the main contemporary ways of looking at the Acropolis, the archaeological, the art historical, the romantic aesthetic, and the political, were invented and introduced during the last two centuries.

***

Within a few years of the advent of photography, more images of the Acropolis had been produced and distributed than in all previous millennia put together.

---

34 A process discussed by, among others, Yannis Hamilakis, *The Nation and its Ruins: Antiquity, Archaeology, and National Imagination in Greece* (Oxford: Oxford University Press, 2007).

The photographers, while purporting to offer images that are direct analogues of reality ('the camera cannot lie'), that the photo-chemical technology appears to guarantee, soon adopted the techniques of fashion, advertising, opera and cinema, to produce imagined but unseeable images, using long ladders and special cameras to shoot from viewing stations that never existed in modern or ancient times. Figures 5.12 and 5.13 are examples of these images, icons of icons, a vision of an Eternal Greece produced for a global viewership.[35] In 'Eternal Greece', there are usually no people, nor any clues to when the images were made. By eliminating contingency, they eliminate time. Some, such as the example in Figure 5.13, are deliberately archaised.

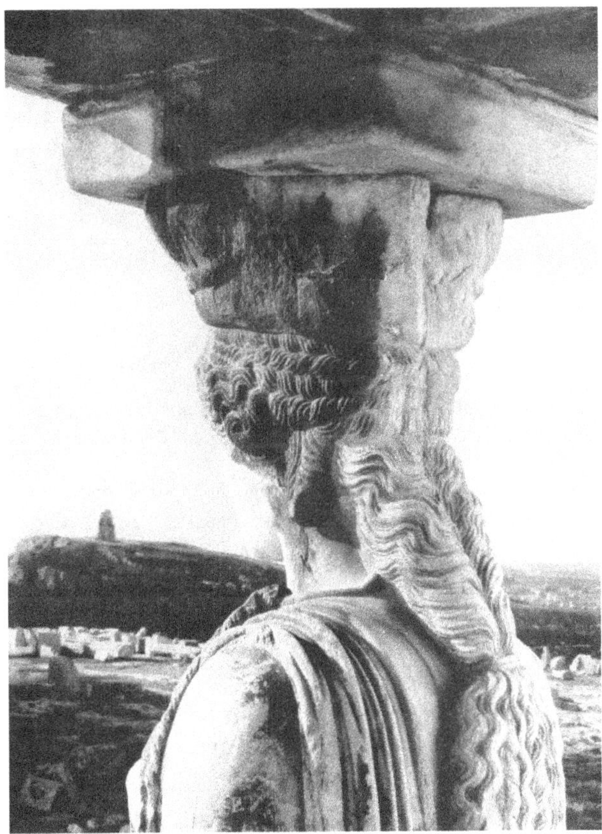

Fig. 5.12 Caryatid looking towards Philopappus, 1929.

---

35 The main pioneers and practitioners of the style from the arrival of photography to the mid-twentieth century include, in rough chronological order, Robertson, Stillman, Bonfils, Gkinakou, Margaritis, Constantine, Boissonas, Sebah of Constantinople, Antoine Bon, 'Nelly', Alnari, Ponten, Boudot LaMotte, Sirén, Hoyningen-Huene, Hege, Hürlimann, Herbert List, Lukas, and for moving images Riefenstahl.

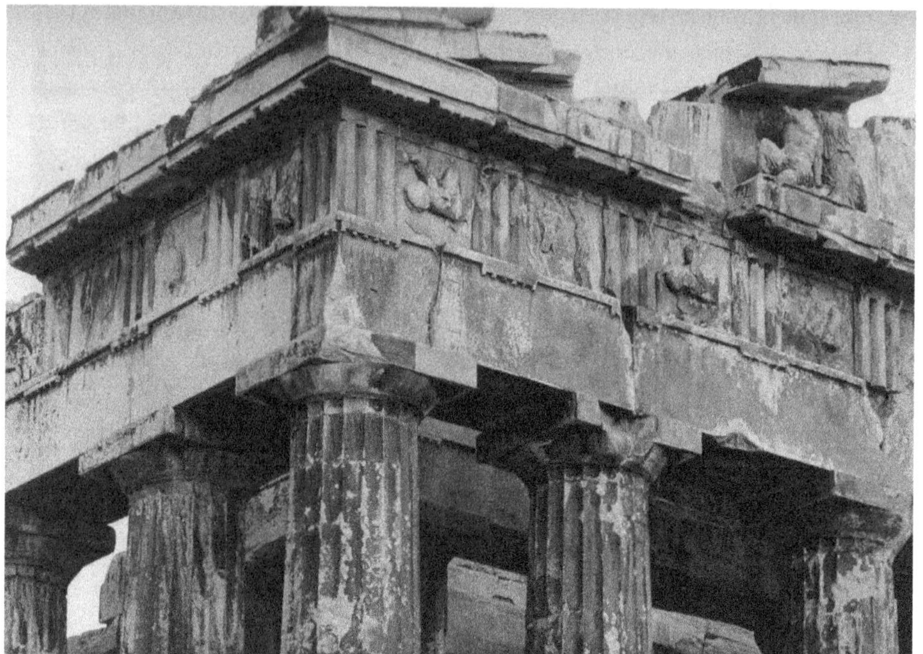

Fig. 5.13 North-west corner of the Parthenon, 1923.

The makers of the modern Acropolis were not only the archaeologists and engineers, but the photographers, publishers, and postcard makers who presented an incorporeal Acropolis, hovering between realism and iconicity. Pan, incidentally, Lucian tells us, complained that, as a plain country god from the Peloponnese, he could not understand words like 'incorporeal' that he often overheard in his cave wafting up from the philosophical academies.[36] It was a word that the satirist knew would always raise a laugh at the expense of the philosophers. In *Timon*, for example, Lucian has the plain-speaking Zeus complain about the philosophers that: 'One must sit with one's ears plugged, if one does not want the drums of them cracked; such long vociferous rigmaroles about Incorporeal Things'.[37] In the eleventh century a small Byzantine Christian church, dedicated to 'the Incorporeals', was built alongside the grand Roman ruin of Hadrian's Library, in which the ancient philosophers had stored their books and conducted their classes in specially designed rooms. The word may have been a Christian attempt to appropriate an ancient word still associated with the locality.

Modern coexisting ways of seeing are caught by the image at Figure 5.14.

---

36 *Double Indictment*, 11. ἀκούω γε αὐτῶν ἀεὶ κεκραγότων καὶ ἀρετήν τινα καὶ ἰδέας καὶ φύσιν καὶ ἀσώματα διεξιόντων, ἄγνωστα ἐμοὶ καὶ ξένα ὀνόματα.

37 Lucian, *Timon*, 9.

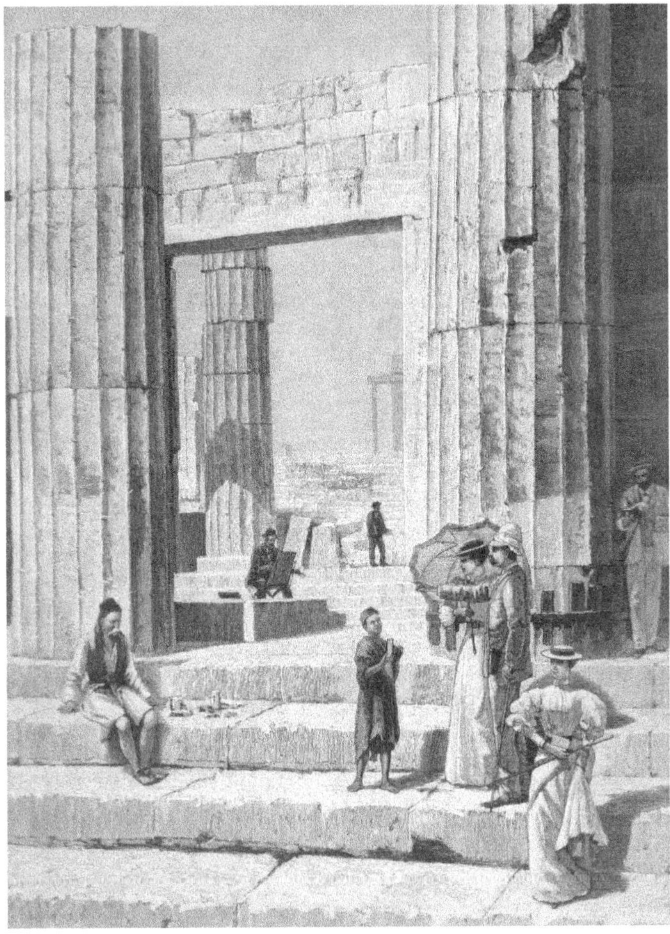

Fig. 5.14 Viewing the Acropolis, c.1898.

This image, that itself has the clarity of a photograph, is probably copied from a photograph of a painting which had itself been composed from photographs rather than from a personal visit by the artist, and there is no viewing station from where the scene could have been seen. A product of illusory realism, the image picks out some of the main ways of viewing since the clearances. We see a western officer, such as Colonel Barry with whom I began, with his ladies, taking charge with his pointing arm. The elderly Greek, one of the former soldiers employed as guards, is lost in his own, possibly philhellenic, thoughts. We see an artist, and a man reading – maybe an ancient author or an archaeological guide-book. And in the background we glimpse another man looking up, who may be internalising Eternal Greece. The lady who rebelliously breaks away represents the viewers who throughout the ages have resisted the mainstream conventions.

Working down to the eighteenth-century layers before the Greek Revolution below we find ways of viewing that were very different. Figure 5.15 is a view of the Acropolis as seen from the town.

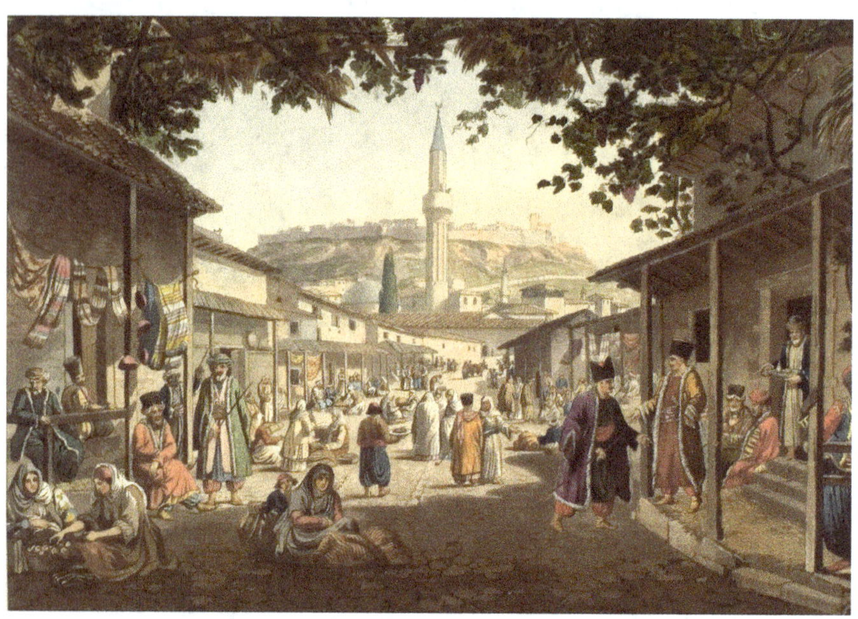

Fig 5.15 The Acropolis as seen from the centre of Athens, by Edward Dodwell, c.1805.

Although Athens was then a town of only about six to ten thousand inhabitants, it contained forty churches, over eighty chapels, and eleven mosques. By its religious buildings, Athens visually presented its political and social organisation into religious communities, the majority Orthodox Christians and about a quarter Muslim. There were also a few hundred Africans. A visitor to Piraeus in 1809 saw only two ships in the harbour, one exporting antiquities for Lord Elgin, the other importing slaves from Africa.[38]

To the surprise of western architects, the classical buildings on the Acropolis mostly lay outside the sightlines from the town. It was only from a distance that the Acropolis appeared as a statue to be wondered at from all sides, in its unique light, as it had been celebrated in antiquity, as some of the eighteenth-century artists tried to capture.

---

38 John Galt, *Letters from the Levant* (London: Cadell and Davies, 1813), p. 127; *Voyages and Travels, in the Years 1809, 1810, and 1811* (London: Cadell and Davies, 1812), p. 185.

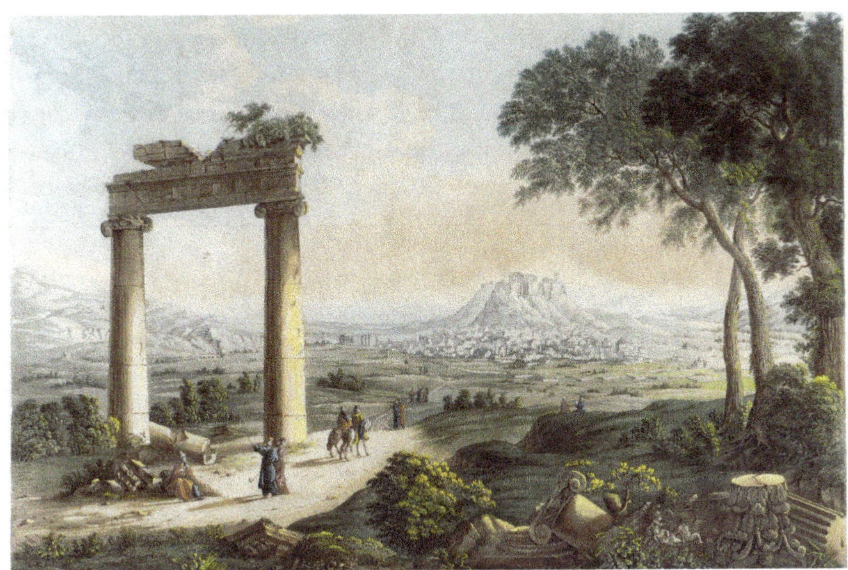

Fig. 5.16 The Acropolis as seen from a distance
by an arriving traveller, c.1800.

Figure 5.17 shows how the entrance to the Acropolis appeared during
the hundred years or so after an Ottoman refortification programme was
completed sometime in the early eighteenth century until the changes
brought about during the Revolution that began in 1821.

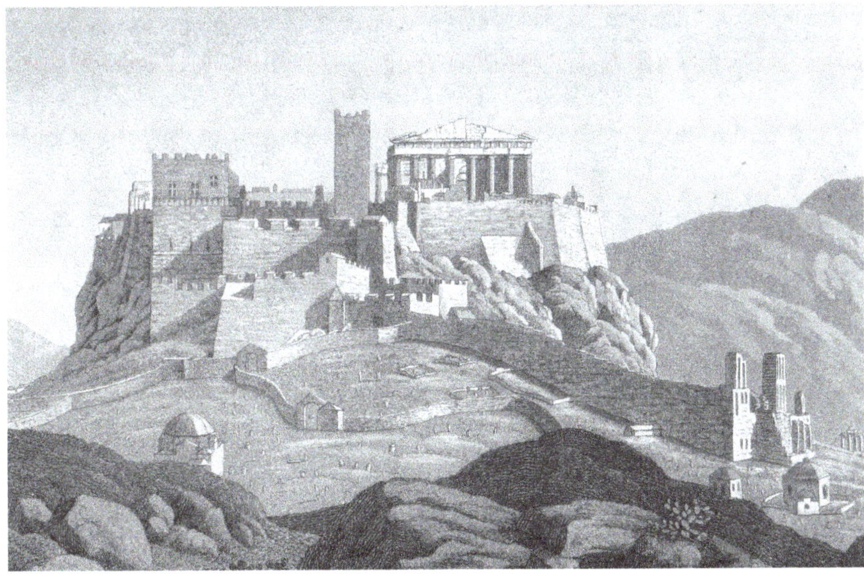

Fig. 5.17 The Entrance to the Acropolis, Heinrich Hübsch, 1819.

What was unignorable was the huge Muslim cemetery with its mosque that proclaimed to every viewer that Athens was part of the Ottoman dominions and had been inhabited by Muslims for four centuries – for as long as Europeans had been settled in North America. In the eighteenth century the Muslim population spoke Greek as their first language.[39]

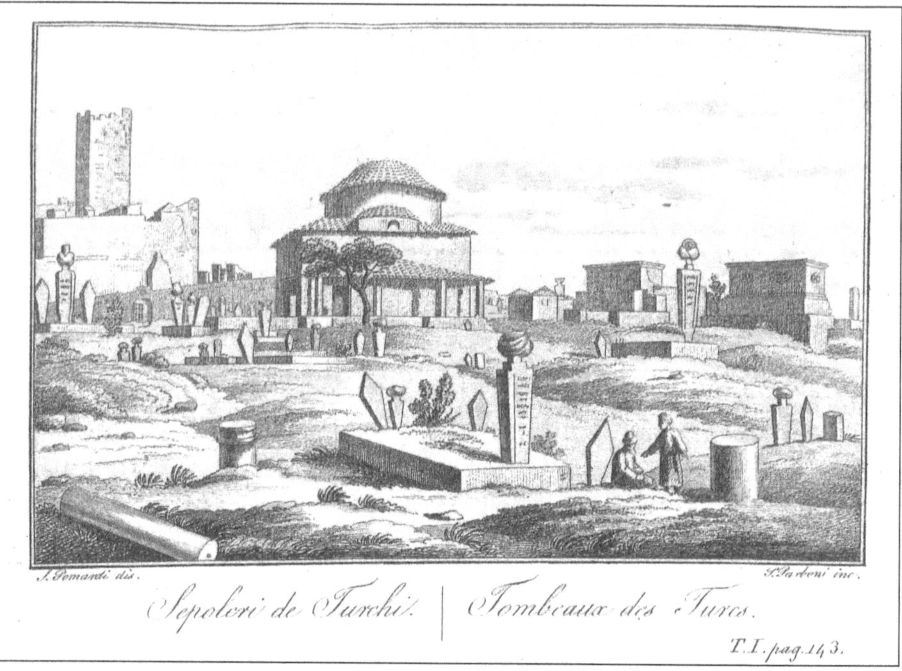

Fig. 5.18 The Muslim cemetery at the entrance to the Acropolis.

In my explorations in the area I have come across a few paving stones apparently made from Muslim tombs, but as part of the Hellenising agenda the cemetery was cleansed from sight, and from memory.

In the long eighteenth century, unlike today, the Acropolis visually presented the continuity of its long past back to mythic times. But here I note two large differences between the experience of local viewers and that of visitors. For hundreds of years, hardly any of the Orthodox Christian community of Athens ever saw inside the Acropolis as it had been a closed military facility since at least the thirteenth century. By contrast, for visitors

---

39 The Turkish language 'in Greece where it is little understood, even by the Musulmans themselves, and where its use is confined to the large cities, and some districts in Macedonia', William Martin Leake, *Researches in Greece* (London: John Booth, 1814), p. iv. According to Sicilianos, 1960, p. 20, 'The Turks who lived in Athens spoke a mixed language, mostly composed of Greek, and had forgotten their own language to such as extent that they could not converse with members of their own race who came from abroad'.

from western Europe, the desire to see the buildings on the summit was their main reason for being in Athens, and they could afford to pay to gain entrance to the site. The second big difference is the availability of expectation-setting mediating images. In 1835 shortly after the Acropolis was handed over to the newly independent Greek state, the authorities began to issue admission tickets, made by lithography. One was a map, the other a picturesque view.

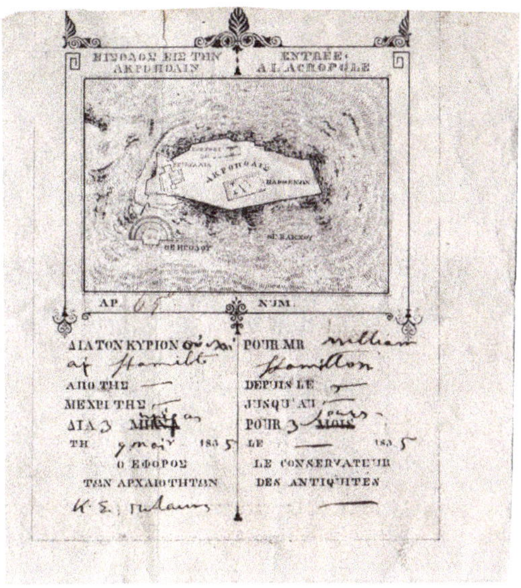

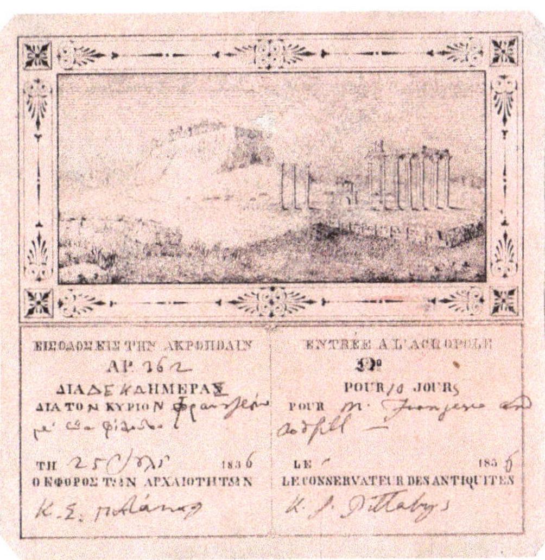

Fig. 5.19 Admission tickets to the Acropolis, mid 1830s.

The map, that only notes the ancient buildings on the Acropolis, looks forward to the time when the town would be removed. The view, by including in its frame both a church and a camel train, keeps continuity.

Figure 5.20 is an engraving of a bronze coin made in Athens during the Roman imperial period.

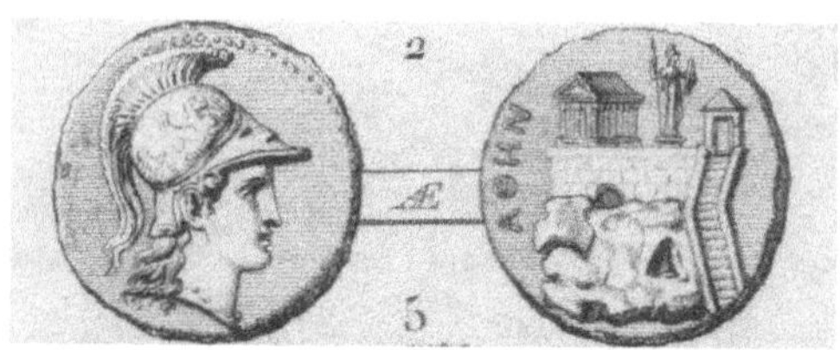

Fig. 5.20 A low denomination bronze coin issued in Athens,
Roman period, probably first century AD.

That coin, catching the viewing experience of the ancient observer, picks out the ancient way up to the Acropolis, past the Cave of Pan, up the steps, and it shows the bronze statue of Athena Promachos, and a classical building – probably the Propylaia not the Parthenon, or maybe just a generic temple. For nearly two thousand years, from the time that this coin was struck until the tickets of 1835, I do not know of a single visual representation of the Acropolis produced locally. And by local I include the whole Byzantine and Ottoman territories.

This absence, we can be certain, was not due to lack of technological or artistic skill. The government that built Haghia Sophia in Constantinople, then the largest building in the world, had plenty of skills, and could import any that it did not have. What we see here – or rather do not see – is the continuing result of the decisions by the early church councils to forbid all but Orthodox Christian art. And in this regard, as in many others, the law of Byzantium did not end with the fall of Constantinople but continued to be applied in Athens until the Revolution of 1821. By contrast, visitors from the west had not only read descriptions of Athens by ancient and modern writers but had been prepared for the experience. And they found that much was indeed as they had been educated to expect. As Byron wrote:

Yet are thy skies as blue, thy crags as wild;
Sweet are thy groves, and verdant are thy fields,
Thine olive ripe as when Minerva smiled,
And still his honied wealth Hymettus yields.

Athena's owls still fluttered round the Acropolis. Every spring and autumn, almost to the day, the storks mysteriously came and went, building their nests on the monuments as shown in Figure 5.21.

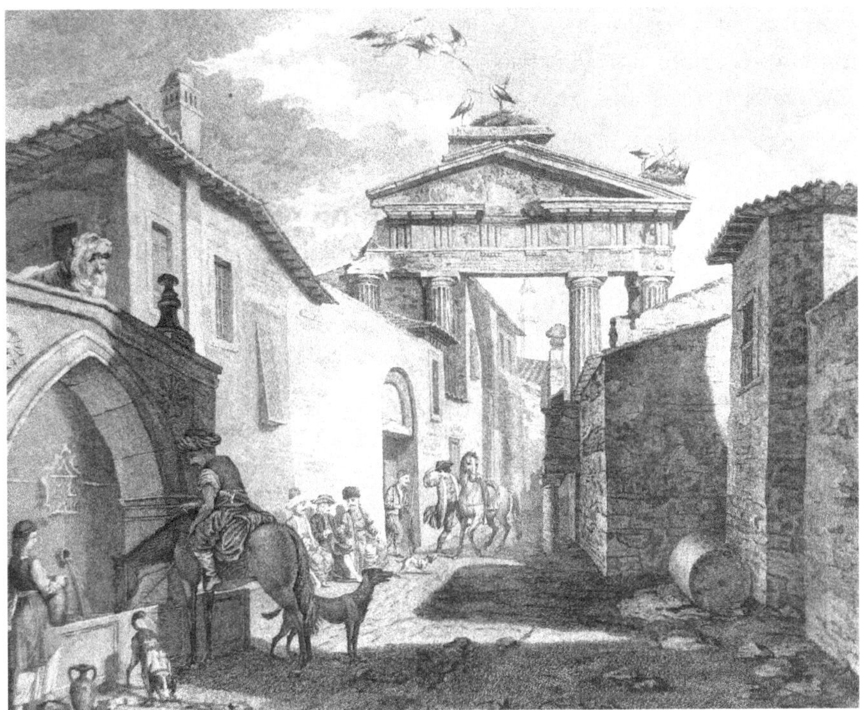

Fig. 5.21 'A View of the Doric Portico at Athens in its present state', c.1751.

In ancient times an enclosed area of the Acropolis slopes had been called 'the place of the storks' ('*to pelargikon*') a verbal slide from '*to pelasgikon*' (the place enclosed by the Pelasgians). It was a 'storkade', as one clever translator has put it, and we cannot fully understand ancient literature without reinserting the storks. For Enlightenment viewers, their acts of viewing, their makings of meanings, were attempts to use their imaginations to fill the gap between Nature, which they perceived as fixed, and the works of Man which were always changing. So the philosopher of history started with the storks. When wheeling high in formation in the sky, the storks had the panoptic view that the human viewer longed to share. The storks had stable government. The older storks looked after the younger ones, who, it was believed, cared for their parents. And in the eighteenth century any storks unable to fly to Africa spent the winter in the Ottoman governor's garden which offered social care, free at point of delivery. Secure in their own little acropolises, generations of Athenian storks had observed the ups and downs of human history with indifference and condescension.

But what were the laws of human history that were so different from the laws of Nature as practised by the storks? And how could they be discovered? The book that most helped to spread and entrench the philosophical way of seeing was *The Ruins* by Count Volney, his meditations on the ruins of empires, first published in French in 1788 on the eve of the French Revolution that he claimed to have predicted when looking at the ruins of Palmyra. As he wrote of his investigative method: 'I will dwell in solitude amidst the ruins of cities: I will inquire of the monuments of antiquity what was the wisdom of former ages'.[40]

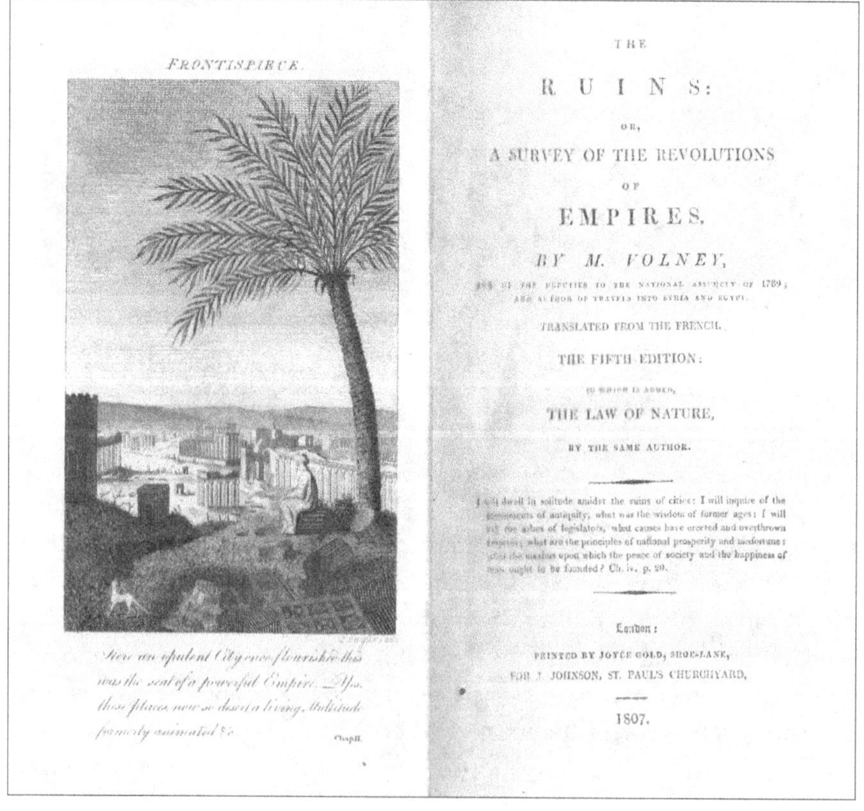

Fig. 5.22 Volney's *Ruins*.

---

40 Quoted on title page of most editions and translations from chapter iv.

In the eighteenth century the Athenian Acropolis was uniquely well suited to the search for unifying theories. More even than Rome, it visually presented a continuous story. Far into the nineteenth century, despite the findings of science and scholarship, many histories start with 'the Creation of the World', as calculated from the biblical texts. They assume a providentialism that takes as given that the course of history is under a divine guidance that punishes as much as it saves. Many books play variations on *Athens its Rise and Fall, Athens, Elevation and Decline, Athens, Grandeur and Decay*. To individuals and to societies, the Acropolis visually presented lessons that were universal, exportable, and relevant to current public policy questions.

Besides perambulating the Acropolis with eyes open, the philosopher therefore spent time reflecting on the totality of his or her experience, following the arguments, weighing the evidence, and fixing the lessons in his memory. The philosopher viewed the Acropolis with his eyes closed.

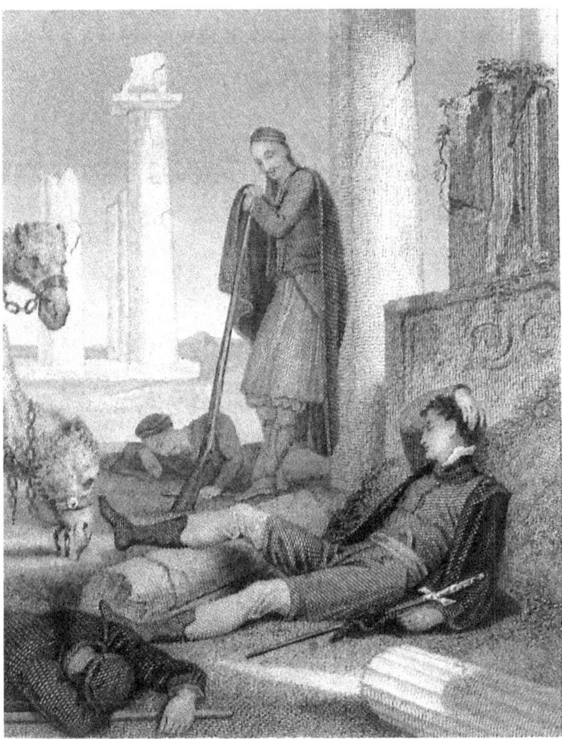

Fig. 5.23 'Byron's Dream', 1819.

But what were these lessons? To account for the achievement of Athens, many applied the theory developed by Hume, Montesquieu, de Staël, and some of the ancients, that the character of a people is an outcome of the natural environment. The Thebans were stupid, the ancients had said, because Boeotia was damp. Byron, picking up that tradition, noted that Lord Elgin came from Scotland, 'a land of meanness, sophistry, and mist; /each breeze from foggy mount and marshy plain / Dilutes with drivel every drizzling brain'.

But the climate of Athens is not always balmy, and its soil is rocky. It was Sparta, which has a more pleasant climate and a more productive soil, that had produced militarism. If the explanation for the achievement did not lie in Nature, it must lie in Man? So was it the institutions of the ancient Athenians that had led to their achievement, was their system of government, their commercial spirit, their democracy resting on a slave economy? But then what about the long decline? For help in meditating on that question, the philosophical viewer was visually assisted by the artistic conventions of the capriccio and the picturesque, and I show just one example of the images that were most frequently encountered at the time, rather than those commonly reproduced today.

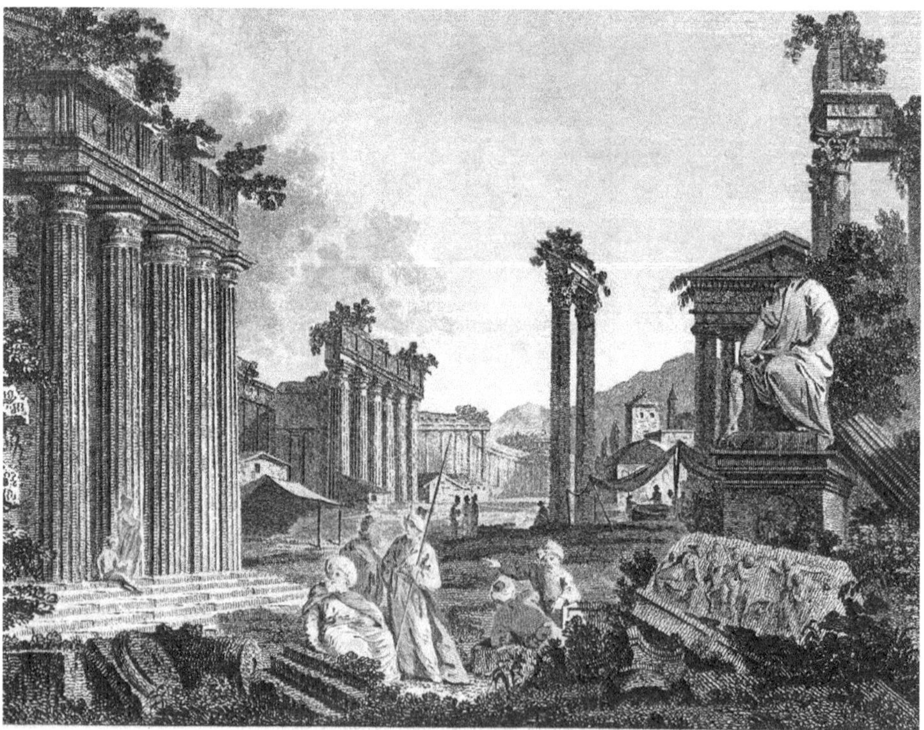

Fig. 5.24 'The Ruins of Athens'.

Textbooks for artists, including a few that advise on how to present Greek ruins, emphasised that accuracy was not important: the depiction of ruins must always have a moral aim. Viewers looking at these images were invited to ask themselves questions such as: why had Athens come to this? Had Athens been punished for its sins by divine providence? Like Sodom and Gomorrah, Nineveh and Tyre, Pompeii, and other ancient cities? And, if so, why had Athens been damned? Maybe too much luxury or free-thinking? And if Athens had it coming, then others had better look out too, as many warned. The explanation that carried most conviction to viewers from the west is that the failure must lie in the essential character of the people. The main early theorist of racism, Robert Knox, drew heavily upon the Acropolis, as shown in his book.

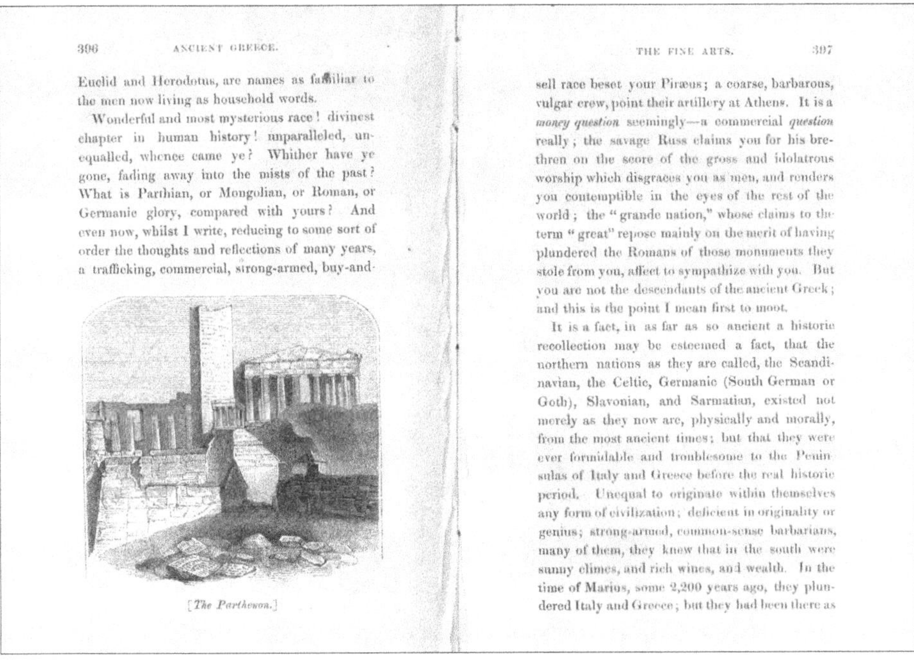

396   ANCIENT GREECE.

Euclid and Herodotus, are names as familiar to the men now living as household words.

Wonderful and most mysterious race! divinest chapter in human history! unparalleled, unequalled, whence came ye? Whither have ye gone, fading away into the mists of the past? What is Parthian, or Mongolian, or Roman, or Germanic glory, compared with yours? And even now, whilst I write, reducing to some sort of order the thoughts and reflections of many years, a trafficking, commercial, strong-armed, buy-and-

[*The Parthenon.*]

THE FINE ARTS.   397

sell race beset your Piræus; a coarse, barbarous, vulgar crew, point their artillery at Athens. It is a *money question* seemingly—a commercial *question* really; the savage Russ claims you for his brethren on the score of the gross and idolatrous worship which disgraces you as men, and renders you contemptible in the eyes of the rest of the world; the "grande nation," whose claims to the term "great" repose mainly on the merit of having plundered the Romans of those monuments they stole from you, affect to sympathize with you. But you are not the descendants of the ancient Greek; and this is the point I mean first to moot.

It is a fact, in as far as so ancient a historic recollection may be esteemed a fact, that the northern nations as they are called, the Scandinavian, the Celtic, Germanic (South German or Goth), Slavonian, and Sarmatian, existed not merely as they now are, physically and morally, from the most ancient times; but that they were ever formidable and troublesome to the Peninsulas of Italy and Greece before the real historic period. Unequal to originate within themselves any form of civilization; deficient in originality or genius; strong-armed, common-sense barbarians, many of them, they knew that in the south were sunny climes, and rich wines, and wealth. In the time of Marius, some 2,200 years ago, they plundered Italy and Greece; but they had been there as

Fig. 5.25 The Parthenon as a symbol of the superiority
of the northern white races.

With the invocation 'wonderful and most mysterious race! divinest chapter in human history! unparalleled, unequalled, whence came ye? Whither have ye gone, fading away into the mists of the past?' Knox, a medical anatomist, who assumed that ancient men and women looked like the ancient statues from the Parthenon that he had studied in the British Museum, uncritically reversing from icon to actual, declared that the Ancient Hellenes were a blue-eyed race directly akin to the modern Germans and Scandinavians. And across the Europeanised world the old idea that the genius of the ancient Hellenes was due to the natural environment merged with the new idea of essential racial differences. For example the Right Rev. J.A. McClymont, who provided what he probably assumed were uncontentious mainstream words to accompany the first popular book to employ colour in prints, remarked: 'The inhabitants belonged to a good stock, the Indo-Germanic, while their geographical position and surroundings were well fitted to develop a high type of manhood'.[41] And the line goes to Nazism, the German occupation of the Acropolis in 1941, and the systematic killing of those regarded as racially inferior.

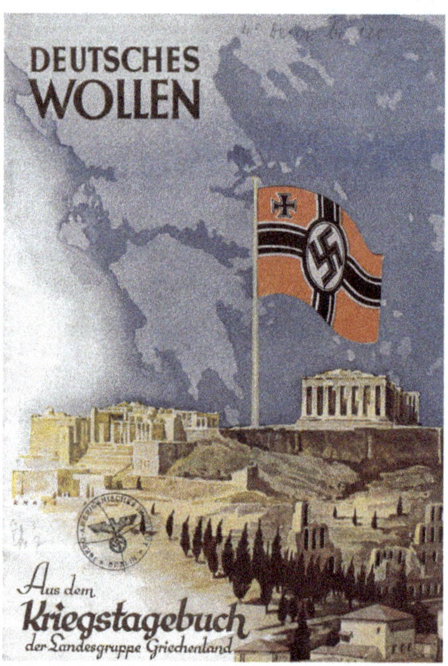

Fig. 5.26 The German flag flying over the Acropolis, 1941.

Nazi racial theories had many roots, of which the Acropolis was not the most important. But it is striking that while during the occupation, the Germans inflicted unspeakable suffering on the people, including mass executions, genocides of the Greek-Jewish community, enslavement, and the burning down of churches and monasteries, they made scarcely a scratch on the Hellenic monuments.[42] Ernst Buschor, a famous professor,

41 John Fulleylove, *Greece Painted by John Fulleylove. Described by Right Rev. J.A. McClymont* (London: Black, 1906), p. 3, and in the editions of the 1920s.

42 The contradictions between the philhellenic admiration for ancient Athens and the

in a book published in Germany during the war, repeated the myth that the ancient Greeks were a Nordic people who had come from the north. In a little book, *War in the age of the Parthenon* that was given out to soldiers and students, he links their struggles to those between Hellenes and centaurs represented in the metopes of the Parthenon, that are indeed, in modern terms an aestheticisation of interracial violence. In a preface, Buschor makes explicit the German claim to be the new Hellenes by dedicating his book to the soldiers 'who have died for the Great Hellenic heritage on the borders of the west'.[43]

Meanwhile, some viewers preferred to turn away from the Acropolis and look instead at the hill of the Areopagos nearby where, according to the author of *The Acts of the Apostles*, Paul had presented his ideas in a seminar of two of the Athenian philosophic schools. In this way of looking, the Areopagos was offered as an alternative – a superior – acropolis, and one which the early Christians had provided with its own mythic associations centred round Dionysius the Areopagite who is only known from one sentence in the *Acts of the Apostles* – but who was given a full biography, an iconic visage, and a large body of pseudonymous writings. The Areopagus is bare. The church and episcopal palace that had formerly stood there, had been destroyed at least once by earthquakes and rock falls, divine providence in this case punishing the Orthodox Christians. Instead, the Areopagus was reimagined as triumphing.

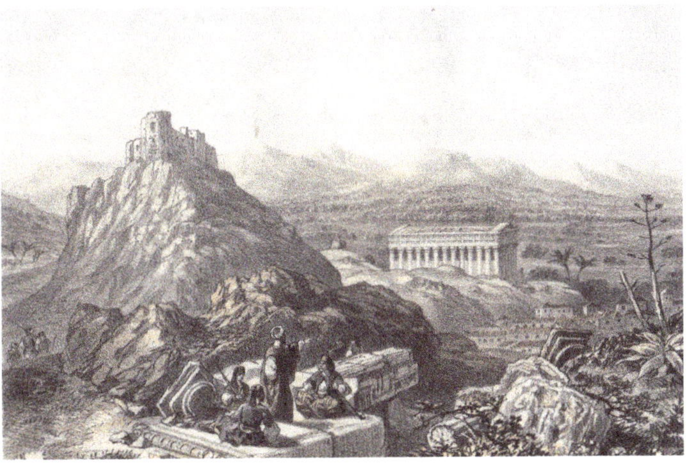

Fig. 5.27 'Mars Hill, Athens'.

German treatment of the Greeks whom they regarded as Slavic, with enslavement and mass killings are described by Mark Mazower, *Inside Hitler's Greece: The Experience of Occupation, 1941-44* (New Haven, CT: Yale University Press, 1993).

43 'die auf griechischem Boden und an anderen Rändern des Abendlandes für das Grosse Griechische Erbe fielen', Ernst Buschor, *Das Kriegertum der Parthenonzeit* (Munich, 1943).

There is a large body of texts of nineteenth-century, mainly western, Christian groups who compare the Acropolis unfavourably with the Areopagus, that is ancient Hellenism with Christianity. Some are fanatical, violent and triumphalist, others forgiving or trying to have it both ways. The counter-Acropolitans, as we can call them, were however united by their hostility to what the classical Acropolis represented, that they described, typically, as 'the very citadel of Grecian paganism' 'all rank idolatry'.[44] Their largely forgotten texts give us, I suggest, an insight into the range of reactions at the end of antiquity, a time when the contest between the values of ancient Hellenism was gradually being won by the incoming Christians, for which the surviving record is heavily weighted towards the point of view of the victorious theocrats.

But before turning to Byzantium I want instead to return to another way of seeing invented in the eighteenth century, the aesthetic. Could it be, some asked, that the buildings of the Acropolis preserved some essence of Hellenism that was independent of their associations? The aesthetic way of viewing, unlike the philosophical, does not need active viewers. On the contrary, it claims to be an autonomous domain of meaning. The aesthetic, being immaterial, is exportable. By the end of the eighteenth century, Europe was already filled with new buildings modelled on the ancient buildings of Athens and North America followed. I show a picture by the architect James 'Athenian' Stuart, who did more than anyone to export aesthetic Hellenism.

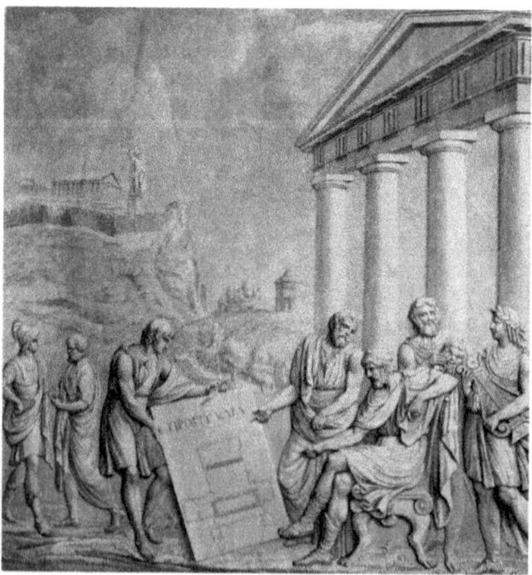

Fig. 5.28 The essence of the Athenian Acropolis exported to England.

---

44 The quotations are from James W. Hott, D.D., *Journeyings in The Old World* (Dayton, OH: United Brethren Publishing House, 1884), p. 221, and *Photograms of an Eastern Tour. ... By Σ. With original illustrations* (London: [Bungay printed], 1859), p. 126.

Stuart imagines the ancient architect Mnesikles showing his plans for the Propylaia to Pericles and the other famous men of the time. The Cave of Pan and the stairs up to the Acropolis – and the usual non-existent view of the Parthenon. The building on the right is a gentleman's library. England, such buildings proclaim, has imported the essence of the classical Acropolis. Britain is the new Athens. And the style in which the ancient values were expressed could be copied. And it was a small step from exporting the incorporeal aesthetic to exporting the actual stones. It is this way of seeing, an attempt to separate the aesthetic from the historical and geographical context, that encourages the collecting of 'unprovenanced' antiquities, that continues to damage our ability, and that of future generations, to recover knowledge of the ancient world. Figure 5.29 reproduces a French lithograph showing Elgin that I only found a few years ago.

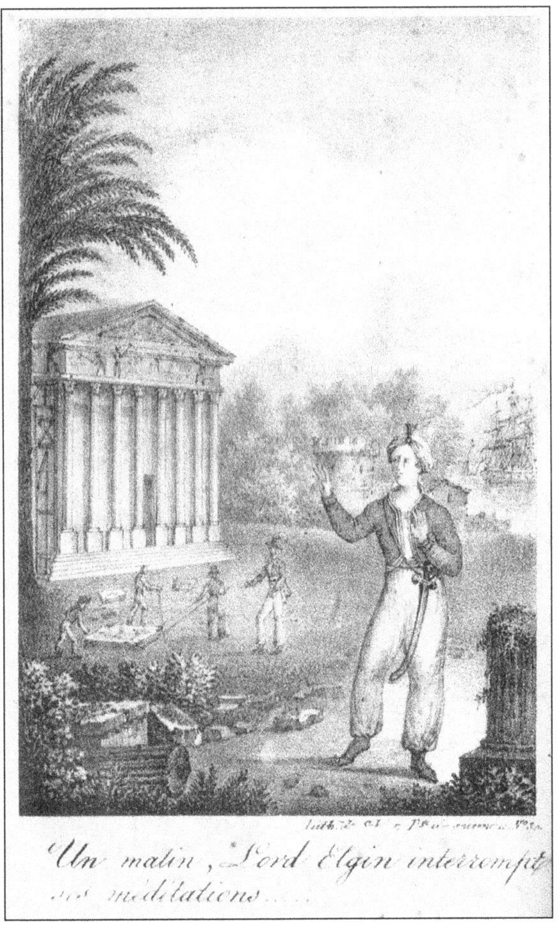

Fig. 5.29 'Lord Elgin interrupts his meditations'.

This illustration nicely captures a transition from the philosophical mode of viewing where the viewer's experience is central, to the aesthetic notion that meaning can inhere in stones.

***

Digging down deeper to the seventeenth century, we see that when the modern scientific on-the-spot study of the Acropolis began in the 1670s, much was immediately re-discovered about the ancient sites and buildings. Scholars from the west, unlike the local people of that time, had access to the printed works of the Leiden scholar, Johannes Van Meurs, known as Meursius, who, half a century before, had patiently collected and published all the references in the surviving works of the ancient authors that had been recovered and printed at the rime of the European Renaissance – a corpus not much enlarged since. And when we dig through to the local layers below the 1670s, we find a curious pattern. During the entirety of the period between the Christian takeover of the eastern empire at the end of antiquity and the encounter that began in the 1670s, not only are there no pictures of the Acropolis made locally in the whole Byzantine and Ottoman territories, but, in the vast surviving literature of Byzantium, mentions of Athens can be counted on the fingers of two hands.[45]

The three that can have any claim to represent local ways of seeing during the long millennium share some characteristics. The authors, or as we should perhaps call them, the story-tellers, know the names of some ancient Hellenic authors, but have no understanding of who they were or of what they wrote. They are all 'philosophers'.[46] Secondly, it is extremely difficult to date the time of composition from internal evidence, with some scholars putting the longest of the three texts as early as the ninth century and others as late as the seventeenth. The problem arises because they make little distinction between what still existed to be seen and what they say had once been there. In this running together of the see-able and the only imaginable, the stories are akin to the 'meaningful history' narratives now classified as post-colonial, that put first the perceived needs of their present. Like the nineteenth-century western Christian viewers of the Areopagus, they are

---

45 Most of those that refer to Athens as a place are noted by Filippomaria Pontani, 'ΕΚΛΕΛΕΙΜΜΕΝΛ ΕΡΕΙΠΙΑ. I Bizantini e le rovine antiche', *Annali della Scuola Normale Superiore di Pisa, Classe di lettere e filosofia. Quaderni*, 4th series, 14, 2002, p. 45. I shall publish another that I have recently discovered in the forthcoming book.

46 In this regard the accounts resemble that of the seventeenth-century Ottoman traveller Celebi, who although highly privileged and by the standards of his cultural group well educated, respects the ancient 'philosophers' but knows little about them beyond their names.

secure in their triumphalism, and it is the places they associate with defeated ideas, notably the outdoor sites where the ancient philosophers held their meetings that they pay most attention to, not quite dancing on their graves, but picking out as 'theatres and schools', meaning, in the Greek, 'things to be looked at and learned from'. Over a thousand years, a Christian theocracy monopolising education and art, had imposed a set of Christian myths on the ancient cityscape, on its buildings, and on its rituals. The long Akathist ['not seated'] Hymn, that is still chanted in Orthodox Churches, composed long before it was adopted into ritual in 626, shows traces of the deep hatred of Hellenic Athens by the early Christians. In one passage, verse 17, not always now sung, the congregation collectively rejoice that their goddess, Mary, has triumphed over the ensnaring logic of the philosophers.[47] And there are other traces of this way of seeing. For example, the church of Saint Philip facing the Acropolis displays a modern image of the mythic visit of one of the disciples of Jesus to Athens where he was said to have confuted the arguments of the philosophers, as shown in Figure 5.30.

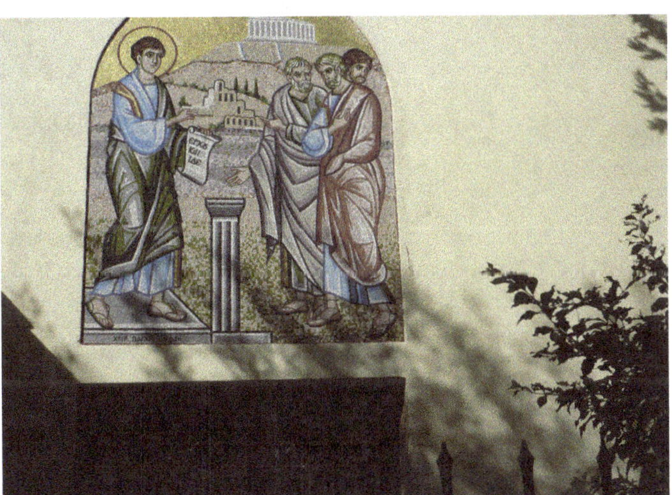

Fig. 5.30 Confuting Hellenism. Mosaic on the church
of Saint Philip facing the Acropolis.

---

47 'Orators most eloquent do we behold mute as fish before you, O Theotokos; for they are at a loss to explain how you could remain a virgin and yet give birth. But as for us, marvelling at this mystery, we cry with faith: Rejoice, Vessel of the Wisdom of God. Rejoice, Treasury of His providence. Rejoice, you who proves the philosophers fools. Rejoice, you who proves the logicians illogical. Rejoice, for the subtle debaters are confounded. Rejoice, for the inventors of myths are faded away. Rejoice, you who breaks the webs of the Athenians. Rejoice, you who fills the nets of the Fishermen'. Translation into English made by Vincent McNabb in 1934: http://www.orthodoxchristian.info/pages/Akathist.htm.

There is space for only a few remarks about how the Acropolis may have been viewed in antiquity – a long period of time but since viewing conventions were long-lived, some general points can, I suggest, be made. First, the ancient perception of the landscape and the cityscape was highly poetic, and so is the art in which landscape and cityscape were presented. Figure 5.31 shows a mosaic of which there are two versions both probably derived from a famous picture.

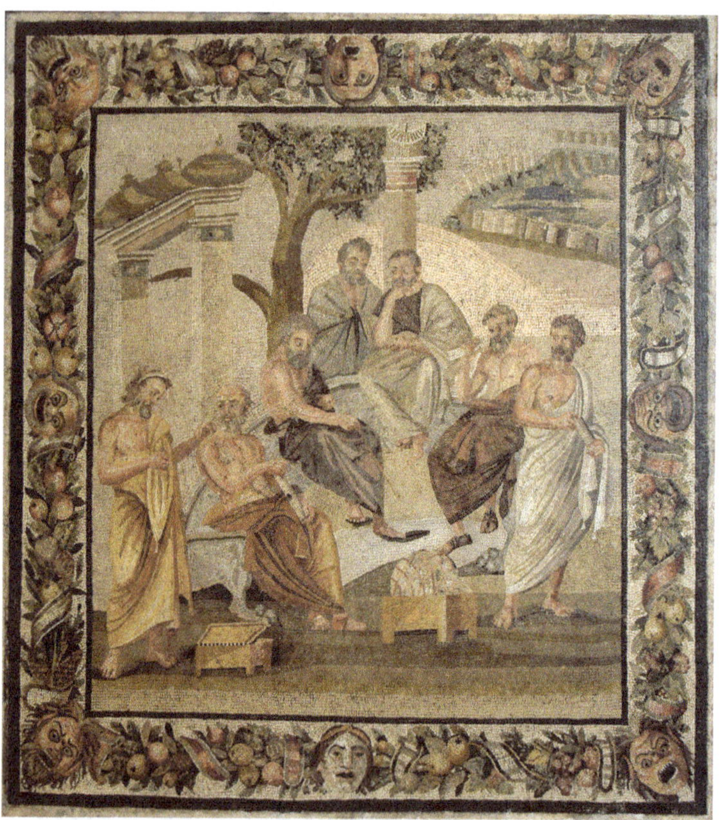

Fig. 5.31 Mosaic of the Villa of Siminius Stephanus.

It shows seven men, probably the Seven Sages, with their human scientific and artistic instruments. In the corner what appears to be a green-walled sanctuary, possibly Delphi or the Acropolis of Athens, is represented as it was encountered by the viewer, as a forest of marble dedications. The border of the mosaic, with gorgons and masks, is a common poetic representation of a physical natural border, like the Acropolis slopes.

In ancient times, to judge from the authors, it was the Acropolis that provided the main interpretative frame, rather than any of the buildings such as the Parthenon. From Julian back to Homer, it is the Acropolis that is appealed to, whether to warn, to shame, to educate or to celebrate. And it is the whole visible Acropolis rock, slopes and summit, myth and history, the natural as much as the man-made. Memory slips away, but memory instantiated in marble, or in literature and ritual, has a better chance. To the ancient Athenians the aspiration was to create not an Eternal Greece, but an Eternal 'Athenianness', a history but especially also an expression of the values of the society, the famous notion of *'paideia'*. And as is made explicit by Aristides, this aspiration was achieved 'by viewing and remembering'.[48]

As the site where the official memory and official values were preserved and displayed, the ancient Acropolis tolerated a good deal of alternative, even of contradiction, provided that it was filtered through the shared system of signs constituted by myth. We see none of that fear of art, and the urge to destroy it, to allow it to be used only for approved purposes, to keep it indoors, to allow two dimensions but not three, and to control both the production and consumption, that is such a feature of the long millennium of theocracy that followed.

***

So what, if any, more general conclusions emerge from this brief summary of the long history of ways of looking at the Acropolis of Athens? As an embodiment of numerous, mostly incommensurate, imagined pasts and ideologies over thousands of years, it offers a uniquely full case for investigating the processes by which the past has been understood, misunderstood, misrepresented, claimed, mythologised, and presented and packaged for the current purposes within different societies. And how it can be drawn into an explanatory, but also often into an allegedly legitimating, relationship with the present and the future. In the richness of its retrievable historical experience, the Acropolis of Athens is an inheritance as precious as the marble.

The read-across questions for those responsible for ancient and historic monuments round the world therefore come tumbling out. Which pasts deserve to be preserved? How should any current generation regard its

---

48 Aristides, *Panathenaic oration*, 154.

responsibilities to its predecessors and its successors? Is it possible, or desirable, to recover the historically typical and not just the unusual? Should preference be given to what is now regarded as valuable, remembering that such judgments change, as the thousand years of hostility, indifference and neglect of the Acropolis vividly demonstrates? How far can those with responsibility offset the modern consumerism that treats the past as a resource to be exploited, for tourism, or for building a sense of community, such as nation or religion, and thus instilling a false view of the past driven by present day ideological objectives? Is there a legitimate place for 'epistemic cooperation', a phrase invented recently to describe an administrative process that ensures that archaeologists, lawyers, 'heritage professionals' and others have a right to be heard in the decision taking.[49] Pragmatic solutions of this kind, however, that sidestep the competition between the truth claims, risk both slipping into relativism and enabling the loudest and politically most powerful voices to force their way.

The dead have no rights nor do I suggest that they should be given any. Indeed much of our knowledge of ancient Hellas comes from excavating graves, setting aside the wishes of those who mourned and commemorated. However, I suggest, we owe it to ourselves and to our children to be as truthful as we can about the past. The Venice Charter was a commendable attempt to devise an inter-generational ethics aimed at saving the materiality of ancient buildings, based on notions of stewardship and respect for the autonomy of the past and of the future. In the modern west we have well-tried protocols for assessing the validity of research into the past, including into myth-making, of which evidence, openness, and free debate are amongst the most important. Perhaps, given the present threats, the time has come to build into that tradition a code of ethics for those who claim to make the mute stones speak?

---

49 The phrase 'epistemic cooperation' is used by Geoffrey Scarre and Robin Coningham, *Appropriating the Past: Philosophical Perspectives on the Practice of Archaeology* (Cambridge: Cambridge University Press, 2013), p. 6.

6. South Asian Heritage and Archaeological Practices

Sudeshna Guha

I

Studies of the histories of heritage inevitably lead us to disciplinary introspection. As with the scholarship of heritage studies elsewhere, research into South Asian heritage has developed from considerations of tangible heritage, and through a focus on the social biographies of historical monuments, built environments and landscape. Academic projects are fed by the non-academic 'heritage industry' in which civilisational histories are routinely invented and used as commercial capital for the global market through the creation, circulation and display of 'historically seminal monuments'. An apt example is the replication of the second-century BC Buddhist *stupa* at Sanchi (Madhya Pradesh, India) as the India Pavilion at the Shanghai Expo in March 2010. This architectural adaptation, which left a 'deep impression' upon one of its more important visitors, the Chinese Premier, was aimed at conveying the 'universalistic values of peace, and the message of healing the harm we bring upon nature'.[1] Such acts of rewriting the forms and meanings of historical topography facilitate the bringing home of 'venerable' heritage from foreign lands, as we see in the case of the recent building of the Taj Mahal at Sonargaon (Bangladesh), and the construction of a version of the Sanchi *stupa* at Louyang (China) between

---

1 'China PM visits India pavilion at Shanghai Expo', *The Times of India*, 31 October 2010, http://timesofindia.indiatimes.com/india/China-PM-visits-India-pavilion-at-Shanghai-Expo/articleshow/6845554.cms

          http://dx.doi.org/10.11647/OBP.0047.06

2008 and 2010. Although each instance of re-evaluation, adaptation and replication of tangible and intangible heritage pursues different aims, all demonstrate the importance of engaging with the history of the reproduction of monuments as the 'performative spaces' within which new meanings of the 'actual objects' are created.[2]

Inevitably, the rewriting of heritage as global capital drives academic study of the 'careers' and 'travels' of objects and monuments. Within the context of South Asia, this scholarship has created an important analytical corpus regarding the ways in which the reproduction of historical monuments shape 'popular imaginaries of the disciplines of archaeology and anthropology' and serve 'as grounds on which professional knowledge came to be configured within new public domains of display and scholarship'. However, the pioneering scholarship focuses exclusively upon the colonial and post-colonial histories of heritage-making, and in historicising the relationship between archaeological practices and the heritage industry, reinforces the theory – unproblematically presented in all histories of Indian archaeology – that the antiquarian study of South Asia through the region's historical monuments, sites and objects was a 'western cognitive entity'.[3] The long pre-colonial histories of heritage-making within the Indian subcontinent not only demonstrate the errors of this thinking, but also throw into sharp relief the fact that British orientalist historiography conspicuously celebrated the 'coming of antiquarianism into India' for denying native historical consciousness.

The orientalist historiography, which was established in the eighteenth century, no doubt inspired the pioneering British archaeologist of India, Alexander Cunningham (1814-93), to establish the history of antiquarian scholarship of India through the statement that 'the study of Indian antiquities received its first impulse from Sir William Jones, who in 1784 founded the Asiatic Society of Bengal'.[4] However, when we reflect upon the amassing of old manuscripts, paintings, curiosities and objects of art within

---

2   B. Kirschenblatt-Gimblett, 'The Museum as a Catalyst', Keynote address, Museums 2000: Confirmation or Challenge, organised by ICOM Sweden, the Swedish Museum Association and the Swedish Travelling Exhibition/Riksutställningar in Vadstena, 29 September 2000, https://www.nyu.edu/classes/bkg/web/vadstena.pdf

3   T. Guha-Thakurta, 'Careers of the Copy: Traveling Replicas in Colonial and Postcolonial India', Firth Lecture, Bristol University, 8 April 2009, http://www.theasa.org/publications/firth/firth09.pdf and *Monuments, Objects, Histories: Institutions of Art in Colonial and Postcolonial India* (New York: Columbia University Press, 2004), p. 3.

4   A. Cunningham, 'Preface', *Archaeological Survey of India: Four Reports Made During the Years 1862-65* (Simla: Government of India Publications, 1871), p. i.

the Mughal Empire, it is apparent that, like the antiquarian scholarship of the British in India, such acts pointed to scholarship of the past, and to the extra-scholarly value of connoisseurship within the politics of imperial self-fashioning. Furthermore, despite the different intellectual genealogies of viewing, collecting, copying and connoisseurship in the seventeenth-century Mughal domain and Britain and Europe, the descriptions of monuments and artefacts from the former were rather similar in nature to the descriptions that were considered essential by the growing breed of self-styled British and European antiquaries to document the incorruptibility of material sources. An example is Emperor Jahangir's description of the Jami Masjid in Ahmedabad, which he saw in his eleventh regnal year, on 6 January 1617/18, and recorded in his *Jahangirnama* as follows:

> This mosque is a monument left by Sultan Ahmad, the founder of the city of Ahmedabad. It has three gates, and on every side a market. Opposite the gate facing the east is Sultan Ahmad's tomb. Under the dome lie Sultan Ahmad, his son Muhammad, and his grandson Qutbuddin. The length of the mosque courtyard exclusive of the *maqsura* is 103 cubits; the width is 89 cubits. Around the perimeter of the courtyard is an arcade with arches four and three-quarters cubits wide. The courtyard is paved in cut brick, and the pillars of the arcade are of red stone. The maqsura contains 354 columns, and above the column is a dome. The length of the maqsura is 75 cubits, and the width is 37 cubits. The maqsura paving, the mihrab, and the pulpit are of marble.[5]

Jahangir's description undermines the assertion of Cunningham's latest biographer that the 'earliest notices and descriptions of Indian monuments, architecture and sculpture are to be found in the writings of sixteenth- and seventeenth-century European travellers'.[6] It also exemplifies Alain Schnapp's contention, based on his research into histories of historical enquiries, that 'in widely differing circumstances, and given similar assemblages, antiquaries may produce similar statements'.[7] The British pioneered archaeological practices within the Indian subcontinent during the nineteenth century, and historians of South Asian archaeology continue to follow Cunningham in tracing archaeology's genealogy

---

5   *The Jahangirnama: Memoirs of Jahangir, Emperor of India*, ed. and trans. W. Thackston (New York and Oxford: Smithsonian Institute in association with Oxford University Press, 1999) pp. 244-45.

6   U. Singh, *The Discovery of Ancient India: Early Archaeologists and the Beginnings of Archaeology* (New Delhi: Permanent Black, 2004), p. 6.

7   A. Schnapp, *The Discovery of the Past: The Origins of Archaeology* (originally in French, 1993), (London: The British Museum Press, 1996) p. 319.

through European views of South Asia's past. Yet identifying antiquarian scholarship in South Asia as a European quest also perpetuates the traditions of colonial historiography, which were developed by the British administrative scholars of the East India Company, and which declared the natives of Hindustan to be historically unconscious because they did not undertake historical enquiries. In this respect, the post-colonial histories of South Asian archaeology, which emphasise the need to research the agency of 'native' scholarship, pose a paradox, as they enshrine the dictates of the colonialist and orientalist historiography, namely that there was little consciousness of historical scholarship within pre-colonial India. The histories asserting a western origin for antiquarianism in the Indian subcontinent have, moreover, been uncritically used to write the grand histories of world archaeology, and as a result the latter wrongly promote the idea that 'systematic antiquarianism did not develop in India prior to the colonial period. Despite impressive intellectual achievements in other fields, Indian scholarship did not devote much attention to political history, perhaps because the Hindu religion and division of socio-regulatory forces between high priests and warriors directed efforts to understanding the meaning of life and of historical events more towards cosmology'.[8]

Beyond the South Asian sphere, most twentieth-century archaeologists, unlike Schnapp, have viewed antiquarian scholarship as a project of modernity within the Enlightened European world. In determining periodisation, they have made a distinction between acts of valorisation of the past in ancient and pre-modern times, and a conscious approach towards historical enquiry through antiquities from the late-sixteenth and early-seventeenth centuries onwards. This periodisation has been widely accepted within the growing twenty-first-century archaeological scholarship of heritage studies, in which the origins of a heritage-conscious society are traced back to the emergence of an educated public sphere in Europe during the seventeenth century, that responded to the milieu of rising national consciousness with efforts to seek out and control the past through laws and objective field explorations.[9] The understanding of rational enquiries and 'proper' histories and history writing as products

---

8   B. Trigger, *A History of Archaeological Thought* (Cambridge: Cambridge University Press, 2006), p. 77.

9   E.g. M.L.S.S. Sørensen and J. Carman, 'Introduction: Making the Means Transparent: Reasons and Reflections', in M.L.S.S. Sørensen and J. Carman (eds.), *Heritage Studies: Methods and Approaches* (London and New York: Routledge, 2009), pp. 3-10.

of the modern western world, which the above periodisation fosters, clearly echoes British colonial histories of antiquarian scholarship in India. However, heritage archaeologists, who rightly promote the intellectual need to interrogate the dominance of 'western' historiographical traditions, have overlooked the glaring borrowings from a historiography they explicitly reject in their own histories of the origins of heritage practices.

In thinking through the histories of heritage-making within South Asia, we become aware that the acts of replicating historical monuments, such as the building of a Taj Mahal and Sanchi *stupa* at Sonargaon and Louyang respectively, may have extended well beyond the widely-known twelfth-century AD example of the Buddhist temple at Bodh Gaya, which was reproduced at Pagan on the orders of the ruler Kayanzittha so that his subjects could worship at their venerable shrine. The repeated reuse of the rock and pillar edicts of the Mauryan Emperor Ashoka (268-31 BC) from the first century, by Mahakshatrapa Rudradaman (c.150 AD), until at least the seventeenth century, by the Mughal Emperor Jehangir (r.1605-27 AD), indicate the disparate histories of conscious acts of memorialisation, and encourage us to look beyond the 'western' historiography of the origins of heritage practices. Furthermore, we also note that the restoration of tombs and mosques, of which there are numerous examples from the Delhi Sultanate (specifically between c.1369 and 1503 AD) and the Mughal dynasties (especially from Aurangzeb's rule 1658-1707 AD), echo many aspects of the nascent nineteenth-century archaeological restoration projects, in that they were political acts aimed at redefining the way sacral and historical spaces were experienced. Also worthy of note, therefore, are the popular perceptions within India regarding archaeological practices during the early twentieth century, when archaeological undertakings and scholarship were both becoming increasingly visible through the conservation work and excavations of the colonial Archaeological Survey. The following remark with which the members of the Delhi Municipal Committee feted the departing Viceroy George Nathaniel Curzon (1899-1905) is representative:

'It would not be too much to say that your Excellency has bridged over the 500 years since the time of the Emperor Feroz Shah Tughlak, who was what would be called in modern parlance as Delhi's first great archaeologist'.[10]

---

10 13 November 1905; *Lord Curzon's farewell to India: being speeches delivered as viceroy & governor-general of India, during Sept.-Nov. 1905* (Bombay: Thacker and Co., 1907).

Curzon remains the principal architect of the archaeological restorations of historical India, which he facilitated through the restitution of the Archaeological Survey of India in 1902. Yet it is only by looking beyond the connected histories of archaeological practices and heritage that we are able to establish more precise cultural histories of history-making and heritage practices within South Asia.

II

In reviewing the archaeological scholarship of heritage we are shown the ways in which inferences are often transformed into material evidence. The British scholarship of Indian archaeology began from the nineteenth century and was initiated with the aim of uncovering ancient India's supposedly pristine 'Buddhist' cultural legacy. Among the early excavations that were undertaken were those by Alexander Cunningham at the Dhamek Stupa in Sarnath near Banaras between 1834-36. Through them Cunningham initiated his 'Buddhist archaeology' of India, which gathered further momentum after the Great War of 1857, largely because of his leadership of the Archaeological Survey of India between 1861-65 and 1871-85. In 1863 Matthew Sherring of the London Missionary Society excavated at Banaras with the aim of demonstrating the presence of Buddhism in the city's foundational history. It is clear from the focus of both Cunningham's and Sherring's excavations at Sarnath and Banaras respectively, that the British launched their 'archaeology of India' to establish a counter-narrative to the prevalent 'Hindu' civilisational history of the natives, which they dismissed as mere Brahmanic propaganda. By establishing archaeological, and hence tangible, evidence of a physically absent religion, the excavators sought to demonstrate that just as Buddhism had disappeared from India despite being the national religion for more than 500 years, so too could Hinduism.

As well as calling into question the place of Hinduism in India's civilisational history, the archaeological finds of Buddhist sites and monuments supposedly ruined and destroyed by the ascendant Muslim rulers from the twelfth century onwards provided visual evidence to support the new Raj's depiction of the Muslims as destroyers of all that was glorious in India's ancient heritage, while also illustrating the relative benevolence of the British towards their heathen subjects. This archaeological history thus demonstrates how historical landscapes are continuously refashioned 'to instantiate particular histories and historicities', and so exemplifies the manner in which archaeological scholarship of ancient civilisations can contribute towards the construction of intangible heritage.[11]

The material evidence of civilisational origins and legacies, and of past perceptions of cultural geographies, identities and traditions, which the archaeological scholarship of 'prehistoric' and archaic civilisations routinely produces, undermines the assumption that heritage is inherently knowable. However, perhaps because of the palpable materiality of archaeological data, the archaeological literature of the history of heritage practices often misleadingly conveys the assumption that heritage can be discovered, recorded, and mapped, despite the fact that many archaeologists now increasingly search for innovative, discipline-specific methodologies to help clarify the ways in which 'interpretations may be constructed from data'.[12] As the theories discussed below regarding the Indus (or Harappan) Civilisation illustrate, the archaeological constructs of civilisational heritage force us to revisit some old-fashioned disciplinary concerns, such as explanations for cultural continuity and change, schema of classifications and periodisation, and the kinds of data that are selected as evidence of cultural boundaries. Critical reviews of the archaeological constructs would show the shifts and transformations over time in notions of valid evidence, and encourage us to reconsider the existing methodologies by which material traits are translated into cultural forms. In this they also remind us of the need to consider the ethical aspects of heritage-making and its scholarship.[13]

III

The object of sustained archaeological study since 1924, the Indus Civilisation physically straddled the border between India and Pakistan, two countries

---

11 N. Abu El-Haj, *Facts on the Ground: Archaeological Practice and Territorial Self Fashioning in Israeli Society* (Chicago, IL: University of Chicago Press, 2004), p. 13. On the nineteenth-century archaeological explorations of Banaras see S. Guha, 'Material Truths and Religious Identities: The Archaeological and Photographic Making of Banaras', in M.S. Dodson (ed.), *Banaras: Urban Forms and Cultural Histories* (London and New York: Routledge, 2012), pp. 42-76.

12 Sørensen and Carman, 2009, p. 4, see also p. 24.

13 The scholarship of heritage ethics is growing. It has provided a critical stance to the practices of archaeology, and concerns with many different issues. For two different approaches to considerations of ethics see L. Meskell, 'Human Rights and Heritage Ethics', *Anthropological Quarterly*, 83(4), 2010, pp. 839-60, and L. Smith and E. Waterton, *Heritage, Communities and Archaeology* (London: Duckworth, 2009).

whose shared cultural histories were officially divided by the partition of 1947. As a result of the partition, the post-colonial scholarship of the Indus Civilisation in Pakistan has been facilitated to a large extent by 'non-native' archaeologists. Therefore, embedded within the historiography of this Bronze Age phenomenon of the third millennium BC, are competitions and contestations regarding the authorship of knowledge and 'important' discoveries, unequal intellectual encounters, disparate claims to 'cultural legacies', and conflicts and tensions regarding the granting of permission to 'foreigners' to dig the 'native soil' of others. The ninety-year-long archaeological scholarship of the Indus Civilisation therefore provides us with a seminal archive of creations, representations and contestations around the ownership of evidence of heritage.

The history of Indus scholarship also highlights the waning influence of British scholarship upon Indian archaeology after the Raj, and the concomitant spread of North American theories and methods within South Asian archaeology. This epistemological shift has left a rich collection of official correspondence, which offers an insight into the spectacular conflicts between the British old guard, some of whom, such as Mortimer Wheeler (1890-1976), continued to serve as diplomats of Indian archaeology, and the young American entrants into the field, such as Walter Fairservis Jr. (1921-94).[14] The numerous examples of professional clashes between the British and American camps demonstrate the fallacy of reducing the power politics of post-colonial archaeological scholarship in South Asia to a simple dichotomy of foreign versus native.

The history of the Indus Civilisation encompasses a remarkable geographical shift around the year 2200 BC, when cities within the Indus valley, including the type-sites of Harappa and Mohenjodaro, declined and new cities, such as Rakhigarhi, Kalibangan and Dholavira, emerged in regions to the east and south-east. This geographical change creates the need to consider the manner in which past perceptions of territoriality have been sourced through the archaeological scholarship, and provokes an enquiry into the way in which archaeologists have established material evidence of the indigenous. The understanding of the Indus Civilisation as 'sub-continental' in its 'roots' and 'style' is a specifically North American contribution to the historiography, and was formally suggested in 1967

---

14 Details in 'Wheeler Papers', Box 459, archives of the British Academy, London.

by Fairservis, who endowed the Civilisation with 'Indian' features by historicising its 'ethos' as village-orientated.[15] Fairservis subsequently stated that 'the story of prehistoric India, which stretches back to a time so remote that it conforms to a Hindu Kalpa of untold generations reaching to a primordial world, nonetheless repeats again and again the pattern which was not to change until the East India Company ships moved up the Hooghly'.[16] Fariservis's view of a uniquely Indian civilisation whose characteristic features – a Hindu society with a village- and caste-based culture – had remained essentially unchanged since time immemorial, followed the trends of contemporary orientalist historiography. However, this view also prevails today within the functionalist and systemic modelling of an overarching construct of 'Cultural Tradition', whereby the Indus Civilisation is now regarded as demonstrating the continuity of an exclusively indigenous cultural history of South Asia.

IV

The archaeological construct of 'Cultural Tradition' was initially developed in the context of studies of the settlement patterns of prehistoric Mesoamerica in order to record cultural change and continuity and measure the processes of cultural integration.[17] It was widely adopted by the processualist school of New Archaeology during the 1960s, and was introduced into South Asian archaeology a decade later by Jim Shaffer through his research on prehistoric Baluchistan. Since the early 1990s, Shaffer and his co-author Dianne Lichtenstein have gradually extended the scope of the model. They now propose an overarching 'Indo-Gangetic Cultural Tradition', encompassing the long-term cultural developments in northern South Asia which link 'social entities over a time period from the development of food production in the seventh millennium BC to the present'.[18] In an earlier model of this theory, which was published in 1995, the authors conceived the continuity as being economically and culturally

---

15 W.A. Fairservis Jr., 'The Origin, Character, and Decline of an Early Civilization', *American Museum Novitates*, 2302, 20 October 1967, p. 19.

16 W.A. Fairservis Jr., *The Roots of Ancient India* (London: Allen and Unwin, 1971) p. 381.

17 See G.R. Willey and P. Phillips, *Method and Theory in American Archaeology* (Chicago, IL: University of Chicago Press, 1958).

18 J.G. Shaffer and D.A. Lichtenstein, 'South Asian Archaeology and the Myth of Indo-Aryan Invasion', in E.F. Bryant and L.L. Patton (eds.), *The Indo-Aryan Controversy: Evidence and Inference in Indian History* (London and New York: Routledge, 2005), p. 93.

focused upon cattle. Now, with due regard for the danger of slipping into orientalist historiography, they insist that by charting an unbroken indigenous cultural continuity for northern South Asia they nonetheless recognise 'significant *indigenous discontinuity*', and do not 'propose social isolation *nor* deny any outside cultural influence'.[19] However, despite all these qualifications and careful nuances, Shaffer and Lichtenstein's 'Indo Gangetic Cultural Tradition' still evokes orientalist and colonialist historiography in the basic assumption that this tradition can be recognised because its core features have remained unchanged over millennia.

Following Shaffer's work, an archaeological narrative of northern South Asia has been established on the basis of constructions of cultural traditions that historicise the indigenous and the foreign as being respectively internal and external to this vast region. Yet such distinctions lead to misleading histories of 'others' and 'otherness', reminding us of the observation of the noted historian B.D. Chattopadhyaya that even the region's Muslim communities were not regarded as 'others' by the Hindus until the twelfth century because 'the notion of territorial outsider in a political sense [was] not compatible with the early cosmological/geographical concept'.[20] We should not forget that the Indus Civilisation was historicised as indigenous by all early excavators, notably John Marshall, who described the authors as being 'born of the soil', and Mortimer Wheeler, who stated that 'the population would appear to have remained more or less stable from Harappan times to the present day. Invasions of these regions, however important culturally, must have been on too small a scale to bring about marked changes in physical characteristics'.[21] Although Marshall and Wheeler established the indigenous nature of the Civilisation with reference to its inhabitants, they explained many of its socio-cultural features as elements of 'borrowing' from the bronze-age cultures of west Asia. They studied the Civilisation at a time when the 'Aryan invasion' of northern India in the second millennium BC was considered an undisputable historical fact, and were hesitant to historicise a sophisticated city-type civilisation, which predated the 'Vedic Civilisation' of the 'Aryans' by more than a thousand years, as an indigenous product of South Asia. The intellectual understanding of

---

19 Ibid.

20 B.D. Chattopadhyaya, *Representing the Other? Sanskrit Sources and the Muslims* (Delhi: Manohar, 1998), p. 90.

21 J.H. Marshall, *Mohenjodaro and the Indus Civilization* (London: Arthur Probsthain, 1931), p. 109; R.E.M Wheeler, *The Indus Civilization*, 3rd edition, (Cambridge: Cambridge University Press, 1968), p. 72.

the Indus Civilisation as indigenous in the twenty-first century arises from the convincing evidence against any 'invasion' of the Indo-Aryan speaking people, which has effectively removed all 'foreign hands' from the cultural make-up of South Asia's ancient past. However, the on-going academic debate regarding the exact physical location of the first perceptible 'roots' of the Indus Civilisation points to the need for greater sensitivity towards the manner in which the archaeological search for evidence of an indigenous civilisation contributes to issues of cultural ownership.

Thus, although the Indus Civilisation is now celebrated as a pure-bred product of South Asian soil, the question of its precise origins remains a contentious topic. In particular, Indian nationalist archaeologists reject the 'Baluchi story' of their North American colleagues who excavate the 'Harappan' sites of Pakistan, according to which the roots of the Civilisation's incipient technologies can largely be traced through the evidence of domestication at Mehrgarh in the Kacchi Plain. Instead, they put forward an alternative origin story focused upon evidence gathered within India, which highlights the origins of rice and millet domestication in the 'Indus-Hakra-Ghaggar alluvium' and the innovations in metal technologies in the 'Aravalli hills during the fourth to mid-third millennium BC'.[22] These assertions have provoked the surprising counter-claim that possible evidence for the indigenous growth of Taxila, Charsada and Peshawar (Pakistan) into important commercial cities by c.600 BC calls into question the 'time honoured models' describing the derivation of 'Indian culture' from 'a Gangetic homeland'.[23] A surprising claim because although the region of Magadha in the Gangetic valley was the heartland of the classical kingdoms of ancient India, it has never been regarded as the 'homeland' of 'Indian culture'. In all models since the nineteenth century the 'homeland' has remained the Sapta Sindhu, believed to be in and around the area of Punjab which is in Pakistan today, where the early Vedic hymns were supposedly composed. The nationalist and counter-nationalist claims may seem childish, but they clearly demonstrate the performative uses to which evidence of the indigenous is put within the scholarship of South Asian archaeology.

---

22 D.K. Chakrabarti, *The Oxford Companion to Indian Archaeology: The Archaeological Foundations of Ancient India, Stone Age to AD 13 Century* (New Delhi: Oxford University Press, 2006), p. 134

23 J.M. Kenoyer, 'New Perspectives on the Mauryan and Kushana Periods', in P. Olivelle (ed.), *Between the Empires: Society in India 300 BCE to 400 CE* (New York: Oxford University Press, 2006), p. 46.

V

Functionalist, adaptive and processualist approaches to culture and cultural change have given rise to numerous inferences about the presence of an incipient caste-based, multi-ethnic population within the Indus Civilisation. However, since archaeologists now also strive to ensure that their scholarship is anthropologically informed, we cannot overlook the fact that their representations of the Civilisation's social structures and ethnicities, which are mainly inferred from specialist craft production technologies and stylistic similarities in artefact types and their decorations, go against the caution of social anthropologists that people 'can't be put into a box anymore'. Moreover, India and Africa are now identified by anthropologists as 'obvious examples' of places that include societies of long-standing superdiversity.[24] The historical fact of this superdiversity – understood as the 'diversification of diversity' – in South Asia leads us to question the way in which archaeological inferences about social identities are forged from artefacts, and to dismiss the assertion, often made by archaeologists, that past markers of identity can simply be uncovered and understood through archaeological fieldwork.

In order to identify continuities between the Indus Civilisation and the subsequent cultural histories of early India, archaeologists of the twenty-first century have also shown a renewed interest in sourcing Sanskrit and Pali texts, many of which are vastly disparate in terms of both chronology and intent, from which to glean the 'idea of an ancient Indian/South Asian Civilisation'. On the basis of comparisons and juxtapositions of patently mismatched textual and archaeological 'sources', we are told that 'the very fact that authorities both in the Harappan and Ganges civilisation expressed their ethos in similar material symbols – various forms of fortification, circumvallation – indicates that the forms of authorities in these two civilisations may have been similar as well', and that the 'deep structure' of the South Asian Civilisation, which developed from the Neolithic period onwards, can be defined by 'five traits; namely, agricultural economy, an orally transmitted code of conduct, an orally transmitted sacred knowledge, an idiosyncratic sociocultural system, and a set of ritual and sacrificial practices'.[25] This new archaeological literature

---

24 J.N. Jørgensen and K. Juffermans, 'Superdiversity', November 2011, http://hdl.handle.net/10993/6656

25 P.A. Eltsov, *From Harappa to Hastinapura: A Study of the Earliest South Asian City and Civilization* (Boston, MA and Leiden: Brill, 2008), pp. 165, 185.

seeks to be politically correct in terms of its intellectual framework, and constitutes the grand civilisational tradition of South Asia since the distant past as one which was multi-ethnic, multi-lingual and religiously diverse. Nonetheless, even this new literature overlooks the blatant essentialism embedded in the idea of a unique South Asian civilisational ethos. After all, few academic archaeologists would care to propose the archaeological history of a unique, age-old civilisational ethos for western Europe, North America, Britain, France, the United States, or any other regional or national domain of the 'western' world.

Processualist archaeology was developed by the New Archaeologists of the 1960s, but had fallen out of favour by the late 1980s, when archaeologists came to recognise that the inherent positivism of the processualist approach encouraged an abject disregard for human agency, and hence also for the basic responsibilities of archaeological scholarship. Although the processualist school of thought has long been out of fashion in theoretical archaeology, its tropes have continued to guide studies of the Indus Civilisation, especially in North American scholarship on the subject since the late 1980s. This outmoded approach, which is most obviously apparent in the schemes of periodisation that are developed on the basis of the functionalist constructs of traditions, eras and phases, takes no notice of the theoretical slippage that occurs in establishing evidence of social identities through evidence of a society's production technologies. Thus, inferences regarding the existence of specialist craftsmen within the Indus Civilisation are routinely drawn upon to show the presence of kin and caste groups, and evidence of the spatial demarcation of the different crafts and manufacturing processes within the cities is presented as evidence of social segregation, and of the possible existence of a caste system.[26] Given that western archaeologists often criticise their non-western counterparts for failing to adopt new theoretical approaches, the continued dominance of the processualist school of thought in the archaeology of the Indus Civilisation is somewhat surprising, and demonstrates the theoretical poverty of even 'western' studies of South Asian archaeology. In this respect, the archaeological construct of a 'Great South Asian Tradition' through the modern scholarship of the Indus Civilisation forces us to interrogate the intellectual and moral obligations of today's 'post-colonial' archaeology.

---

26 For an early example see K.K. Bhan, M. Vidale and J.M. Kenoyer, 'Harappan Technology: Theoretical and Methodological Issues', *Man and Environment*, 19, 1994, pp. 141-57.

7. The Ethics of Digging

Geoffrey Scarre

[W]hile the Workmen made several Ditches, they fell upon divers Urnes, but earnestly, and carelessly digging, they broke all they met with, and finding nothing but Ashes, or burnt Cinders, they scattered what they found.[1]

Sir Thomas Browne

Sir Thomas Browne's account of the chance discovery and thoughtless destruction of Roman sepulchral urns near Brampton in Norfolk is the stuff of archaeologists' nightmares. Fortunately, this particular story had a happy ending: following the antiquarian knight's arrival on the scene several more urns were unearthed, which Browne carefully described in what amounts to an early example of an archaeological report. We can only speculate how much of the English archaeological record disappeared in similar incidents over the centuries but vast quantities of ancient material must have been destroyed by the ignorant or the uninterested. The rise of antiquarianism in the eighteenth century and its gradual transmutation into a professional and scientific archaeology were of inestimable importance in stemming this loss of objects and the information to be obtained from them. And scholarly excavators not only preserved the archaeological riches but became increasingly adept at reading the messages they conveyed. By the mid-twentieth century, university-trained archaeologists had understandably come to see themselves as the primary stewards of the archaeological heritage. For they, more than others, had the knowledge and

---

1   Sir Thomas Browne, 'Concerning some Urnes Found in Brampton-Field, in Norfolk, Anno: 1667', in *Religio Medici and Other Writings* (London: Everyman's Library, 1969), p. 142.

        http://dx.doi.org/10.11647/OBP.0047.07

skills to extract maximum information from an often partial and imperfect record. Archaeology, which had formerly been a pastime for amateurs, had evolved into a business of experts.

Yet professionalism in archaeology, as in some other scholarly fields once dominated by laymen, is not an unmixed blessing. If the past and the things of the past are our common heritage (as the familiar mantra runs), then the privileging of the expert over the amateur in the practice of archaeology raises certain questions about equity. Where professionals rush in, amateurs may fear – or more often be forbidden – to tread. At worst, professional archaeologists may look on untrained amateurs as interfering nuisances, to be kept at a distance; at best, amateurs on excavation sites are treated as unpaid assistants to the experts, useful pairs of hands to carry out the dirty work. If all of us are equally heirs to the past, then it seems that some heirs are more equal than others. But if the relegation of amateurs to subsidiary roles is to some extent an inevitable effect of the ever-increasing dependence of archaeological research on sophisticated technology and analytical techniques (even in the world of supposedly post-processual archaeology, with its greater tolerance of alternative narratives), there are other exclusionary effects of professionalisation that may be more avoidable. Archaeologists who claim to be stewards of the archaeological heritage on behalf of everyone doubtless speak sincerely. But not everyone accepts that archaeologists are the best people to manage that heritage or to construe its meaning. Thus, many indigenous people in North America, Australia, New Zealand and elsewhere protest at the disturbance by archaeologists of the sites at which their ancestors lived and died, which they see as disrespectful and intrusive; or they are highly sceptical about the truth, or the relevance to themselves, of the accounts of the past that archaeologists deliver.

In the latest edition of their textbook *Archaeology: Theory, Methods and Practice*, Colin Renfrew and Paul Bahn assert that 'the fundamental purpose of archaeology must be to provide people with a better understanding of the human past'.[2] This statement appears in a chapter on archaeological ethics bearing the significant title 'Whose Past?' At one level, this is a question about who has the right to decide what is removed from the ground, how it should be handled, whether it should be retained or reburied, and who should ultimately have control of it. At another level, it raises subtler issues

---

2 C. Renfrew and P. Bahn, *Archaeology: Theories, Methods and Practice*, 6th edition (London: Thames and Hudson, 2012), p. 540.

about identity, allegiances and social continuity: about who is entitled to speak about the past of a community whose sense of itself is founded in certain beliefs (which may be true or false) about its own origins. Few of us enjoy having our identity defined for us by others, and we may be still more resentful when outsiders tell us that our own favoured stories about our roots are wrong. Nevertheless, archaeologists cannot and should not be expected to compromise their professional standards of evidence when conducting excavations or interpreting their finds. Archaeology is a scholarly discipline, not a spinner of myth, a servant of ideologies, or a rubber stamp for popular opinions. Archaeologists need to be rigorously scientific in their methods while avoiding the academic bullishness that so naturally offends others. This is not an easy ethical nut to crack.

In the survey that follows I look briefly at some of the moral responsibilities that professional archaeologists, and particularly those engaged in the excavation and interpretation of sites, must bear on their shoulders. Knowing how to behave as a virtuous archaeologist is difficult when the responsibilities in question pull in divergent directions, as they often do. For convenience's sake, I shall divide the discussion somewhat arbitrarily into three sections: 1) Responsibilities to People; 2) Responsibilities to Things; 3) Responsibilities to the Profession. (These labels do not, of course, identify entirely disparate categories of issues.)

1. Responsibilities to People

In recent years there has been increasing recognition of the variety of 'stakeholders' in the archaeological enterprise – that is, the different sets of people whose interests are actually or potentially affected by the activities of archaeologists. A short-list of those who have been considered stakeholders includes (in no order of precedence, and allowing for overlap): a) archaeologists; b) the general public; c) local (including indigenous) communities; d) genetic and/or cultural descendants of the subjects under investigation; e) tribal associations; f) religious affiliates, or claimants to that status; g) national or local governments; h) owners of land or property on which excavation is carried out; i) planners and developers; j) the dead (if, as some philosophers believe, some kind of 'moral estate' can be ascribed to people after their death). In addition to *present* people who are affected by the activities of archaeologists, there are also potential effects on *future* ones to be considered. So (to state the obvious) a site which is excavated today will not be available as a virgin site for later generations of archaeologists and their public.

Satisfying the particular, and sometimes sharply conflicting, interests of such a variety of groups can produce hard dilemmas for archaeologists. Larry Zimmerman emphasises that while archaeologists claim to act as stewards on behalf of the public, that public is far from homogeneous and may contain members who 'have a substantially different view of stewardship of the past than archaeologists'.[3] Given the diversity of interests and viewpoints, even archaeologists who acknowledge their accountability to the public might sometimes be stumped to answer the question 'What public?' In the notorious controversy over the disposal of Kennewick Man in the north-west USA, members of the Umatilla tribe argued that the only respectful mode of caring for the extremely ancient remains in question was to rebury them, a mode of 'stewardship' which archaeologists who wished to preserve them for further research rejected with horror. There may also be people whose paramount interest is not in stewardship of *any* kind, sometimes for perfectly legitimate reasons. A town council or construction company which wants to build a school or social housing on an archaeologically sensitive site may reasonably argue that the land cannot be frozen forever in the past, and that present needs must sometimes trump the case for preservation. (Fortunately, in many such cases some compromise is possible, whereby a portion of the site is preserved or a 'rescue dig' by archaeologists is commissioned before the developers move in.)

The interests that need to be considered when archaeological excavation is in prospect vary considerably from place to place. Generally speaking, the investigation of the site of a deserted medieval village in the British countryside is less ethically sensitive than a project to excavate the dwelling site of an indigenous community in North America or Australia. Digging a settlement in rural Yorkshire or Oxfordshire to learn more about the former inhabitants is likely to be welcomed by the local residents as a way of making connections with their forbears, bringing the past to life and fostering a sense of trans-temporal community. (However, not all contemporary Britons feel ethically relaxed about the practice of archaeology. In the last few years the Society for Honouring the Ancient Dead (HAD) has argued for the adoption in Britain of a default procedure of reburial of human

---

3   L.J. Zimmerman, 'When Data Become People: Archaeological Ethics, Reburial, and the Past as Public Heritage', *International Journal of Cultural Property*, 7, 1998, p. 70.

remains discovered in the course of research – a proposal that has been met with resistance by much of the archaeological community.) By contrast, the excavation of a former tribal occupation site on the American Great Plains by archaeologists trained in western techniques of scientific analysis grounded on Enlightenment epistemology, may be seen by a present-day Indigenous community as an act of intellectual and moral arrogance that treats people – their people – as mere data for research.

In the USA, the passing of the Native Graves Protection and Repatriation Act in 1990, which mandates that tribes be consulted before human physical remains or associated funerary objects are removed from tribal or federal land, and establishes the right to demand the return of those that have previously been removed, has set the framework for generally improved relations between archaeologists and indigenous groups. But even before the enactment of NAGPRA, changing conceptions of their role by archaeologists, including a wider and more generous recognition of their responsibilities to other stakeholders, were producing a less imperious mode of conducting research, in which purely academic considerations no longer alone ruled the roost. What Colwell-Chanthaphonh and Ferguson have called an 'ethic of collaboration', that emphasises a cooperative role for native communities in deciding research questions, selecting sites for analysis, managing excavations, and publishing and publicising results, is fast becoming a standard component of cultural resource management in the USA.[4]

While it would be hard to deny that cooperation and consultation among stakeholders is highly desirable on both moral and on practical grounds, it would obviously be too sanguine to suppose that consensus will invariably be the outcome of such practice. It is not always possible to reconcile the different interests, still less the underlying ideals that may be at issue; it can also be hard to decide just who the relevant stakeholders are, or who is entitled to speak for them. The fifth principle of the World Archaeological Congress's First Code of Ethics calls on archaeologists '[t]o acknowledge that the indigenous cultural heritage rightfully belongs to the indigenous descendants of that heritage'.[5] Yet the prima facie justice of this principle ought not to obscure the fact that an unwillingness to

---

4   C. Colwell-Chanthaphonh and T.J. Ferguson, 'Virtue Ethics and the Practice of History: Native Americans and Archaeologists along the San Pedro Valley of Arizona', *Journal of Social Archaeology*, 4, 2004, p. 23.

5   World Archaeological Congress, *First Code of Ethics*, 1990, http://www.world archaeologicalcongress.org/site/about_ethi.php

share one's cultural heritage is not always defensible on the ground that such sharing would be a threat to that culture's integrity. Moreover, if the principle implies that indigenous owners have the ultimate say over what happens to their cultural heritage, then it may inadvertently warrant even such acts of wilful destruction as the Afghan Taleban's dynamiting of the Bamiyan Buddhas in 2001 or the current spate of destruction of cultural heritage by Islamic fundamentalists in Mali. Such cases evince a total, but surely disputable, rejection of the idea that there may be other people with a legitimate interest in the heritage in question. (It is also worth noting in this connection that conventional legal notions of property, which mostly accord owners the right to do what they like with whatever belongs to them, are inadequate tools for thinking about the ethical responsibilities of the finders, managers or controllers of sites or objects of cultural interest)[6] In the contemporary global village, people increasingly care about sites of cultural interest wherever in the world they are. As Atle Omland writes, 'The [UNESCO] World Heritage concept rests fundamentally on the idea that cultural heritage can be held in common'.[7] But while this view has evident attractions, determining the relative weight of different stakeholder interests and finding modes of conflict-resolution that are acceptable to all parties are not always simple.

2. Responsibilities to Things

When archaeologists speak about the 'archaeological record', they are sometimes referring to the material sites and objects located within them, and sometimes to the knowledge obtainable from that material by the application of appropriate investigative techniques. This ambiguity is not entirely harmless. For archaeologists may persuade themselves that they are 'preserving the archaeological record' when they write up their excavation reports, where their investigations have actually damaged or degraded the material record. Brian Fagan sounds a salutary warning note:

> [I]n an era when the archaeological record [in the material sense] is under threat everywhere, the first concern of any research project should be

---

6   T. Allen, 'Legal Principles, Political Processes and Cultural Property', in G. Scarre and R. Coningham (eds.), *Appropriating the Past: Philosophical Perspectives on the Practice of Archaeology* (New York: Cambridge University Press, 2012), pp. 239-56.

7   A. Omland, 'The Ethics of the World Heritage Concept', in C. Scarre and G. Scarre (eds.), *The Ethics of Archaeology: Philosophical Perspectives on the Practice of Archaeology* (Cambridge: Cambridge University Press, 2006), p. 243.

the maintenance of the site and the stakes of all those concerned with its conservation – be they archaeologists, local land-owners, tourist officials, or indigenous peoples.[8]

Fagan's proposal may seem the merest common sense. Yet the only way of wholly conserving a site is to leave it completely alone. Even light-touch investigation which creates minimal disturbance causes permanent changes to a site. Attempts to restore it to its previous condition at the close of a dig often consist in little more than a cosmetic replacement of its previous covering of earth. Although the visual *status quo ante* may be restored in this way, signs of previous activity will still be apparent to later investigators who reopen the excavation. Objects of significance found at the site will have been removed, reducing the informational basis available to subsequent researchers. In some cases, exposure by archaeologists to the light and air of what has been long buried actually serves a sentence of destruction. (One of the most tragic examples is the fading away of hundreds of painted frescoes and inscriptions at Pompeii since they were first uncovered by diggers in the nineteenth century.) Clearly, archaeologists must be willing to put up with some loss of the material record in the creation of the knowledge-record; yet there can seem something oddly conflicted about a science that is willing to destroy the very thing it loves.

Still, without digging there would be no data, and most archaeologists consider that some amount of dislocation and destruction is an acceptable, if regrettable, price to pay for making the material record speak. But justifying the pretension to stewardship requires that a maxim of 'excavational economy' is adopted whereby a site is disturbed no more than is necessary to realise the basic research objectives. Collecting items that are surplus to requirements, and that will be left to gather dust in the storerooms of museums or archaeology departments, is academically pointless and morally irresponsible. Investigators need also to ensure that maximum benefit accrues to stakeholders from the work that has been carried out, by publishing and disseminating their analyses, facilitating public access to the site where practicable, and exhibiting the finds. (An exception to this publicity condition may be made where revealing the details of an archaeological site is liable to attract the attention of professional or amateur looters.) Last but not least, archaeologists must

---

8   B. Fagan, 'Foreword', in V. Cassman, N. Odegard and J. Powell (eds.), *Human Remains: Guide for Museums and Academic Institutions* (Lanham, MD: AltaMira Press, 2007), p. xvii.

interest themselves in the proper curation of objects that are removed in the course of excavations. Michael Trimble and Eugene Marino complain that many archaeologists continue to be negligent concerning the future of the objects collected once their own research questions have been answered. In their view, 'These collections should be valued, curated, and studied, not just by archaeologists, but by everyone with a professional interest and the results of those studies should be made widely available'.[9] If a particular institution lacks the facilities to look after objects properly, either it should not have acquired them in the first place or it should now transfer them to another location where they can be better studied, enjoyed and protected.

To speak about archaeologists' responsibilities to things is a way of acknowledging the value they have as objects created by and associated with our ancestors. This, of course, is quite different from their financial value in the commercial market; the earthenware funerary urns that so excited Sir Thomas Browne would have been of no interest to treasure-hunters on the trail of gold and silver. Nor is it identical with beauty or artistic value, as many objects without these (including human remains) can provide important information to the specialist. But the value that old objects possess for us is not entirely a function of what they can tell us about past lives. Much of the thrill of gazing on an ancient coin or pottery vessel or textile fragment derives from the very fact of its association with people who were once as real and vital as we are. In *A Treatise of Human Nature*, David Hume speculates that the 'esteem and admiration' we feel for very old objects stems from the sense of awe aroused in us when we contemplate vast passages of time.[10] But while Hume may be right that objects can fascinate by virtue of age alone, we are less likely to be deeply moved by ancient things that lack the human connection. The oldest stone tools or earthenware pots are vastly younger, for instance, than the fossilised tree-ferns that we blithely burn on our fires in the form of coal, yet only the former evoke our 'esteem and admiration'. Human remains, which have an even more intimate relationship with our forebears than the things they made or used, are naturally the most intriguing and evocative objects of all.

---

9 M.K. Trimble and E.A. Marino, 'Archaeological Curation: An Ethical Imperative for the Twenty-First Century', in L. Zimmerman, K. Vitelli and J. Hollowell-Zimmer (eds.), *Ethical Issues in Archaeology* (Walnut Creek, CA: AltaMira Press, 2003), p. 99.

10 D. Hume, *A Treatise of Human Nature*, ed. L.A. Selby-Bigge (Oxford: Oxford University Press, 1888), pp. 432, 433.

3. Responsibilities to the Profession

Archaeology is unusual among the sciences in that it can easily become a victim of its own success. Too much archaeology, or too many archaeologists, and the future of the subject is endangered by the sheer depletion of its source material. There are only so many ancient cities, sites and landscapes awaiting the archaeologist's spade, and the understandable desire of researchers to engage with the more before the less interesting means that the richest plums will tend to be selected first. When the richer sites are exhausted, archaeologists turn their attention to those of more marginal interest until they, too, are worked to the point of exhaustion. According to Fagan, 'Today there are hundreds, if not thousands, of researchers who are mining sites, often without reference to all the potential stakeholders involved, to answer purely academic – and often very insignificant – questions'.[11] It might be countered that such sites provide useful training-grounds for young archaeologists in places where they can do relatively little harm; also, that even minor academic questions may be worth answering in order to add small pieces to the larger jigsaw of the past. (But the questions really must be answered, and the answers published in appropriate places and within a reasonably short period of time, otherwise the disturbance of a site is indistinguishable from vandalism.) However, John Locke's principle that a resource may be appropriated only on condition that there is 'enough, and as good left in common for others' is difficult to apply in archaeology.[12] It looks as though future archaeologists will be forced to make do with the leavings from the current archaeologists' table.

Some archaeologists judge this picture to be needlessly alarmist. So long as human societies exist there will always be something new to excavate, as fresh generations go the way of their ancestors, leaving behind their own material traces. Larry Zimmerman pertinently asks: 'Archaeologists promote the idea that archaeological sites are non-renewable resources, but aren't humans creating new archaeological sites all the time?'[13] If archaeology aims 'to develop general principles about human behaviour', then sites of recent creation should be equally productive of information

---

11 Fagan, 2007, p. xvi.

12 J. Locke, *Two Treatises of Government*, ed. P. Laslett (New York: New American Library, 1963), p. 329.

13 Zimmerman, 1998, p. 78.

as older ones.[14] As one obvious example, in Britain and other early industrialising centres there is now a lively 'industrial archaeology' whose raw material is frequently less than a century or two old. In a few generations' time, archaeologists may be enthusiastically excavating the remains of our own civic centres and shopping malls. According to Zimmerman, there could in principle be a fruitful 'archaeology of five minutes ago'.[15] But while this is so, archaeologists who are fascinated by more ancient things – those who wish to study the origins of man, or the migrations of long-gone peoples, or the development of early technologies, or the rise of early civilisations – will eventually face a much more straitened choice of unexcavated locations. Do present archaeologists treat their successors unjustly by removing the opportunities for research that they themselves enjoy?

Depriving future archaeologists of similar opportunities to those enjoyed by present ones to excavate sites of prime importance may not seem a particularly grave evil in the greater scale of things. And if professional courtesy (to rank the moral obligation no higher) of current archaeologists to future ones dictates that they should reserve for them some potentially significant sites, there are other stakeholders in the archaeological enterprise whose interests may be less well served by such a self-denying ordinance. A rural community wanting to learn more about the history of their village, a people who wish to know who their ancestors were and where they came from, or members of the public who value the feeling of closeness to the past that archaeological discoveries can provide, may think it a poor reason for waiting to have their curiosity satisfied that future archaeologists will need to have something to do. Resolving this particular tension is challenging, but once again much may be achieved by mutually respectful and tolerant consultation among the various stakeholders concerned, and by a willingness to give and take. By encouraging the idea of an 'archaeology for all', professional archaeologists not only show themselves sensitive to the interests of those outside the profession, but benefit their own and later generations of archaeologists as well. By getting the public on their side, archaeologists are better placed to secure for their discipline the popular, political and

---

14 Ibid.

15 L.J. Zimmerman, 'Social Problems and Creating an Archaeology of "Now", Not Just "Back Then"', Address to World Archaeological Congress, WAC-6, University College, Dublin, 29 June – 4 July 2008.

financial support that is necessary to ensure its long-term prosperity. In the long run, the self-interest of the profession and the interests of other stakeholders may be less divergent than they may first have appeared. And if that is true, it is good news for everyone.

III

OWNERSHIP
AND RESTITUTION

8. 'National' Heritage and Scholarship

John Boardman

The debate over the handling and publication of ancient artefacts acquired through channels other than official excavation has raged for over fifty years. The 1970 UNESCO Convention on the Means of Prohibiting and Preventing the Illicit Import, Export and Transfer of Ownership of Cultural Property[1] has effectively increased the value of objects known before 1970 but done nothing to halt the acquisition and marketing of objects 'recovered' since that date, although there are a few inhibitions about the way they are marketed. Robbing graves probably ranks alongside other 'oldest professions' of the world, although nowadays it is often accidental, and since 'recycling' is generally perceived as being a civilised activity, it could readily be defended. More general recognition of national responsibility for the preservation of the evidence of ancient cultures in or on its soil is now in place and selectively acted upon, except where issues of greater political or economic force prevail. We can probably not expect more. But it is still not uncommon to hear the term 'national heritage' being used, and this can easily lead to a more casual approach to some aspects of the problem. Better by far to speak of 'global heritage', the 'heritage of man' or even just 'heritage', and whether it has to be 'cultural' or not may be a moot point.

The use of the word 'national' carries with it implications of moral or legal claims by any country on artefacts found on or in its soil. The implication is

---

1 See http://portal.unesco.org/en/ev.php-URL_ID=13039&URL_DO=DO_TOPIC&URL_SECTION=201.html

 http://dx.doi.org/10.11647/OBP.0047.08

that the modern nation has a responsibility, which is not contested, but that is based on some positive link between the modern and ancient cultures that the land sustained. Where this is clearly lacking, problems arise. It is easy to see where 'national' interests have been counter-productive, even in recent years – the destruction of Buddhist monuments by an Islamic state, the destruction of Islamic monuments by a Christian state, the destruction of anything that gets in the way of any sort of 'development' that is deemed more important.

Sometimes the argument for possession is more subtle or complicated. A fine Athenian vase made in about 500 BC was immediately exported to Italy where it was soon put into an Etruscan (non-Greek) grave and in modern times recovered 'unofficially' and taken to display in an American museum. It is a Greek product, its use was as an Etruscan grave offering, and its major period of display for admiration and study has been in a New World museum. It has been returned to Italy because it was found there, not because it was made there or because it might be a better demonstration of the quality of Greek art there. Objects of scholarly rather than aesthetic (i.e. for a modern public) importance are more easily judged and accommodated where they are best understood and appreciated, which is not always where they were found.

The restitution of 'works of art' to their country of origin might be held to depend on whether it is thought that they are in fact best appreciated there. We could hardly wish for the dispersal of collections of diverse post-antique world art, and should treasure all the more those galleries of ancient art composed from widely different sources – the British Museum, the Louvre, the Metropolitan Museum in New York, countless smaller galleries worldwide – which give the public the opportunity to judge and compare.

In all this, 'nationalism' need and should play no part. Genetic and/ or cultural continuity in populations is often too easily assumed and the markers for it (language, script) sometimes overvalued. Sometimes the differences are obvious – as in the Americas with their native and immigrant populations. Britain's genetic past is so variegated that it poses no serious problems of this type. For Greece the alphabet provides the strongest link with the past since even the ancient physical type – tall, fair-haired, blue eyed – is at some variance with the modern Balkan (Christian) aspect, much adjusted by contacts east and west. The fact that, whatever is alleged, there are very few countries whose modern populations have any serious genetic or cultural links with their distant past, should not be ignored – a problem which is (understandably but nonetheless mistakenly) not much favoured in modern political and historical scholarship.

The classical world is one in which the problem of restitution of monuments to their former physical position (not just environment) is at stake. Yet no one would put the Elgin marbles back on the rebuilt Parthenon where they would be barely visible, over forty-feet up. The marbles, which have been on display in the British Museum in London for nearly two centuries, have already proved their worth in the shaping of classicising arts as well as in general education for visitors from all over the world, through their juxtaposition with prime works from Egypt and the Near East. There must surely sometimes be a case to be made for not letting the past get in the way of the future.

While many 'source' countries take their responsibilities seriously, there are many shortcomings. To understand the past we need access to all the evidence, *in corpore* or in publication, yet, for the classical world, both Greece and Italy have very poor records indeed in the matter of publishing their own excavations, and in providing scholars with access to the evidence gathered in the process. Not that they are alone, there are still western museums which choose to be selective of whom they allow to study their material, on nationalistic grounds. This is not simply a matter of laziness or indifference. The remark that 'they want to steal our material' can still be heard, as well as manifest examples of scholars 'sitting on' what they perceive as 'their' material indefinitely, indifferent to whatever regulations there may be about the period for which they might claim priority. Jealousy seems a very strong motive in many cases, often abetted by extreme views about what 'copyright' entails.

For learned journals to restrict or ban publication of 'doubtful' objects is simply a censorship of scholarship indefensible on any grounds. Our attitude to the past, including that of scholars for whom it is a subject of intense interest and also often a living, can even verge on the superstitious. The worst example of this is the feeling that unprovenanced objects should not be studied by scholars, should not be published, should not be conserved, should perhaps even be destroyed – an approach which would not make the slightest difference to the discovery of objects, to a 'trade' and interest in collecting and display that is immemorial, and which reveals at the same time an indifference to the integrity of evidence and scholarly freedom, an attitude which is frankly itself unscholarly. That the American Institute of Archaeology takes some such views impugns its scholarly status. The German Institute is wary since the freedom of action by its foreign institutes might be jeopardised. Some scholarly journals are also wary, and they also thus betray their scholarly responsibilities.

'Ownership' of the past does no doubt need closer definition, not least of the responsibilities which it carries with it – to display, educate and publish. Alongside this we need recognition that scholarship devoted to the past should be one human activity that should on no account or for whatever reason be subject to censorship or suppression.

9. *Fear* of Cultural Objects

Tom Flynn

The terrible Buddha priests want their revenge! They seek me and they
will also find me! There is no escape from their secret power![1]

This paper seeks to read some of the current disputes about the collecting of cultural heritage through an analysis of *Furcht* (*Fear*). This little-known silent film of 1917 by the German director Robert Wiene (1873-1938), who went on to make *The Cabinet of Dr Caligari* (1920), is regarded as one of the most influential examples of German expressionist cinema. In *Fear*, a wealthy German Count returns home from India with a statuette he has stolen from a temple and thereafter gradually descends into a state of guilt-ridden paranoia over his acquisition.

The fear to which the title refers is ostensibly generated by the repercussions flowing from the Count's illicit acquisition of the statue and the fear of his own imminent death, foretold by a phantom Buddhist priest who visits his home. The relationship between the collector and the mysterious representative of the source community from which the object was removed echoes the encounter between powerful European nations and the peoples and communities they subordinated during the colonial era. The film also works on a psychological level, expressing the 'deep and fearful concern with the foundations of the self' that has been identified as a core preoccupation of early twentieth-century

---

1   Bruno Decarli as Count Greven, *Furcht*, directed by Robert Wiene, 1917.

       http://dx.doi.org/10.11647/OBP.0047.09

German cinema.[2] As Siegfried Kracauer has suggested, the political circumstances of the period immediately after the First World War prompted the contemporaneous imagination towards the ancient concept of Fate – 'Doom, decreed by an inexorable Fate was not mere accident but a majestic event that stirred metaphysical shudders in sufferers and witnesses alike'.[3]

Released in 1917, just prior to the German Revolution and the establishment of the Weimar Republic, Wiene's narrative, played out in the film through the experiences of the wealthy collector, might also be interpreted as prefiguring Germany's surrendering of its colonies that became a condition of the Treaty of Versailles. *Fear*, I suggest, can thus be read as a symbolic enactment within the cultural sphere of the castration anxiety articulated almost contemporaneously by Freud. It might also stand as an early example of what Anton Kaes has described as 'shell shock cinema' – films that 'evoke fear of invasion and injury, and exude a sense of paranoia and panic'.[4] Wiene's own *Dr Caligari* remains one of the pivotal examples of this sub-genre, and while *Fear* may not partake of the 'fragmented story lines, distorted perspectives … abrupt editing and sharp lighting' that Kaes identifies as the defining characteristics of shell shock cinema between 1918 and 1933, the film does rehearse another of that category's core preoccupations. The soldier's return from the front in a psychologically altered state from that in which he left – 'he has come home, but the war has come with him'[5]– is a theme mirrored in the plight of *Fear*'s Count Greven who returns from his travels psychologically disturbed, or as the intertitle has it: 'Two years ago a happy cheerful man went abroad – and what sort of man came home?'

While these aspects of film history and film criticism are fruitful routes into an appreciative understanding of *Fear*, I want instead to focus here on the film's frame story about the acquisition and collection of cultural objects. Wiene's ambiguous treatment of fear also provides

---

2   S. Kracauer, *From Caligari to Hitler: A Psychological History of the German Film* (Princeton, NJ: Princeton University Press, 1974 [1947]), p. 30.

3   Ibid., p. 88.

4   A. Kaes, *Shell Shock Cinema: Weimar Culture and the Wounds of War* (Princeton, NJ: Princeton University Press, 2009), p. 3.

5   Kaes, 2009, p. 2.

a lens through which to read the ideologically loaded discourses that cluster around cultural heritage issues today. It is an unusual theme for a film of that period and in a sense we might see it as the venerable initiator of a cinematic 'cultural heritage' category that embraces everything from Chadi Abdel Salam's thoughtful *Al Mummia* (*The Night of Counting the Days*) of 1969, and Jules Dassin's heist caper *Topkapi* (1964), to the popular *Indiana Jones* and *Lara Croft: Tomb Raider* franchises.

Vestiges of the anxiety dramatised in *Fear* can still be detected today in attitudes expressed towards the 'encyclopaedic' museums of Europe and North America by source nations seeking to recover objects appropriated during the era of colonial conquest. Conversely, the combative positions adopted by some museum directors in their attempts to ward off repatriation requests appear to express another kind of anxiety – a fear of 'the floodgates' opening[6] – leading to the wholesale denuding of museums and the loss of the reassuring material plenitude that is a legacy of Enlightenment-era collecting.

Wiene's film hinges on the overpowering sense of foreboding felt by a wealthy aristocrat whose acquisitive impulse has driven him to commit a cultural crime. Whether the emotions he manifests on arriving home with the statue are intended to signify tremors of colonial guilt, Wiene leaves the viewer to decide. Is the fear experienced by his protagonist a response to some genuine objective danger, or the delusions of a deranged mind – a real fear or a neurotic fear, to use Freud's typology?[7] Wiene's father is said to have suffered from mental illness towards the end of his life,[8] which has been considered a possible source of the psychological themes explored in his later *Dr Caligari*. Released in 1917, *Fear* provides an even earlier point of reference for those concerns.

***

The film opens with the return to his ancestral home of the wealthy Count Greven (Bruno Decarli) from a 'foreign journey of several years'.

---

6 T.-L. Williams, 'Cultural Perpetuation: Repatriation of First Nations Cultural Heritage', *University of British Columbia Law Review*, 29, 1995, pp. 183-201.

7 S. Freud, 'The Uncanny' (1919), in *Art and Literature* (London: Penguin, 1990).

8 U. Jung and W. Schatzberg (eds.), *Beyond Caligari: The Films of Robert Wiene* (New York and Oxford: Berghahn, 1999), p. 66.

As his carriage pulls up outside the castle, numerous manservants are on hand to attend to his luggage. Once inside, the Count, visibly distraught, instructs his servants to lock all the doors and bolt all the gates to the estate, announcing: 'I never want to see a strange face again!' He makes his way upstairs to his private quarters, passing through rooms full of Chinese porcelain, Old Master paintings and antique furniture. Some moments later his servants enter, carrying a large rectangular wooden trunk he has brought back from his travels. After dismissing them, the Count furtively unlocks the trunk and removes a metal statue of a Buddhist deity, which he begins passionately to embrace, before returning it to the box and locking it. When night falls, the Count returns to the box, removes the statue and carries it to another room where he installs it on a pedestal in a specially designed niche behind a glass door concealed by a curtain.

In the days that follow, the Count becomes increasingly agitated, skulking around his castle at night with a lighted candle, constantly looking over his shoulder, peering nervously out of the windows and into darkened recesses. Aware of his master's mounting anxiety, the Count's butler seeks help from the village minister, who offers to visit (we later learn he is the Count's former teacher and mentor). The Count confides in the minister, telling him, 'You know that I am driven by an unhappy passion for collecting rare works of art, which drove me into the world to see the most beautiful art objects'. He then reveals how, 'one day, deep in the heart of India, I heard about the holy Buddha image in the Temple at Djaba, whose beauty made the sick well and the sad happy … I had to see it'.

The film then cuts to a flashback in which the Count, dressed in full colonial regalia of pith helmet and white three-piece suit, is shown creeping stealthily into a temple interior where he eavesdrops on a ritual conducted by a Buddhist high priest (Conrad Veidt) involving a small statue. After the priest and his acolytes have left, the Count approaches the statue and swoons in front of it, before snatching it from its niche and departing. The priests return to the temple and are enraged to find their sacred object missing.

Back in his castle, the Count tells the minister, 'Since that day I have had no peace. The terrible Buddha priests want their revenge! They seek me and they will also find me! There is no escape from their secret power!'

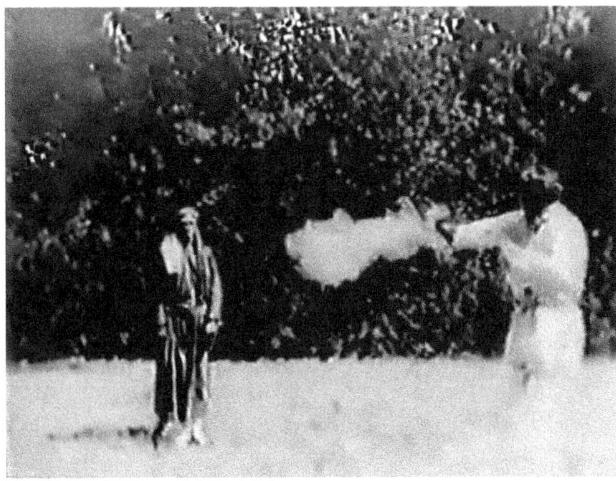

Fig. 9.1 Count Greven shoots the Buddhist priest.

That night, an exterior shot of the castle gardens reveals the Buddhist priest standing statue-like on the lawn, staring up at the Count's window. Lying in bed, but suddenly aware of the proximity of a sinister presence, the Count rises and takes a pistol from under his pillow. From his window he sees the figure of the priest and in an agitated state proceeds out into the garden to confront him. Without entering into a dialogue with the man, the Count fires three shots. The priest remains standing, evidently unharmed, at which point the Count collapses before him and pleads to be put out of his misery: 'Take my life! Death will be a release for me!' The priest calmly shakes his head and replies:

> Then I would take something of no value to you! Instead you must live and learn to love life. Then today seven years hence you will die at the hand of one who is dearest to you.

Stricken with fear, the Count returns upstairs to the cabinet in which he has placed the statue and is unsettled to find pinned to the plinth a handwritten note confirming the curse – 'Do not forget … today seven years hence!' Seemingly reconciled to his fate, the Count decides to live life to the full, hosting elaborate soirées, gambling, drinking and dancing through the night with his friends. One evening, still troubled by his approaching death, he abruptly calls a halt to the partying. He banishes the revellers and thereafter embarks upon a series of scientific experiments in his basement laboratory. Yet even after discovering a means to convert nitrogen into protein – 'which could do away with hunger in the world forever' – the Count smashes his scientific equipment and decides to divert his energies towards something new. This time it is love that preoccupies him. A romantic interlude ensues in which he woos a young woman (Mechtildis Thein), escorting her around the castle ramparts, frolicking with her beside the lake, enfolding her in passionate embraces. And yet, despite the 'days full of sunshine and happiness', the Count knows time is running out and soon plunges back into a state of near delirium. Convinced the statue is the source of his torment, he takes it to the lake and casts it into the water. On returning to the castle he is suddenly overcome by a dark intuition and approaches the cabinet, only to discover to his horror that the statue has mysteriously reappeared – 'The suffering!'

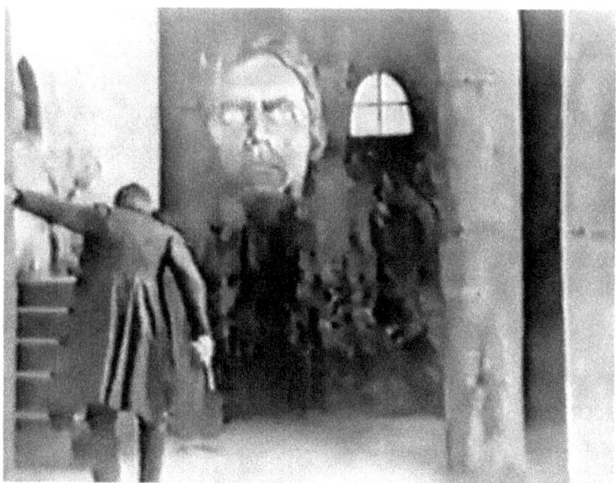

Fig 9.2 Count Greven encounters the ghostly face of the priest in his cellar.

Fearing imminent death, the Count begins to perceive danger everywhere and even accuses his butler of poisoning his tea. He then enters his study to find his lover idly fondling a dagger. This reminds him of the curse – 'The hand of the one who is dearest to you'. He promptly takes out his pistol and fires at her, but misses. 'I hate the world!' he declares. 'I hate life! There is no hand that is dearest to me!'

The camera now reveals the Buddhist priest has returned to the garden and is seated on the lawn in the lotus position, hands clasped over his breast, head bowed. Inside the castle, the Count descends to the cellar, gun in hand, where he begins to lurch about in suicidal panic. Finally, when the ghostly face of the Buddhist priest appears in the air before him, he slowly turns the gun towards his own heart and fires.

In the closing sequence, a series of double-exposure shots convey the spectral image of the priest rising from the lawn and entering the castle.

He climbs the stairs to the cabinet room, retrieves the statue and solemnly carries it away.

***

Rarely has the restitution of cultural property been so melodramatically enacted. While the film could be read as a symbol of the neurotic *Weltanschauung* of the German nation at the end of the war, it also comments on the psychology of colonial collecting. A closer examination of the film's symbolism and narrative arc reinforces the relevance of both interpretations. The Weimar Republic, established a year after *Fear* was released, ushered in a cultural environment of what the historian Peter Gay has described as 'exuberant creativity and experimentation', and yet one tempered by 'anxiety, fear and a rising sense of doom'.[9] Wiene's film mirrors these apparent cultural contradictions as Count Greven veers between irrational dread and the rational impulse towards scientific research (the village minister who comes to counsel him concludes: 'You don't need a priest, you need a doctor'.) Wiene had dealt with the idea of threatened rationality in a number of his films of this period.[10] *Fear* might thus be seen as an example of what the cultural historian Richard Brantlinger has described as 'Imperial Gothic', a literary topos that 'combines the seemingly scientific, progressive, often Darwinian ideology of imperialism with an antithetical interest in the occult'.[11]

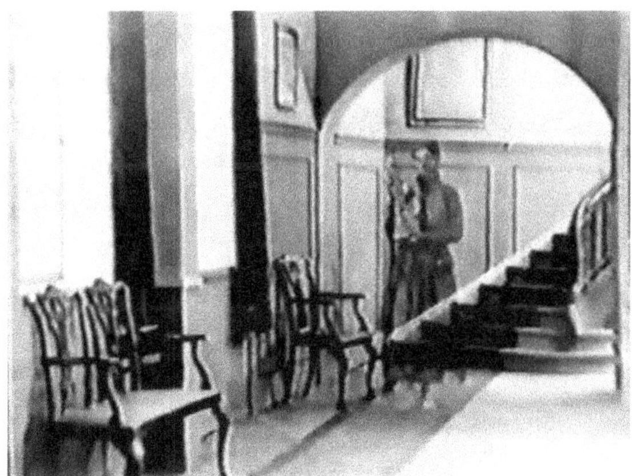

Fig 9.3 The spectral image of the Buddhist priest departs
with the recovered statuette.

---

9   P. Gay, *Weimar Culture: The Outsider as Insider* (London: Norton, 2001 [1968]), p. xiv.

10 Jung and Schatzberg, 1999.

11 P. Brantlinger, *Rule of Darkness: British Literature and Imperialism, 1830-1914* (Ithaca, NY: Cornell University Press, 1990), p. 227.

The 'haunting' of Count Greven provides a useful metaphor through which to explore more recent developments in the 'culture wars' between source nations and western collectors (be they so-called encyclopaedic museums or private individuals). Underpinning many of these disputes are various strains of fear. On the one hand, it is clear that some European and North American museum directors fear that the increasingly vocal and determined calls for repatriation of objects acquired during earlier eras – indeed still being acquired in 1917 at the time Robert Wiene directed *Fear* – could lead to a serious stripping-out of western museums.[12] This was most clearly articulated in the 'Declaration on the Importance and Value of Universal Museums' issued by the Bizot Group of museum directors in 2002, which proved divisive and controversial within and beyond the international museum community.

The emotional response to rising demands for restitution of objects can be contrasted with the fear felt by some developing nations who interpret European and North American museums as tyrannical symbols of imperial greed. As Kavita Singh has noted, the knowledge that significant amounts of other nations' cultural patrimony is languishing in the basements of these museums, much of it uncatalogued and neglected, has engendered a view of encyclopaedic museums as 'terrifying places with insatiable appetites for works of art'.[13]

Count Greven's castle, with its grand salons brimming with Dutch Golden Age portraits, Imari vases, Indian sculptures and heavy antique furniture, might be seen as a symbol of the western museum complex. The Count, having admitted to an unquenchable desire to seek out the world's most beautiful works of art, struggles to reconcile his acquisitive impulse with a nagging awareness of the unethical nature of his collecting. Returning home with the Buddhist statue looted from the Indian temple at Djaba, the Count places it on a stand in a glazed cabinet concealed behind heavy curtains. The object is thus immediately 'museified', 'pedestalised' – that is, decontextualised, marked out. Its symbolic power as a synecdoche of a

---

12 See, for example, J. Cuno, *Whose Muse? Art Museums and the Public Trust* (Princeton, NJ: Princeton University Press, 2004); J. Cuno, *Who Owns Antiquity? Museums and the Battle over our Ancient Heritage* (Princeton, NJ: Princeton University Press, 2010); J. Cuno, *Museums Matter: In Praise of the Encyclopaedic Museum* (Chicago, IL: University of Chicago Press, 2011); J. Cuno, *Whose Culture? The Promise of Museums and the Debate over Antiquities* (Princeton, NJ: Princeton University Press, 2012).

13 K. Singh, 'Do we really want the freer circulation of cultural goods?', *The Art Newspaper*, 192, June 2008, http://www.theartnewspaper.com/articles/Do-we-really-want-the-freer-circulation-of-cultural-goods?/8581

mysterious and unknowable Orient becomes apparent from the moment the Count arrives home, telling his servants, 'Lock the doors, bolt the gates! I never want to see a strange face again!' The reference to the temple at Djaba is clearly a fictional confection, although in Hindu traditions djaba refers to a particular social group and means literally 'outside'.[14]

Credited as the film's writer as well as director, Wiene may have drawn on his own collecting interests in creating his original script for *Fear*. Wiene was himself a collector of Benin sculpture, a significant amount of which was dispersed through the international art market following the sacking of the Benin kingdom of west Africa by the British Punitive Expedition of 1897. This was a classic instance of pith-helmet subjugation, the British ransacking the Benin Kingdom in retaliation for the killing of some of their soldiers during an earlier mission undertaken ostensibly to form a trade agreement with the Benin people.[15] The Punitive Expedition sent the Oba of Benin into exile and looted the kingdom of its cultural heritage, including carved ivory leopards and the extraordinary ancient brass sculptures that had for centuries adorned the Oba's royal residence. The Benin objects almost immediately became enveloped by controversy, chiefly on account of the circumstances of their acquisition. Many of the brasses found their way into the British Museum, others entered museums in Chicago, Boston, Berlin, Hamburg, Dresden and elsewhere, while still others were bought at auction by European private collectors or through dealers who acquired them on the secondary market. Wiene, it seems, was one such collector, although exactly when and how he took possession of his own examples is unclear. Dr Hans Feld, former editor of the influential German film magazine *Film Kurier*, who knew Wiene during the director's time in London in the mid-1930s, recalled of his frequent visits to Wiene's flat in Maida Vale:

> Wiene and his wife offered a home away from home. He took personal interest in the daily lives of his guests and with his smiling scepticism he created some balance. His art collection – mainly Benin sculptures – was a reminder of a world which most of us had forgotten.[16]

---

14 K.P.H. Koentjaraningrat (ed.), *Villages in Indonesia* (Kuala Lumpur, Jakarta: Equinox Press, 2007 [1967]), pp. 221-24.

15 R. Bacon, *Benin: City of Blood* (Memphis, TN: General Books, 2009 [1897]).

16 Jung and Schatzberg, 1999, p. 19.

Forgotten, perhaps – certainly largely overlooked by a museum-going public who at that time would still have seen them as 'primitive' or 'tribal'[17] – the Benin sculptures have subsequently come to figure among the most contested objects in the uncompromising stand-offs between source nations and encyclopaedic museums. They are now widely recognised as evidence of the worst excesses of colonial aggression and thus symbols of the imperial underpinnings of the 'universal', or encyclopaedic, museum. Was Wiene motivated to write *Fear* as a result of his own experience of owning a sculpture that had been illicitly removed from a weaker nation? That question may never be settled, but how prescient his film now seems in the light of later developments in the fractious politics of cultural heritage collecting.

The encyclopaedic museum has its roots in the princely collections of Renaissance Europe which held that the ordered arrangement of objects could amount to a legible representation of the wider universe. That tradition was developed during the era of the European Enlightenment when the museum emerged as an expression of the rational impulse to order and classify, to contain the whole universe beneath one roof. More recent analyses, however, have come to view the museum's universalising strategies as fundamentally irrational and illegible, not to say unsustainable. As Eugenio Donato has observed:

> The set of objects the Museum displays is sustained only by the fiction that they somehow constitute a coherent representational universe ... Such a fiction is the result of an uncritical belief in the notion that ordering and classifying, that is to say, the spatial juxtaposition of fragments, can produce a representational understanding of the world.[18]

Count Greven's collecting is presented as an irrational, obsessive activity as opposed to the rational, reflective pursuit of knowledge through classification.[19] His private, almost fetishistic relationship with the statue is signalled from the moment he removes it from its box. Jealously guarding it from the eyes of others, he embraces it, fondles it, clutches it to his breast with an amorous passion.

---

17 J. Clifford, *The Predicament of Culture: Twentieth Century Ethnography, Literature and Art* (Cambridge, MA: Harvard University Press, 1988).

18 E. Donato, 'The Museum's Furnace: Notes towards a Contextual Reading of Bouvard and Pécuchet', in J. Harari (ed.), *Textual Strategies: Perspectives in Post-Structural Criticism* (Ithaca, NY: Cornell University Press, 1979), p. 223.

19 Clifford, 1988, p. 219.

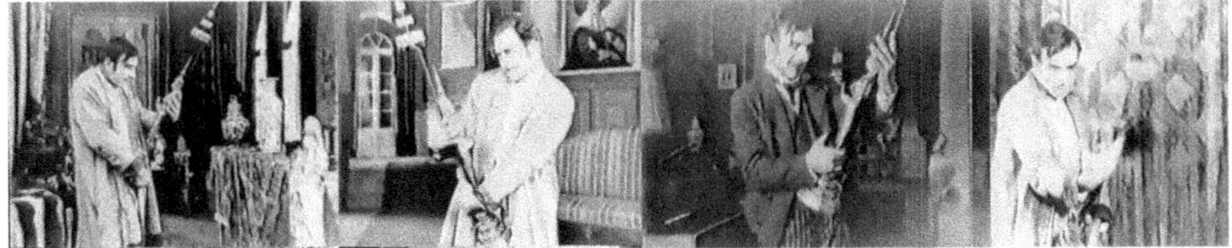

Fig 9.4 Count Greven with the object of his desire.

The phallic connotations are apparent in almost every frame in which the statue is shown: the Count holds it before him like an erect penis, his scopophilic fixation coexisting with the dread that it will be taken away from him. The psychoanalytic roots of this kind of anxiety are well documented in Freud's work, but there are fictional precedents too. French author Maurice Leblanc's popular Arsène Lupin mysteries, almost contemporaneous with *Fear*, echo the torment experienced by Wiene's obsessive collector. In *Arsène Lupin in Prison* (1907), Leblanc writes:

> Baron Satan leads a life of fear. He is afraid, not for himself, but for the treasures which he has accumulated with so tenacious a passion and with the perspicacity of a collector whom not even the most cunning of dealers can boast of ever having taken in. He loves his curiosities with all the greed of a miser, with all the jealousy of a lover.[20]

From the opening frames of the film, the life of fear led by Wiene's Count Greven is marked out in relation to the statue and seems to be generated by a consciousness of his guilt in having stolen it. In a key moment in the film, the Count fires his gun at the figure of the priest who remains unharmed – the first suggestion that he may be merely a figment of the Count's imagination. The Count falls at the priest's feet and begs to be put out of his guilt-ridden misery. 'I want to die', he cries, as if the ultimate punishment at the hands of this 'terrible Buddha priest' is the only way to end his torment.

The theft or unauthorised extraction of cultural heritage, even in its most fragmentary form – and the guilt such acts can engender in the perpetrator – is also a theme in twenty-first-century art practice. British artist Andy Holden's *Pyramid Piece* (2010), fashioned out of panels of knitted yarn and upholstery foam over a steel armature, takes the form of a huge lump of rock. It represents an enlargement of a tiny piece taken from the Great Pyramid

---

20 M. Leblanc, *Arsène Lupin in Prison* (Whitefish, MT: Kessinger Press, 2012 [1907]).

of Giza by Holden while visiting Egypt with his family as a young boy. 'It became for me, at the age of ten, this kind of strange guilt object', Holden has said of the piece he stole. 'I couldn't really understand why I wanted to take something authentic rather than buy a replica'.[21] Fifteen years later he returned to Egypt to try and locate the exact place on the pyramid from which he had taken the fragment. The knitted sculpture, then, is merely a pretext for the articulation of an inexplicable desire to possess the object and the experience of its removal and eventual return.[22]

The unexpected effect an illicitly acquired object or fragment can have on its possessor is an abiding theme in literature and film. Wilkie Collins' *The Moonstone* of 1868 set a benchmark for mystery narratives centred around disputed cultural heritage. Like the Buddhist statue in *Fear*, the moonstone has been taken from its rightful home by a European traveller (a British army officer) and, as in *Fear*, it becomes the focus of a quest for repatriation by Indian priests. It is eventually returned to the statue from which it was originally removed.

Guilt – or the anxiety induced by illicit ownership – seems also to have motivated the return of a fragment of the Colosseum removed by an American couple while on holiday in Italy in the 1980s. Regretting what she eventually came to see as a thoughtless and selfish act, Mrs Janice Johnson of North Carolina posted the fragment to Rome's archaeological office with a covering letter in which she confessed: 'I have been bothered by the fact that we took something that did not belong to us and am now returning it. I have felt badly about it whenever I would see this rock sitting on our shelf among our other artefacts from trips taken over the years of our lives'.[23] The not uncommon tendency to assign some metaphysical quality to inanimate objects in cultural heritage cases was illustrated by the Johnsons' closing request to the Roman authorities that the fragment be returned to the Colosseum 'so it may again be at rest back where it belongs'.[24]

The guilt experienced by individuals like the Johnsons can be contrasted with the attitudes of stubborn indifference adopted by encyclopaedic

---

21 Andy Holden, *Tate Shot: Art Now: Return of the Pyramid Piece*, 10 April 2010, https://www. youtube.com/watch?v=mr5WCSziG28

22 Described by Holden in the associated video work, *Return of the Pyramid Piece*, https:// www.youtube.com/watch?v=mr5WCSziG28

23 'US tourists return Roman artifact 25 years later', *The Guardian*, 7 May 2009, http://www. guardian.co.uk/world/feedarticle/8495017

24 'US couple return ancient artifact to Rome after 25 years', *The Telegraph*, 8 May 2008, http://www.telegraph.co.uk/news/newstopics/howaboutthat/5293725/US-couple-return-ancient-artifact-to-Rome-after-25-years.html

museums seeking to deflect calls for return. Expressions of remorse or regret – accompanied by an official apology – have occasionally been articulated by governments or heads of state on behalf of nations seeking to heal historical wrongs, often inflicted during the imperial age. In the case of the Parthenon Marbles in the British Museum – the appropriation of which by Lord Elgin is also widely viewed as an act of cultural desecration, the Ottoman permission to remove them notwithstanding – opinion polls consistently show a majority of the public in favour of return.[25] In this respect, the British Museum and many of today's larger museums who face similar cases, are failing to act in accordance with the wishes and sensibilities of the people they purport to represent. Might it be the case that they have come to see the prospect of mass returns as a form of punishment for the acquisitive activities of earlier generations. Fear of punishment was not what drove Mrs. Johnson to return the fragment of the Colosseum, she merely felt it was the ethical thing to do. But guilt seems to have been a motivating factor, as it was in the case of Andy Holden's returned pyramid piece. In *Fear*, Count Greven's attempt to banish his sense of guilt lead him to try and dispose of the stolen statue by throwing it in the lake. The theme echoes Picasso's attempt a few years earlier to dispose of an ancient Iberian sculpture in his collection, which had been sold to him by an associate of his friend Apollinaire, a Belgian named Géry Pieret, who had stolen it from the Louvre in 1911.[26] Under suspicion for the theft, Picasso and Apollinaire considered throwing the sculpture in the Seine to deflect suspicion away from themselves and, presumably, thereby to remove the burden of fear and guilt.

Freud saw guilt as the most important problem in the evolution of culture, maintaining that 'the price of progress in civilisation is paid in forfeiting happiness through the heightening of the sense of guilt'.[27] Moreover, in his clinical studies Freud found that 'the sense of guilt expresses itself in an unconscious seeking for punishment'.[28] Throughout *Fear*, Wiene provides plentiful hints that what we are witnessing are the phantasms of a psychotic mind – the ghostly apparition in the garden; the magical reappearance of the statue in its cabinet after the Count has thrown it in the lake; the

---

25 The issue of 'restitution' is discussed by Sir Mark Jones in Chapter 10 in this volume.

26 S. Loreti, 'The Affair of the Statuettes Reexamined: Picasso and Apollinaire's Role in the Famed Louvre Theft', in N. Charney (ed.), *Art and Crime: Exploring the Dark Side of the Art World* (Santa Barbara, CA: Praeger/ABC-CLIO, 2009), pp. 52-63.

27 S. Freud, *Civilization and its Discontents* (Eastford, CT: Martino Fine Books, 2010 [1929]), p. 123.

28 Freud, 2010/1929, p. 125.

presence of the handwritten note decreeing the seven-year curse; and the substitution of the priest for the carriage driver as the Count is preparing to flee the castle (foreshadowing the demonic coach driver who crops up just a few years later in F.W. Murnau's *Nosferatu*). All these combine to deliver an aura of the uncanny, the *Unheimlich*, that characterised so much German expressionist cinema of this period.[29]

The fear that a wronged people – often configured as the dead or half-dead – will somehow return to wreak ghastly vengeance on the living is an enduring trope of the Gothic genre (the Buddhist priest who cannot be killed also prefigures the zombies beloved of later Hollywood horror). To suggest that the vengeful Other of the imperial age has now returned to haunt the encyclopaedic museum might be to stretch the metaphor. What is undeniable, however, is that the increasingly clamorous demands by source nations for return of their cultural property is beginning to present an existential challenge to these institutions.

Tellingly, at the end of Wiene's film, although Count Greven has killed himself, the image of the 'terrible Buddhist priest' – previously presented as a probable symptom of the Count's psychotic state – survives in film time to reclaim his temple statue. Wiene thereby genuflects towards that strand of counter-Enlightenment metaphysics upon which the cinematic art has always thrived. Thus, while ostensibly a psychodrama about an obsessive collector, *Fear* is also a disquisition on film itself and our fascination with the threshold between fantasy and reality and the monsters lurking beyond the boundaries of the rational mind. Meanwhile, the increasingly persistent calls on European and North American museums for the return of cultural objects are not issuing from some spectral being. They are a reality. If, like Count Greven, we feel fear, it is entirely of our own making.

---

29 Freud, 1990/1919; S.S. Prawer, *Caligari's Children: The Film as Tale of Terror* (Cambridge, MA: Da Capo, 1980).

10. Restitution

Mark Jones[1]

In considering the thorny questions of restitution it may be helpful to begin with some recent examples of restitution in action, to see if the practice and principles enunciated to support, or implicit in, these cases have a bearing on the yet more controversial areas in which claims for restitution remain contentious.

On St Andrews Day 1996, a rectangular block of sandstone, 'The Stone of Destiny', was formally installed in Edinburgh Castle.

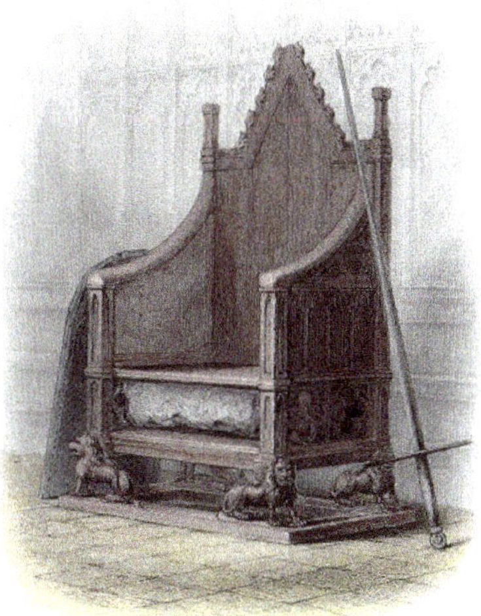

Fig. 11.1 The Coronation Chair of Edward I, 1296,
with the Stone of Destiny.

---

1   A version of this essay appeared in *The Art Newspaper*, 250, October 2013, pp. 67-70.

                    http://dx.doi.org/10.11647/OBP.0047.10

This act of restitution was intended symbolically and really to undo the actions of Edward I of England 'Hammer of the Scots' who, seven hundred years earlier in 1296, had instructed that the Stone of Destiny, the coronation stone of the Kings of Scots, should be taken from Scone Abbey and carried south to Westminster Abbey. There it was placed in the King of England's coronation chair, 'King Edward's Chair', in Westminster Abbey, thus symbolically asserting and reinforcing England's claim to sovereignty over Scotland.

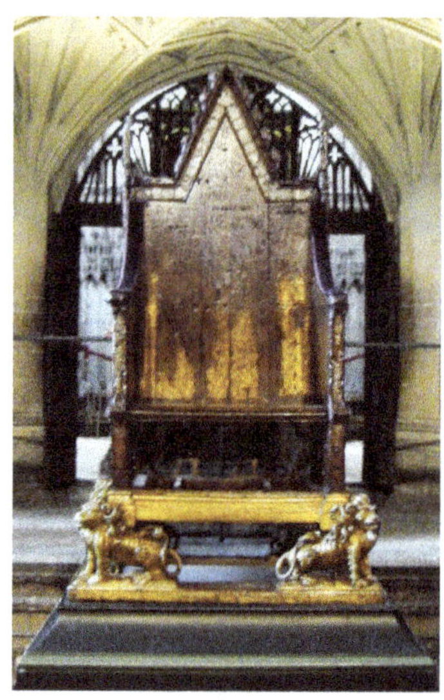

Fig. 11.2 King Edward's Chair, Westminster Abbey, England.

The Scots were not alone in believing that objects had the power to confer and confirm legitimacy in the exercise of power. St Stephen's Crown, for example, not only conferred legitimacy on the kings of Hungary, but ruled in their place during the regency that followed the First World War. Similarly, the royal treasures held at the Abbey of St Dennis had a crucial part in the inauguration of the Kings of France and the London Stone had a similar function for those who ruled London. For many cultures across the globe (e.g. Maori taonga in New Zealand), objects can acquire sacred or symbolic power which makes them much more significant to people's sense of themselves and their history than their often unimpressive physical appearance might suggest. It is the symbolic significance of possession and relinquishment, their close association with perceptions of power and status, that makes restitution and return so difficult and emotionally charged.

The return of the Stone of Destiny was initiated by a desperately unpopular Conservative Secretary of State for Scotland, Michael Forsyth (now Baron Forsyth of Drumlean), who presumably hoped that its return would persuade Scottish voters that Scotland's nationhood would remain proud and intact under Conservative administration, without devolution (the re-creation of a Scottish parliament) and within the United Kingdom. It was not a success: the Conservatives lost all their Scottish seats in the following elections.

Surprisingly few questions about this act of restitution were raised at the time. But the Irish and the English have, if we can derive a theory of restitution from the generality of current cases, a better claim to the Stone than the Scots. It is often maintained that objects should be returned to their place of origin: this is one of the bases of Italian, Greek, Turkish and Egyptian claims for the return of antiquities. Yet the 'origin' of the authentic Stone of Destiny is, according to legend, not Edinburgh or Scone but Tara in Ireland. It is sometimes also claimed that it is the length of association with a particular place or culture that is important. But the Stone of Destiny has been in Westminster Abbey for longer than it was at Scone Abbey.

To complicate matters further the Stone's authenticity is questionable. Alex Salmond (First Minister of Scotland and Leader of the Scottish National Party) is one of many who have publicly doubted it.[2] It can hardly be true that the stone is, as legend would have it, the coronation stone of the Kings of Tara in Ireland, brought by King Fergus to Scotland in the late fifth century. Geologists have identified the stone from which it is made as coming from the vicinity not of Tara but of Scone in Scotland. Nor does it look like the seat on which John Balliol was crowned in 1292. Walter de Hemingford, who attended Balliol's coronation, described this as 'hollowed and made in the form of a round chair'.[3] Perhaps the Abbot of Scone gave Edward's men something else altogether and hid the authentic chair. But if so, why was the authentic stone not used for the coronation of Robert the Bruce? And why did the Scots want it back badly enough to make its return one of their objectives in negotiating the Treaty of Edinburgh/Northampton in 1327-28 (Edward III issued a royal writ requiring its return, but it was never carried out). In 1950 four young nationalists stole the stone from Westminster Abbey. It was broken in the process and Alex Salmond is not alone in suggesting that the stone returned in 1951 could have been one of the copies made by Bertie Gray, the Glasgow stonemason to whom the stone was taken for repair. But

---

2   Auslan Cramb, 'Stone of Destiny is fake, claims Alex Salmond', *The Telegraph*, 16 June 2008,   http://www.telegraph.co.uk/news/newstopics/howaboutthat/5293725/US-couple-return-ancient-artifact-to-Rome-after-25-years.html
3   This suggests that it was similar to St Winifred's seventh-century throne, the 'Frith Stool', in Hexham Abbey, which is made in exactly this way.

would Scots therefore regard an English claim for the permanent return of the Stone to Westminster with indifference? Almost certainly not; at least until a more convincing and better preserved version turns up.

It begins, I hope, to be apparent that discussion of restitution within the United Kingdom raises many of the key issues in a context which, precisely because it is domestic – and therefore somewhat less fraught than restitution claims involving disputes between states as well as nations – helps us to understand that these issues are universal.

There are many other examples of restitution debates within the UK. In May 1999 the leading Scottish Nationalist Winnie Ewing was quoted in the Glasgow Herald: 'Not only have we seen the return of the Stone of Destiny to Scotland, but another part of our history is returning'.[4] She was referring to the Dunkeld Lectern which is said to have been made in Italy in 1498 and given by Pope Alexander VI to George Crichton when he became Bishop of Dunkeld in 1526 (rather confusingly since Alexander VI died in 1503).

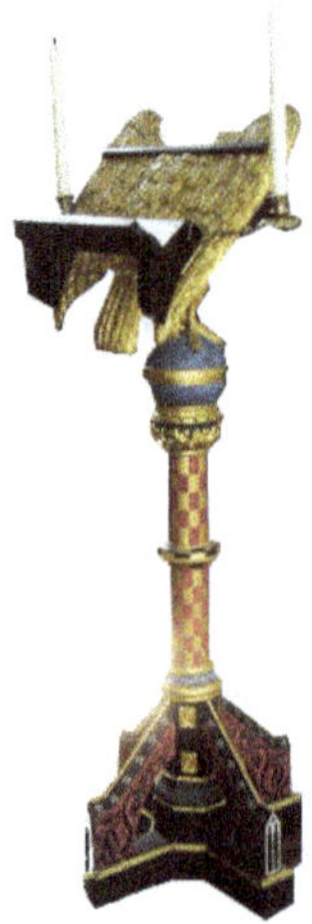

Fig. 11.3 The lectern at St Alban's, Copnor.

William Galloway, a Scottish antiquarian writing in 1879, suggested that the lectern, which bears George Crichton's name and arms, and which had been found in St Stephen's Church, in the English town St Albans, when the Montagu family tomb was opened in 1748, might have been given to

---

4   Raymond Duncan, 'A lost Scots treasure emerges from hiding Dunkeld Lectern makes capital return', *The Herald*, 3 May 1999, http://www.heraldscotland.com/sport/spl/aberdeen/a-lost-scots-treasure-emerges-from-hiding-dunkeld-lectern-makes-capital-return-1.293750

the church by Sir Richard Lee.[5] It is known that Lee looted a brass font from Holyrood Abbey during a punitive expedition launched against the Scots by Henry VIII in 1544, which he gave to the Abbey Church (now cathedral) in St Albans and which was melted down during the English Civil War, so Galloway suggested that the lectern might also have been looted and demanded its return to Scotland.

The lectern's loan to the exhibition 'Angels, Nobles and Unicorns' in 1982 aroused strong nationalist feelings in Scotland and it was stolen from St Stephen's church in 1984. Happily it reappeared, after extended negotiations between the Church of England and the Church of Scotland, during my time as director of the National Museums of Scotland in the 1990s, and eventually went on display in the Museum of Scotland as an icon of Scottish History.

But again, on the basis of the accepted story, the lectern originated not in Scotland but in Italy and has been associated with St Stephen's Church, St Albans for more than 400 years (from roughly 1544 to 1984) – much longer than with Dunkeld (less than 20 years). To add to the confusion, a census of eagle lecterns of this type demonstrates that they are overwhelmingly found in churches north of London, in East Anglia and central England, and it seems probable that they were made in England or the Low Countries. So it must be the historic wrong, Sir Richard Lee's putative pillage, that motivated the Church and others to work for, or accept, its return to Scotland, rather than anything particularly Scottish about the object.

Other contested British objects recently in the news include the Lewis chess pieces, the Lindisfarne Gospels and the Great Bed of Ware.

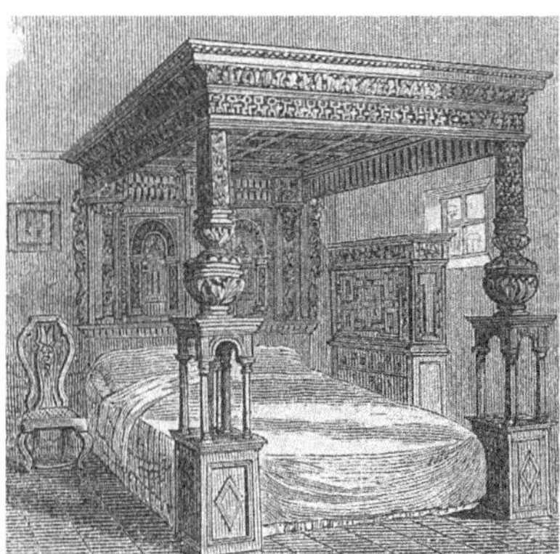

Fig. 11.4 Great Bed of Ware.

5   William Galloway, 'Notice of an ancient Scottish Lectern of Brass, now in the Parish Church of St Stephen's, St Albans, Hertfordshire', *Proceedings of the Society of Antiquaries of Scotland*, 13, 1878-79, pp. 278-301.

The Great Bed of Ware was made around 1590 to attract custom to the White Hart Inn in Ware. Subsequently in other inns in Ware, it was sold in 1870 to the owner of Rye House, Hoddesdon, before being bought by the Victoria and Albert Museum in 1931. Some argue that the Great Bed 'belongs' in Ware, although there is nothing obviously contestable about the chain of ownership. Its return to the town for a year from April 2012 to April 2013 has been generally welcomed, though even with the publicity generated by this historic event only about 25,000 people saw it during its year there, perhaps a tenth as many as would have seen it in the V&A over the same period. The experiment has perhaps dampened the sometimes excessive expectations about the consequences of a 'return' while at the same time reinforcing understanding that there can be multiple legitimate interests or stakeholders in a historically resonant object, particularly when that object is in a public collection and therefore in some sense owned by 'the people' as well as by a particular institution.

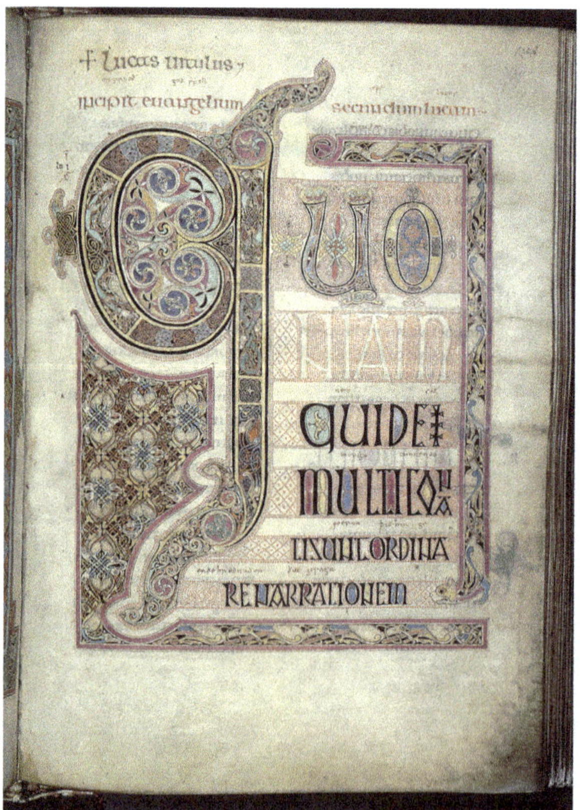

Fig. 11.5 The opening of St Luke's Gospel in the Lindisfarne Gospels.

The Lindisfarne Gospels, made by Eadfrith, Bishop of Lindisfarne (699-721), has been in the British Museum/British Library since its foundation in 1753, given by the heirs of Sir Robert Cotton (1570-1631) who acquired it in the early seventeenth century, after its removal from Durham under Henry VIII in the 1530s.

Its return to the north-east of England has been vigorously campaigned for, a campaign that is supported by the former Bishop of Durham, now Archbishop of Canterbury, Justin Welby. He was quoted in the *Northern Echo*: 'I think something that comes from here should be part of the life of the region'.[6] John Danby of the Northumbrian Association took a less nuanced view: 'They should be restored to their rightful home'.[7] It remains to be seen to what extent the loan of the Lindisfarne Gospels to Durham from July-September 2013 satisfied local opinion.

The Lewis chess pieces bring us back to Scotland, but in this case the issues surrounding them are as much intra as inter-national.

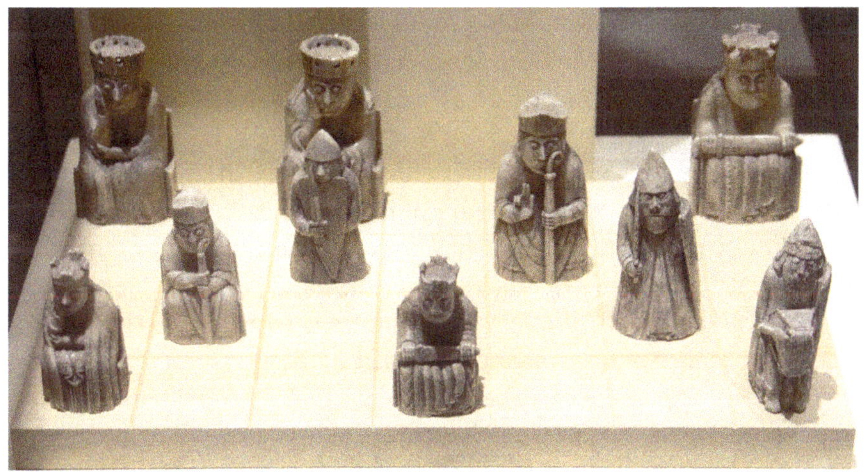

Fig. 11.6 Chess pieces from Uig, Lewis, now at the
National Museum of Scotland, Edinburgh.

These walrus ivory and whale tooth chess and gaming pieces, made in the late twelfth century, were found in a kist, or container, in the dunes

---

6   Mark Tallentyre, 'Church's new leader calls for Lindisfarne Gospels' return', *Northern Echo*, 12 November 2012, http://www.thenorthernecho.co.uk/news/local/northdurham/10040266. Church_s_new_leader_calls_for_Lindisfarne_Gospels__return/?ref=arc

7   'Petition demands return of Lindisfarne Gospels', *The Journal*, 16 March 2006, http://www.thejournal.co.uk/news/north-east-news/petition-demands-return-lindisfarne-gospels-4581288

at Uig on Lewis in 1831. Eighty-two are now in the British Museum and eleven in the National Museum of Scotland, Edinburgh.[8] When I was director of the National Museums of Scotland in the 1990s there were strongly stated demands for their return to Lewis – whether to Stornoway or Uig was a matter of debate. There seemed to be a real risk that the pieces could be 'kidnapped' if returned to Lewis, but regular loans to the Museum of the Western Isles, initially from the British Museum and the National Museums of Scotland, and in subsequent years from the NMS alone, created a reasonably harmonious partnership which then extended to other exchanges.

In 2007-8 there was a new campaign for their return. Linda Fabiani, Scottish Minister for Europe, External Affairs and Culture said 'it is unacceptable that only 11 Lewis Chessmen rest at the National Museum of Scotland while the other 82 remain in the British Museum in London', thus appearing to suggest that 'return' should be to Edinburgh rather than Lewis. Margaret Hodge, then Minister for the Arts in Westminster responded 'It's a lot of nonsense isn't it?',[9] while Bonnie Greer, deputy chairman of the British Museum 'absolutely' believed that they should stay in London. A renewed loan to an exhibition that toured Scotland in 2009-11, and an agreement that six chess pieces from the British Museum will go on long-term loan to the new museum in Lews Castle in 2015[10] seemed to restore a degree of harmony. No claim to the chess pieces has yet been lodged by Norway, although the balance of scholarly opinion is that they were probably made in Trondheim.

What can be learnt from the five examples cited here? First, that there is a strong tendency for well-known objects associated with a place to be claimed for that place. Sometimes the claim is that a historic wrong should be put right: Henry VIII's despoliation of the monasteries or English looting of a Scottish church. Sometimes there is a sense that objects are significant to the culture, history or society of the place, region or nation in question. Their absence leaves something important incomplete: repossession will restore the community's identity and make it whole. There are economic arguments too: tourism would be generated and the local economy boosted by possession of the contested objects. In no case is the argument for 'return' – and I put return in inverted commas because this is the term

---

8   Given by the Society of Antiquaries of Scotland in 1888.

9   *Sunday Herald*, 3 February 2008.

10 Frank Urquhart, 'Lews Castle to house Western Isles museum', *Scotsman*, 27 November 2013, http://www.scotsman.com/lifestyle/arts/news/lews-castle-to-house-western-isles-museum-1-3210848

most widely used even though strictly four out of five cases do not involve return to the putative place of origin – based on what would generally be regarded as a coherent set of generally agreed principles. And yet in every case the argument is deeply felt, often widely supported and, in terms of public reception and results, quite effective.

Indeed, if we look solely at the effects of the restitution claims cited here, it could be argued that they are on balance positive. The Lewis chess pieces are much better known, have been more thoroughly studied and seen and enjoyed by many more people than would have been the case if they had remained uncontroversial. The same is true of the Lindisfarne Gospels which, though on display in the British Museum for many years when I worked there, attracted very little public attention. The return of the Stone of Destiny meant a lot to many Scots, but there has been no comparable and offsetting sense of loss in England. Active and valuable partnerships have been created around several of these objects, partnerships which would not have come into being without the stimulus of controversy. Although there are unattractive, dog-in-the-mangerish aspects of all these claims, the overall outcome has, so far, been beneficial for all concerned. So might restitution claims be a good thing, to be encouraged rather than feared?

Certainly the climate of opinion has changed significantly over the last fifty years. When I first worked in the British Museum in the 1970s, it was regular practice to take in and study coin hoards which had been illegally excavated and exported. The argument was that there would be a significant loss to our knowledge of the past if these hoards went unrecorded. This was true of course, but when it became obvious that the countries from which these hoards came regarded this as unethical and unacceptable, and a boycott of offending museums was threatened, policy changed. Since then the British Museum has taken the view that museums must not give encouragement or legitimacy to illegal excavation and trade by acquiring, exhibiting or researching objects which do not have a legitimate history going back to the date of signature of the UNESCO Convention on the Means of Prohibiting and Preventing the Illicit Import, Export and Transfer of Ownership of Cultural Property 1970,[11] and has encouraged others to follow suit.

I took part in the debates on this issue in the Bizot Group of directors of the big international art museums in the mid-2000s. Philippe de Montebello, then Director of the Metropolitan Museum of Art in New York and James

---

11 For the text of this convention see http://portal.unesco.org/en/ev.php-URL_ID=13039&
URL_DO=DO_TOPIC&URL_SECTION=201.html

Cuno, then Director of the Art Institute of Chicago, were among those who argued that the acquisition of unprovenanced works could be a moral duty. If great works of art, however discovered, were not acquired by reputable museums, they would be lost to scholarship and the edification and appreciation of the public. Against that it was argued that by apparently legitimising the collection of unprovenanced works, museums would give out the message that private collection of such pieces would, eventually, be approved not deprecated. Collectors would know that, after the passage of a suitable number of years, they could proudly show their collection in public and perhaps end up by acquiring the prestige accrued from the gift of important and valuable works to great public museums. This tended to sustain the illegal trade which does so much damage to archaeological sites and the artefacts found there, and deprives us all of the invaluable information that only proper excavation can provide. Now all major museums agree on this: indeed, having been actively pursued through the courts by the Italian government, the Getty and the Metropolitan Museums have returned illegally traded objects to Italy. As a result, the value of unprovenanced material has reduced in comparison with provenanced material and restitution is now regarded as right and proper where it can be shown that objects have been illegally excavated or traded. Interestingly though, few museums are undertaking active, systematic provenance research to see if their collections do in fact contain such objects.

This chimes with other areas in which ethical questions about the process of acquisition or the propriety of retention have been raised. Holdings of human remains, which remained uncontroversial until the 1980s, became the focus of increased anxiety and distaste in the 1990s and were the subject of UK government legislation to enable their return in 2004. The Department for Culture, Media and Sport (DCMS) 'Guidance for the Care of Human Remains in Museums' issued in October 2005, with the explicit support of the National Museum Directors' Conference and the Museums Association recognised that 'some [human remains] were acquired between 100 and 200 years ago from Indigenous peoples in colonial circumstances, where there was a very uneven divide of power', and recommended meticulous provenance research with open public access to the resulting information.[12] It also provided a step by step guide to dealing with claims for return.

---

12 http://webarchive.nationalarchives.gov.uk/+/http://www.culture.gov.uk/images/publications/GuidanceHumanRemains11Oct.pdf, p. 8.

In the USA, the Native American Graves Protection and Repatriation Act, which was signed into law by President George Bush in November 1990, requires federal agencies[13] and institutions that receive federal funding to return Native American 'cultural items' to lineal descendants and culturally affiliated Indian tribes and Native Hawaiian organisations. At the same time, the American Art Museum Directors (AAMD) have in their own words 'taken a leadership role in restitution of art and other property stolen by the Nazis'. Accepting that the historic wrongs done during the period of Nazi rule in Germany (1933-45) should be undone wherever possible, they published guidelines in June 1998 which became the basis of the Washington Principles agreed later that year. These committed museums to careful and detailed analysis of the provenance of all objects that changed ownership in Europe during the period in question. The importance the AAMD attaches to this is evident from its website which states:

> The AAMD promulgates fundamental standards by which art museums should be governed and managed. ... the AAMD's commitment to these core values and the success of its members in the identification, recovery and restitution of works seized by the Nazis have ensured that America's art museums are among the most trusted and respected public institutions in the world.[14]

British museums, led by Sir Nicholas Serota, followed suit and in both countries meticulous provenance research has been undertaken and a number of claims for restitution have been successful: settled by return of objects to earlier owners or their heirs or by the payment of agreed compensation. Interestingly, many of them have turned out to be cases in which the works were not in fact stolen or seized, as envisaged by the AAMD, but sold under pressure. The Stuttgart Staatsgallerie's recent 'return' to Canada of a *Virgin and Child*, formerly attributed to the Master of Flémalle, righted the wrong done when the picture dealer Max Stern had to sell the painting in order to raise the money needed to buy an exit visa from Nazi Germany for his mother.[15] Where compensation has been agreed, it is based on the value of

---

13 http://en.wikipedia.org/wiki/List_of_United_States_federal_agencies

14 'Art museums and the identification and restitution of works stolen by the Nazis', *Statement on standards and practices issued by the Association of Art Museum Directors*, May 2007, https://aamd.org/sites/default/files/document/Nazi-looted%20art_clean_06_2007.pdf

15 David D'Arcy, 'Canada under pressure over potential Nazi loot', *The Art Newspaper*, 3 April 2013, p. 3.

the work now, not on an estimate of the difference between the price actually obtained and the true value then. So this is a generous and comprehensive approach, but it so far applies only to the Nazi period in Europe. Attempts to extend it to victims of the Armenian genocide (1915-18 and 1920-23) have made some progress in California, but it remains to be seen whether the case brought against the J. Paul Getty Museum by the Armenian Apostolic Church for the return of seven manuscript pages from the Zeyt'un Gospels will succeed. The case has already had some impact though: the Getty has begun discussions with the Matenadaran, the Armenian museum that hold the rest of the Zeyt'un Gospels.[16]

While a member of the Bizot Group, I had the slightly surreal experience in 2003 of seeing a chorus of nodded agreement from my international museum colleagues to the proposal by Italian museum directors that the Group should take a public stand against the return of the Axum Obelisk to Ethiopia.

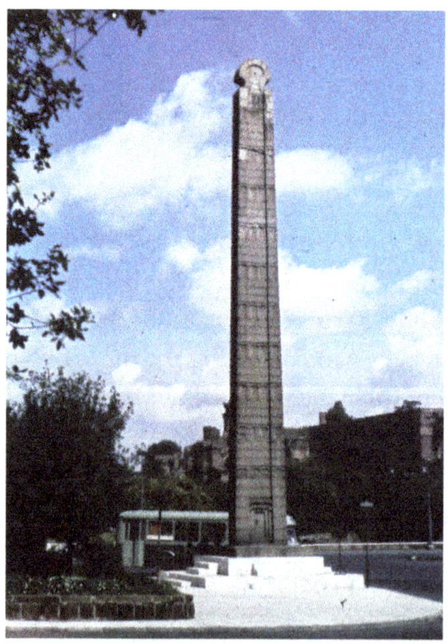

Fig. 11.7 The Axum Obelisk (also known as the Roman Stele) in Rome, where it stood in front of the UN Food and Agriculture Organization's headquarters until 2005.

Fortunately, assent evaporated when it was explained not only that Mussolini had taken the obelisk as war booty in 1937 and erected it in

___

16 Laura Gilbert, 'Restitution to get harder in California?', *The Art Newspaper*, 4 April 2013, p. 4.

Rome as a sign of imperial conquest, but also that at the conclusion of the Second World War Italy had formally agreed its return in 1947. The Bizot Group risked being seen to apply one standard to those of European origin who had suffered loss in the period 1933-45 and quite another to Ethiopia. The obelisk was in fact returned in 2005 and re-erected in 2008.

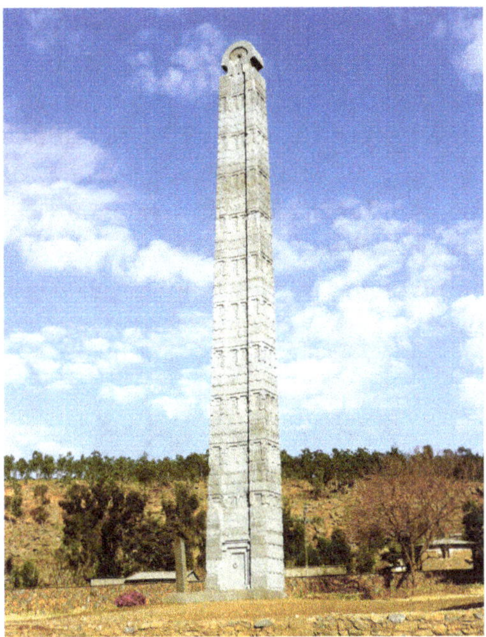

Fig. 11.8 The Axum Obelisk in Axum.

Two other relevant examples of return both concern manuscripts. The manuscripts of Icelandic sagas were systematically sought out and collected by antiquarians in the seventeenth and eighteenth centuries and taken to Denmark for preservation and study. Danish recognition of the central importance of these manuscripts to Icelandic culture was ratified by legislation passed in 1961, which led to a gradual transfer back to Iceland of a significant proportion of the manuscripts over the period 1971-97. Initially contentious this became a focus of scholarly collaboration between the Árni Magnússon Institute in Reykjavik and the Arnamagnean Institute in Copenhagen (which retains a significant collection of saga manuscripts) and a warm point in Danish-Icelandic relations. The consensus built around this return contrasts with the bitter feelings engendered by France's return of manuscripts looted by a French punitive expedition which raided Korea in 1866 after the execution of a number of French Catholic missionaries.

Return was first agreed by President Mitterrand during a visit to Seoul in 1993 and was widely believed to be connected with the award of a very large contract to build a high-speed rail link to the French bidder. Mitterrand, overriding the protests of the then director of the Bibliothèque Nationale, Emmanuel Le Roy Ladaurie and the relevant curators, took one manuscript with him: returned according to the Koreans, lent according to the French. Despite a strong campaign, led by curators in the Bibliothèque Nationale, who pointed out that alienation of objects in French public collections is illegal, President Sarkozy decided to honour the agreement. A formal agreement was made between President Lee Myung-bak of South Korea and President Sarkozy of France that the remaining 297 volumes should be returned on the basis of a five year renewable loan. The manuscripts went back to Korea in 2011 and nobody expects that they will return to France, except as occasional reciprocal loans. The National Museum of Korea held an exhibition in the autumn of that year which in the words of their website 'celebrated the homecoming of *uigwe*, which were looted from their rightful place … in 1866'.[17]

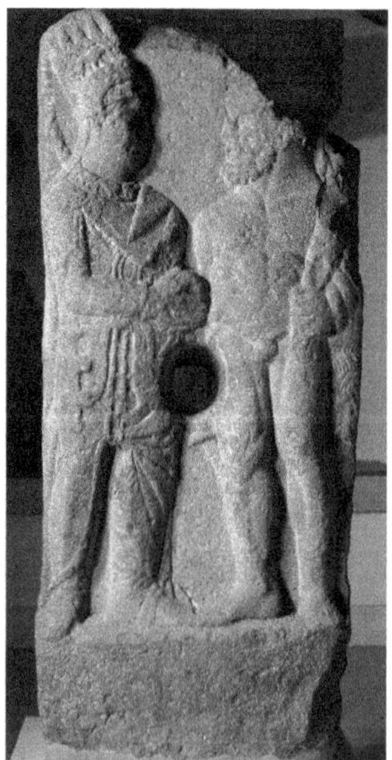

Fig. 11.9 Basalt stela with a relief of Antiochus I Epiphanes.

The issues raised here are of particular importance to museums in Britain since they, like American and French public collections, are responsible

---

17 http://www.museum.go.kr/program/show/showDetailEng.jsp?menuID=002002002 &searchSelect=A.SHOWKOR&pageSize=10&showID=4620

for significant numbers of contested objects. Turkey has recently claimed the return of a number of objects from museums around the world, most publicly the Stele of Antiochus I from the British Museum.

The British Museum has responded by pointing out that the stele was acquired by Leonard Wooley in 1924 with permission from the French authorities in Syria, where the artefact was then stored. It has expressed willingness to discuss a loan for temporary exhibition but concluded its April 2012 press release by stating that 'The Trustees of the British Museum cannot consent to the transfer of ownership of the stele and firmly believe that it should remain part of the British Museum's collection where it can be seen in a world context by a global audience'. A consequence of this dispute has been that Turkey now refuses to lend to the British Museum which also has problematic relations with Greece over the Parthenon Marbles, and with Egypt. This is an uncomfortable and potentially damaging situation for one of the world's greatest museums of the ancient Mediterranean. The problems faced by the British Museum are far from unique.

The Victoria and Albert Museum, like all museums with significant international collections, faces similar dilemmas. To start with a little known example, it emerged in the early 2000s that a Spanish monstrance in the V&A's collection might have been stolen from a monastery in Spain in 1885. Careful research demonstrated that the stolen object and the one in the V&A really were one and the same. The museum faced a problem. Legally the V&A could retain the artefact as the monstrance had been left to the museum by someone who had good title to it under English law. The National Heritage Act 1983, governing the V&A, does not allow it to dispose of objects unless they are duplicate or useless. The monstrance was neither. So it was agreed by the V&A trustees in 2003 that the object should be returned, subject to certain assurances about its care. With the help of the then British ambassador to Spain, an agreement satisfactory to both sides was reached and the monstrance was returned to Spain, to the treasury of Zamora Cathedral, in 2005.[18]

Another case that arose during my time at the V&A concerned the Ethiopian treasures taken from the Emperor Theodore after his defeat at the Battle of Magdala in 1868.

W.E. Gladstone, who was Prime Minister at the time, told the House of Commons that 'he deeply lamented, for the sake of the country, and for the sake of all those concerned, that those articles, to us insignificant, though probably to the Abyssinians sacred and imposing symbols, or at

---

18 Minutes of the Board of Trustees, 17 April 2003 – 23 June 2005.

least hallowed by association, were thought fit to be brought away by a British Army'. He went on to say that 'with that just and kindly spirit which belonged to him, Lord Napier said these articles, whatever the claim of the Army, ought not to be placed among the national treasures, and said they ought to be held in deposit till they could be returned to Abyssinia'.[19] The V&A received a letter from the then President of Ethiopia asking for their return. But a reasonably positive response which asked among other things for information about the gold crown returned in the 1930s received no reply. One complication is that as a result of the 1983 Act, the ownership of these objects – which had originally been a government loan – was vested to the V&A into the property of the Trustees.[20]

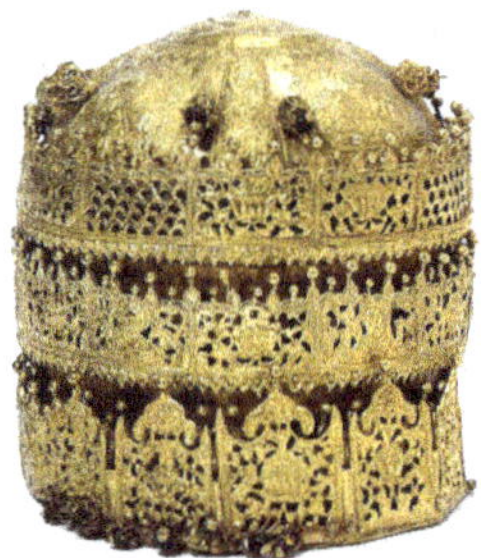

Fig 11.10 Crown, Ethiopia, 1740.

Towards the end of my time at the V&A, two other issues arose. One concerned a small marble head of a child taken by the archaeologist Sir Charles Wilson from the Sidamara Sarcophagus, a third-century Roman tomb which he excavated in 1882 and which is now in the Archaeological Museum in Istanbul.

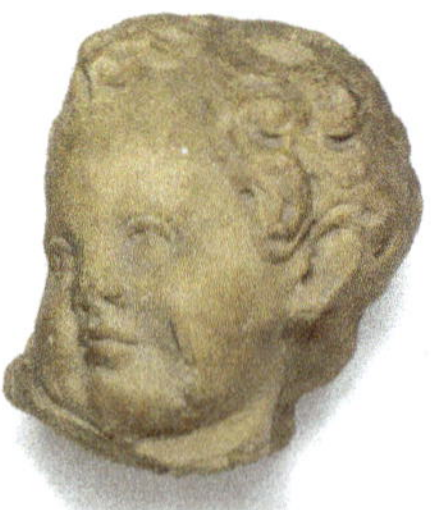

Fig. 11.11 Carved marble head of a child, third century, excavated in 1882.

---

19 30 June 1871.
20 Trustees minutes, 20 October 2005.

The head was subsequently left to the V&A by his daughter. It seemed evident to me, my colleagues and the trustees who I consulted that it should be returned. Actually, this had been agreed in principle by the V&A in the 1930s, but never executed. The head does not fit with the collections of the V&A, which has no classical antiquities, and serves no useful purpose there. But it clearly does belong with the sarcophagus from which it was taken. I hope that its return will not be long delayed. It would be particularly unfortunate if it were argued that return would set a dangerous precedent. To suggest that the rectification of an obvious anomaly of this kind would prejudice the case for the retention of the Parthenon marbles or other antiquities would be to accept that there are parallels where there are really none – and so weaken not strengthen the case for retention.

I well remember the claim made for the return of what were then known as the Elgin Marbles in the early 1980s, the then director David Wilson's sturdy assertion that they legally and legitimately belonged to the British Museum, and his mixture of pleasure and annoyance at the visit of the then Minster for Culture of Greece, the charismatic Melina Mercouri. Following that episode, there was a period when the Greek government was willing, even eager, to discuss recognition of the British Museum's legal ownership of the marbles on the condition that the Greek stake in them was also recognised and they were in practice shared between London and Athens. It seems a shame that that offer was not taken up and that it was subsequently withdrawn, just as it is a shame that the risk that any sculpture lent might not be returned was not properly weighed against the risk that a failure to create partnership around the Marbles might eventually make the British Museum's tenure of them unsustainable.

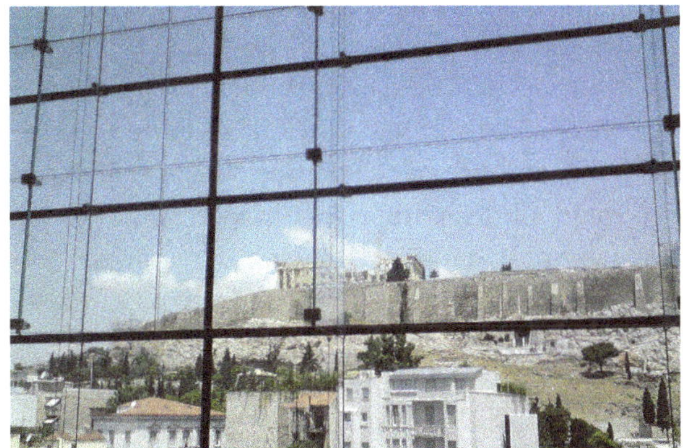

Fig. 11.12 View of the Acropolis from
the interior of the New Acropolis Museum.

The last case I had to deal with was that of the objects looted from the Summer Palace (and elsewhere) during the European invasions of China in 1860 and 1900.

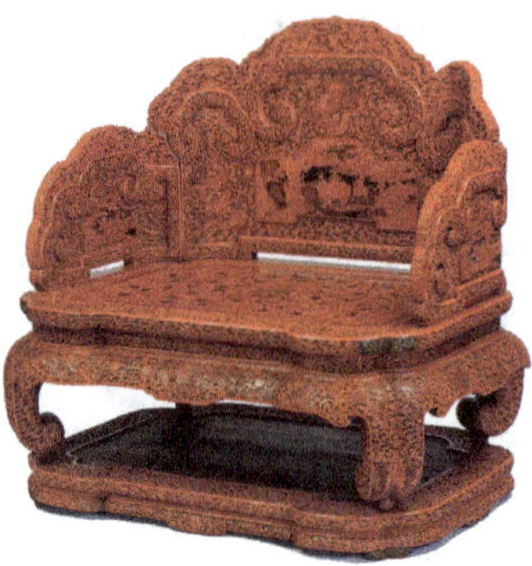

Fig. 11.13 Chinese Imperial throne, carved lacquer on wood
depicting five clawed dragons, Qing dynasty, 1775-80.

On a visit to China in 2010 with Neil MacGregor, Director of the British Museum, I suggested that we propose a programme of serious and sustained joint provenance research with our colleagues in the Palace and National Museums of China, so as to ascertain, as far as possible, the history of the objects in the two museums' collections. I was very pleased when, at a joint press conference in Beijing the following day, Neil MacGregor put forward this suggestion on behalf of the British Museum and the V&A. It seemed to me that this would be a good way to begin the process of deciding the long-term future of the looted objects. François-Henri Pinault's recent decision to return the rat and rabbit bronze heads from the Summer Palace with the statement that 'the family ... strongly believe they belong in their rightful home', which reflects both the importance of the Chinese market to a luxury goods group like Pinault-Printemps-Redoute and the significance of this gesture to Franco-Chinese relations, confirms that the issue needs to be addressed urgently.[21] A report on their return to the National Museum of China quotes a worker surnamed Zhao: 'As a Chinese I hope all those other antiques scattered throughout the world will be returned to China too, but it will depend on how powerful China becomes'.[22]

---

21 Scheherazade Daneshkhu, 'Symbols of amity', *Financial Times*, 27/28 April 2013, p. 4.
22 Kathrin Hille, 'Pinault gives bronze rat and rabbit back to China', *Financial Times*, 29 June 2013.

What has emerged, I hope, is that we now have abundant examples of practice, good and not-so-good, in the field of restitution. Museums in America and Europe have publicly committed themselves to the principle that restitution, or return, can and should be used to right past wrongs. We can see from the numerous examples available to us that engaging with the problems posed by contested objects has had beneficial consequences. Even the Getty Museum, having lived through the trauma of the Italian trial of its former curator of classical antiquities Marion True, has established better relations with the Italian authorities than it had before – although it might have done still better had it responded positively when the issue was first raised.[23]

The same standards must apply universally. We cannot have one rule for Scotland or Spain and another for Turkey or Nigeria. We cannot rectify wrongs wrought in Europe and ignore those committed elsewhere. We cannot proclaim that objects belong in the British Museum 'where they can be seen in a world context by a global audience' without recognising that Istanbul (like Beijing and Shanghai or Delhi and Mumbai) can also claim to be a 'world city' with a 'global audience'.

There are real risks in action, not least to the preservation of the objects, as the return of some of the Benin bronzes in the 1950s and the Ethiopian Crown in the 1930s demonstrate. But these risks are not as great as some imagine. The number of genuinely contested objects is small in number and tiny as a proportion of total museum collection. Inaction is riskier still: time is not on the side of those responsible for contested objects. A price, in terms of the unrealised benefits of collaboration, is already being paid. More serious are the risks of future confrontation over objects which could and should be productive of partnership and good feeling. China has not yet asked for the return of looted objects. Mitterrand and Sarkozy's negotiations with South Korea give us an idea of what might happen if it does. And it will of course, it is just a question of when.

Proponents of an active approach to the resolution of disagreement around artefacts are often accused by those in the museum profession of naiveté, of not fully understanding the situation. My own conclusion, after a lifetime working in some of the museums most affected by these claims, is that the risks of action are overestimated and the risks of inaction are underestimated. But most important for me is that we owe it to our proud tradition of museums serving the public interest to see where something is wrong and take steps to set it right.

---

23 Hugh Eakin, 'The great giveback', *New York Times*, 26 January 2013, http://www.nytimes.com/2013/01/27/sunday-review/the-great-giveback.html

IV
MANAGEMENT AND PROTECTION

11. The Possibilities and Perils of Heritage Management

Michael F. Brown

After two decades of spirited debate about the fate of cultural heritage in a shrinking, commodifying world, a few things seem settled. One is that the unsanctioned appropriation of cultural assets by outsiders is unjust and unethical, especially when undertaken by a more powerful group. It perpetrates an economic injustice because the stewards of an ancient song, art form, or useful element of traditional knowledge are denied whatever profits those cultural resources may accrue in the marketplace. Worse still, the act of tearing cultural elements from their original context may change their meaning, even to those who created them. When the source community is an embattled minority, the resulting distortion is especially damaging.

Many critics of cultural appropriation hoped that the framework of intellectual property (IP) law could be modified to curb such injustices. IP law's attraction was that it was already in place as a global system with well-established precedents. The prospect of co-opting international copyright and patent laws, often portrayed as engines of cultural theft, had a transgressive appeal to those who campaign for robust heritage-protection policies. Yet aside from a few modest improvements here and there, IP has proven to be a fickle ally. Patents and copyrights are time-limited forms of protection. Eventually their term expires, and they revert to the public domain, where they are available to anyone. This time-limited quality is objectionable to source communities that wish to shield their intellectual and cultural property forever. IP's transformation of sacred

http://dx.doi.org/10.11647/OBP.0047.11

forms of human expression into the language of property often offends the people it is ostensibly trying to help.

The multiple deficiencies of an IP-based model have led the heritage-protection movement to cast about for more promising frameworks. This has fuelled growing interest in so-called 'geographical indications' as a way to defend local traditions. Closely related to this is the emergence of formal certifications of virtue. These consist of administrative structures that designate something – a building, an art style, a craft, a genre of traditional music, a ritual – as meriting protected status because of its transcendent cultural importance. An obvious example of the latter is UNESCO's system for identifying and certifying World Heritage Sites.[1]

Legal experiments in heritage management that have been implemented to date tend to follow a similar script. They inevitably give expression to what can be called the 'administrative mind'. The greatest student of the administrative mind was Max Weber (1864-1920), the German sociologist whose analysis of bureaucratic logic remains a touchstone for subsequent work in the field. In the highly rationalised world of bureaucratic administrators, Weber observed, problems are dealt with by carefully defining their properties, establishing fixed rules for dealing with them, subdividing authority among trained experts, and doing everything possible to squeeze awkward exceptions into existing procedural categories. Systems of this sort have become nearly universal because they manage complex systems predictably and, often enough, efficiently. What works well when manufacturing widgets in a factory, however, swerves toward absurdity when applied to more subjective dimensions of human life. A familiar example is the current enthusiasm for auditing the performance of university professors. Asked to judge teaching ability or scholarly merit in a precise way, administrators resort to dubious metrics of success in the name of objectivity. Even more vexing problems arise when attempting to manage something as elusive as culture in the name of protection.

Consider the following case which, although hypothetical, closely tracks emerging strategies to protect traditional crafts in many parts of the world. Let us say that a nation such as India or Ecuador or Kenya has a distinctive, localised, artisanal textile industry of some renown. The national government wants to protect this industry from imitators,

---

1   On certificates of virtue, see Michael F. Brown, 'A Tale of Three Buildings: Certifying Virtue in the New Moral Economy', *American Ethnologist*, 37(4), 2010, pp. 741-52.

especially industrial firms that can easily appropriate traditional designs. To accomplish this, the government creates a geographical indication unique to that tradition, such that no outsider can claim to make 'X fabric' or even 'X-style fabric' without violating national law. So far, so good.

For this law to have teeth, the government must define several things with great precision. First, what *is* X fabric? In other words, what are the boundaries of its design palette, raw materials, thread count, and the like? Next, what are the boundaries of the production zone protected by the new geographical indication? Within that formally defined area, who will be recognised as a certified artisan? Who will do the certifying? How much of the cost of administering the certification system will be passed along to the producers themselves?

One can readily imagine various unintended consequences of this scheme despite its apparent simplicity. The smallest producers may lack the financial resources or literacy skills to file the relevant forms and pay the inevitable fees, thus forcing them to merge with larger, better-established producers who have already achieved certification. Innovative artisans pushing the boundaries of an official style may find their legitimacy questioned by more conservative producers, risking loss of certification. Over time, such rigidity could turn a lively tradition into an inert museum-piece. As Winston Churchill once said of art, 'without innovation, it is a corpse'.

A growing roster of news stories and case studies shows that my hypothetical example only begins to inventory the unintended consequences that may arise from the application of the administrative mind to the challenge of protecting heritage. In 2009, for example, a noisy dispute broke out between Bolivia and Peru over a costume worn by Miss Peru in the Miss Universe Pageant. In the portion of the competition devoted to each nation's folklore, Miss Peru crossed the stage dressed in a costume linked to *La Diablada* ('Dance of the Devils'), which is performed in the Andean *altiplano* region shared by Peru, Bolivia, and Chile. It happens, however, that Bolivia's version of the dance – specifically, the version performed in the town of Oruro – has been certified by UNESCO as a 'Masterpiece of the Oral and Intangible Heritage of Humanity'. For reasons known only to UNESCO, the same dance as performed in Peru and Chile lacks such certification. Thus Bolivia, which sees the designation as an important draw for international tourism, protested that by wearing the costume of *La Diablada*, Miss Peru had pilfered its national patrimony. The colourful scrimmage between Andean nations echoes an earlier dispute between China and South Korea over stewardship of the Duanwu Festival, celebrated in the fifth lunar month in both countries.[2]

Another example is provided by the American Indian Arts and Crafts Act (1990), a US law with the straightforward goal of protecting consumers from false claims that a given piece of artwork has been created by a Native American. The law says that for a work to be legally portrayed as Indian-made, the artist must be an enrolled member of a federally- or state-recognised tribe or Alaska Native community. The doctrine of tribal sovereignty that applies in the United States, however, gives tribes great latitude in their enrolment practices. Some are expansive in their standards, others quite restrictive. The result is that certain artists widely regarded as Native American by fellow Native Americans cannot advertise their work as Indian-made, whereas others with more tenuous links to Native American society are free to do so. Admittedly, these problems arise around the edges of an otherwise effective law, but they illustrate the difficulties that arise when cultural definitions – in this case, of tribal membership – become concretised in formal bureaucratic practice.[3] More troubling still, the law is virtually powerless in the face of products that imitate Native American art but make no explicit claim of Native origin. A morally complex instance of this would be the inexpensive 'Southwestern-style' rugs made by indigenous Zapotec weavers in Mexico, which turn up with great frequency in Native American arts shops in the United States, where they compete with more expensive rugs made by Navajo weavers.

In the arena of traditional music, the ethnomusicologist Javier León has documented the effects of formal certification on Peruvian musicians of African descent. In 2001, Peru's National Institute of Culture declared an instrument called the cajón to be the 'Cultural Patrimony of the Nation'. As the name implies, the cajón is a wooden box that has long been used as a percussion instrument by Afroperuvian musicians. Whether the cajón is unique to Peru is disputed, although exposure to Peru's version of the instrument has unquestionably led to its recent adoption by performing artists in Spain, Cuba, and Mexico. Peru's claim on the instrument has various motivations: national pride, the possible benefits to cultural

---

2   Matt Moffet and Robert Kozak, 'In this spat between Bolivia and Peru, the details are in the devils', *Wall Street Journal*, 21 August 2009, http://online.wsj.com/article/SB125081309502848049.html. On Duanwu, see 'Paying more attention to cultural heritage', *Financial Times*, 18 May 2004.

3   William J. Hapiuk Jr., 'Of Kitsch and Kachinas: A Critical Analysis of the Indian Arts and Crafts Act of 1990', *Stanford Law Review*, 53, 2001, pp. 1009-75.

tourism, and, according to León, the attraction of 'reaping any revenue that such ownership might yield'.[4] One comes away from his study with the sense that declaring the instrument to be an item of national patrimony has produced as much divisiveness as pride among musicians by fostering disputes over whose use of the cajón is more authentic. In a similar analysis of policies designed to protect the musical heritage of the Seto minority group in Estonia, Kristin Kuutma concludes that the 'discursive impact of the concept and perspective of intangible heritage paves a battleground of celebration and contestation among those entangled in the process of heritage production'.[5]

The administrative mind is not the only source of trouble when heritage is redefined as a resource amenable to bureaucratic supervision. Equally vexing is the role of the state. With few exceptions, nation states consider themselves the proper stewards of heritage resources found within their borders, a premise that the charters of organisations such as UNESCO are obliged to honour. Yet the state's interests and those of internal cultural communities often diverge. In the interest of national unity, the state may choose to emphasise some aspects of heritage and suppress others. States may wish to promote certain traditions and heritage sites because they attract tourists, whereas local communities may value a way of life that residents see as irreconcilable with an ever-increasing number of visitors. More often than not, state institutions such as national museums and archives exercise control over heritage resources in ways that are deeply resented by source communities – in recent years prompting calls for the 'liberation' of culture from the iron grip of distant bureaucrats.

More subtle but no less profound implications of state insertion into local heritage practices have been documented by Lorraine Aragon and James Leach in their research on Indonesia's efforts to implement laws that shield traditional arts from exploitation by outsiders. Among their findings is that 'bureaucrats' best-intentioned legal plans do not easily encompass artists' complex aims for art production processes and transgenerational reciprocity'.[6] In other words by reframing local heritage in international

---

4   Javier F. León, 'National Patrimony and Cultural Policy: The Case of the Afroperuvian *Cajón'*, in A.N. Weintraub and B. Yung (eds.), *Music and Cultural Rights* (Chicago, IL: University of Illinois Press, 2009), p. 129.

5   Kristin Kuutma, 'Who Owns Our Songs? Authority of Heritage and Resources for Restitution', *Ethnologia Europaea*, 39(2), 2009, p. 36.

6   Lorraine V. Aragon and James Leach, 'Arts and Owners: Intellectual Property Law and the Politics of Scale in Indonesian Arts', *American Ethnologist*, 35(4), 2008, p. 608.

legal terms, the state is changing local cultures in ways that the alleged beneficiaries find unsettling and even destructive.

Ethnographic fieldwork in certified heritage sites likewise offers a picture of local dissatisfaction simmering under the surface of an upbeat, culture-affirming label. Consider, for instance, the Pelourinho neighbourhood of Salvador de Bahia, Brazil, which was declared a World Heritage Site by UNESCO in 1985. The anthropologist John Collins has assessed the process by which this former red-light district and its primarily Afrobrazilian residents were converted into national patrimony. In order to conform to the state's idea of acceptable heritage, those inhabitants have been subjected to coercive government reform efforts. Collins finds that 'the Bahian state arbitrates "correct" markers of ethnic identity and national history that qualify bearers for political rights while residents who exhibit incorrect behaviours face exile on Salvador's periphery'.[7]

Different concerns are voiced by residents of another World Heritage Site, the mud-brick city of Djenné in Mali. The rigorous preservation protocol developed by UNESCO prevents the people of Djenné from altering the structure or appearance of their houses in any way. Those who wish to increase the size of rooms or renovate them to accommodate plumbing and modern appliances are prohibited from doing so. The inevitable frustrations seem to be turning citizens against the tourism-promoting authenticity from which only a few derive direct benefits.[8]

I could continue piling up examples of what Lisa Breglia, in a study of local attitudes toward Mayan archaeological sites in Mexico, memorably calls 'monumental ambivalence', but the contours of the problem should now be readily apparent.[9] Even thoughtfully designed heritage-protection laws and policies tend to be flawed affairs. Their imperfections arise from two sources. First, most are creations of the nation state, whose interests are likely to diverge from those of subcultural communities struggling to maintain a degree of distinctiveness. Even when the state is not aggressively trying to redefine local cultures and heritage sites to suit a nationalist narrative, a predilection for centralised control is likely to put too much

---

7 John Collins, '"But What if I Should Need to Defecate in Your Neighborhood, Madame?": Empire, Redemption, and the "Tradition of the Oppressed" in a Brazilian World Heritage Site', *Cultural Anthropology*, 23(2), 2008, p. 312.

8 Neil MacFarquhar, 'Mali City rankled by rules for life in spotlight', *New York Times*, 9 January 2011, A4, http://www.nytimes.com/2011/01/09/world/africa/09mali.html

9 Lisa Breglia, *Monumental Ambivalence: The Politics of Heritage* (Austin, TX: University of Texas Press, 2006).

power in the hands of credentialed experts far removed from the everyday interactions that keep heritage alive.

Equally problematic is the transformative power of law itself. As various legal scholars have noted, by its nature law imposes uniformity. In contrast, cultural heritage embodies flexibility and highly contingent ways of doing things, both of which are anathema to law's search for procedural regularity. Indeed, a great irony of the heritage-protection movement is that it advances globally uniform approaches to the defence of heritage said to be threatened by globalisation. Law not only encodes meanings, it retools them in ways that change social practice.

An example that comes readily to mind is the impact of the concept of 'repatriation' encoded in a celebrated US law called the Native American Graves Protection and Repatriation Act of 1990, better known by the acronym NAGPRA. NAGPRA provides for the return of human remains and objects of religious patrimony to Native American communities from which they were taken, subject to specific conditions. Ethnographic studies of the repatriation process have shown that the law has in some cases transformed Native American notions of cultural ownership: tribes now regard themselves as the proper owners of objects that once belonged to individuals, families, or sub-tribal units. This is not necessarily a bad thing – surely it is preferable to having sacred objects of doubtful provenance remain in the hands of museums – but it should not be mistaken for the preservation of tradition. It has changed that tradition in innumerable ways. Moreover, NAGPRA's success in rectifying historic wrongs has inspired supporters of indigenous rights to demand the 'repatriation' of *intangible* heritage – recordings of songs, photographs of rituals, digital images of indigenous art – to source communities. In a digital age, however, intangible heritage does not answer to the logic of the material objects covered by the terms of NAGPRA. Digitised heritage may reside in thousands of places simultaneously. It can be diced into partial elements and distributed instantly around the world. Recovery, reassembly, and sequestration of these scattered shards is an unlikely prospect, however much we might wish it. Leakage of the legal concept of repatriation into a domain where it doesn't readily apply has sometimes made it harder to find effective solutions to the circulation of elements of cultural heritage over which source communities have long sought control.[10]

---

10 On the complex interaction between law and culture, see especially Naomi Mezey, 'Law as Culture', *Yale Journal of Law and the Humanities*, 13, 2001, pp. 35-67.

Twenty years of watching the world struggle with questions of heritage and its preservation have drawn me to the tragic view of human ambition embraced by the literary critic Terry Eagleton. As Eagleton puts it, 'Tragic protagonists ... acknowledge that flawedness is part of the texture of things, and that roughness and imprecision are what make human life work'.[11] However noble our desires, however much we strive to advance the cause of justice, the outcome of this human effort will be marked by imperfection. Such a perspective need not produce ethical paralysis, but it does call for humility and a willingness to change course when evidence warrants. A willingness to laugh at human folly helps, too.

Cultural heritage, whether embodied in places or stories, is a shape-shifting, protean thing whose contours may be contested even by those who create it. For centuries the powerful have tried to define its shape and the uses to which it is put. Now that it has become a commodity, the stakes have risen further. The cultural heritage of formerly isolated communities has gained value in markets hungry for novelty. This coincides with a democratic opening that in many parts of the world has empowered minority communities to reassert their cultural distinctiveness. The resulting convergence of economic interests and identity politics – to say nothing of the spiritual idioms in which heritage-protection demands are often couched – makes for an ethical landscape of great complexity. So what is to be done?

One useful step would be to revisit the broader context that gave rise to the current passion for protecting heritage. The expansion and tightening of global IP rules that began in the 1990s sparked a moral panic about cultural theft. The response has been an effort to defend heritage with new laws that sometimes outstrip copyright and patent law in the degree to which they commodify culture and downsize the public domain. Is emulating the worst features of IP the best way to hold it at bay? Perhaps it is time to re-energise public efforts to roll back expansive IP laws. After all, if corporations find it harder to privatise public knowledge, they will focus their acquisitive attention elsewhere. A promising tactic to undermine predatory IP law has been employed in India, where the creation of a publicly accessible Traditional Knowledge Digital Library has made it more difficult for bioprospectors to secure patents on products derived from Ayurvedic medicine. IP law says that patents may only be issued for

---

11 Terry Eagleton, *After Theory* (New York: Basic Books, 2003), p. 186.

products that demonstrate novelty. By putting ancient medicines in the public domain, India pre-emptively refutes claims that pharmaceutical products based on Indian tradition qualify as 'new'.

Operating on the fringe of the heritage-protection movement are scrappy outsiders whose creativity gives me hope for the future. Among the best is Mukurtu (www.mukurtu.org), a not-for-profit group of anthropologists, programmers, and indigenous thinkers who have created archival software that allows communities to preserve, study, and use their own digital heritage. The program's architecture can be customised to serve a community's changing needs and preferences. Mukurtu isn't a total solution, nor does it aspire to be; this is one of its strengths. Diversity sustains diversity; uniformity stifles it. The steadily growing list of independent museums and cultural centres in the United States, Canada, Australia, and elsewhere is a hopeful sign of local resistance to the imposition of a single set of global solutions. This isn't to say that international treaties such as the Convention for the Safeguarding of Intangible Cultural Heritage, approved by UNESCO in 2003, cannot serve a useful purpose.[12] They focus attention on heritage and, one hopes, help to mobilise public enthusiasm for its preservation. But to the extent that international agreements provide justification for top-down policies and centralised management, they may do more harm than good.

An unavoidable lesson of recent experience is that cultural heritage is most likely to thrive when shielded from the administrative mind's managerial impulse and the suffocating embrace of formal law. When controls are warranted, they should be developed by source communities rather than state bureaucrats. The state's remit should be limited to providing advice, financial support, and appropriate enforcement mechanisms for locally created controls. Such an approach honours culture's dual identity as a verb as well as a noun. For cultural heritage to survive, it must be cultured by its proper stewards.

---

12 For the text of the 2003 Convention see http://portal.unesco.org/en/ev.php-URL_ID=17
716&URL_DO=DO_TOPIC&URL_SECTION=201.html

12. Values in World Heritage Sites

Geoffrey Belcher

1. Introduction

It is helpful to begin with an explanation of the concept and evolution of 'World Heritage' as adopted by UNESCO, the United Nations Environmental, Social and Cultural Organisation which is 'building peace in the minds of men and women'.

In the late 1950s, after the building of the Aswan Dam flooded the Nile Valley, destroying many ancient sites, international concern about places of world significance focused on Egypt. Among the country's countless historic sites, the most famous was the temple of Abu Simbel, with its four giant statues of the great pharaoh Rameses II. As a result of the concerns raised by the flood, international aid was gathered to fund an ambitious scheme to cut the temple's stonework and relocate it to higher ground away from the rising waters. The archaeological and aesthetic legitimacy of this action may have been questioned in subsequent years, but the event did ignite a process that eventually led, via an initiative in the United States, to the establishment in 1972 of the UNESCO Convention Concerning the Protection of the World Cultural and Natural Heritage.[1]

The World Heritage list was readily drawn up in these early years to include the most obvious places of world interest such as the Taj Mahal in India, the Mesa Verde National Park in the USA, and the Galapagos Islands

---

1   See   http://portal.unesco.org/en/ev.php-URL_ID=13055&URL_DO=DO_TOPIC&URL_SECTION=201.html

   http://dx.doi.org/10.11647/OBP.0047.12

in Ecuador. As the idea of the list has evolved, a greater variety of Sites has been added, whilst the process of inscription and management of these World Heritage Sites has become much more rigorous.

Today, a Site can only be inscribed on the list if the World Heritage Committee agrees that it meets one or more of the ten criteria listed in the World Heritage Convention Operational Guidelines (2005),[2] which can be paraphrased as follows:

   (i)   To represent a masterpiece of human creative genius.

   (ii)   To exhibit an important interchange of human values.

   (iii)   To bear a unique or at least exceptional testimony to a cultural tradition.

   (iv)   To be an outstanding example of a type of building.

   (v)   To be an outstanding example of traditional human settlement.

   (vi)   To be directly or tangibly associated with events or living traditions.

   (vii)   To contain superlative natural phenomena.

   (viii)   To be outstanding examples representing major stages of Earth's history.

   (ix)   To be outstanding examples representing significant on-going ecological and biological processes.

   (x)   To contain the most important and significant natural habitats.

The first six of these criteria may be considered to apply to cultural Sites, and the remainder to natural Sites, although some Sites are in the dual category of 'cultural landscape'. As we will see, UNESCO have broadened their approach to inscription over the last few years, and as a consequence the World Heritage list now includes 'properties' of hugely varying character, from places of great architectural beauty such as the Taj Mahal to places linked with significant historical events, including Auschwitz-Birkenau in Poland and Hiroshima in Japan. Natural Sites, meanwhile, include places ranging from the Great Barrier Reef and Shark Bay in Australia to Yellowstone National Park in the USA.

Participating nation states (State Parties) may put forward one cultural and one natural Site for World Heritage status annually, but the UNESCO Conservation Committee's selection process is by no means straightforward. The United Kingdom has had to withdraw nominations for Charles Darwin's Cultural Landscape in Kent, and Wearmouth and Jarrow in the county of Tyne and Wear (associated with the Venerable Bede) in the last few years because the cases, which relied strongly on association with an

---

2   See http://whc.unesco.org/archive/opguide05-en.pdf

important historical figure, were not considered robust enough. At present the number of UK locations listed as World Heritage Sites remains at 28.

The individual characteristics of each Site mean that their management varies and may involve a wide range of issues. At present UNESCO World Heritage Sites have little status in national heritage-protection legislation, and as a result management plans, which are a UNESCO requirement for the protection of the Sites, have only a limited statutory basis. Moreover, many Sites contain private land and enterprises, and so must include elements of a business plan. These issues will be discussed further below.

2. The Wider Value of Heritage

The modern appreciation of the value of historic sites can be traced back to the Renaissance, when architects began to adapt classical ruins in order to develop new architectural styles. Subsequently, in the eighteenth century, the Grand Tour of Italian and Greek archaeological sites became *de rigueur* for young aristocrats. Unfortunately, plundering of artefacts by these eighteenth-century tourists was rife, but their experiences also encouraged the use of classical elements in the 'Palladian' style, which produced buildings of great elegance. The nineteenth century, meanwhile, saw the introduction of a more formal concern with the protection of the historical legacy, and the founding of the Society for the Protection of Ancient Buildings represents a milestone in this regard. Throughout the heritage world, a more rational approach was increasingly taken to the recording of historic sites and objects both above and below the ground. In the case of field archaeology, this meant the establishment in the early twentieth century of highly rigorous excavation procedures designed to prevent the cavalier treasure hunting and consequent destruction of the historic context of such 'finds' that had been widespread since the eighteenth century.

In Britain, the value of historic buildings was further recognised with a number of studies, such as the on-going 'Survey of London' (founded in the 1890s), which documented buildings of historic interest, often shortly before they were destroyed to make way for development. By the twentieth century, historic towns had become an accepted part of the British national culture, although without any specific designation. Ironically their recognition at an international level in the Baedeker guides (founded in 1827) led to some of them (Bath, Norwich, Exeter) being targeted by the Luftwaffe in the early bombing raids of World War II. It appears that these initial raids were aimed at places of cultural rather than military significance, indicating the Nazis' assumption that heritage occupied a special place in the British psyche.

In the wake of the Second World War, innovations in town planning in the UK were driven by a generation sick of the restrictions of war, fed on the 1930s dream of a 'modern' life of convenience and leisure. Their approach to town planning was shaped by the 'Brave New World' visions of Le Corbusier's designs for new cities, including Paris, as well as the more prosaic example of the 'Arts and Crafts' Garden Cities of Welwyn and Letchworth. The establishment of the Town Planning Act in 1948 introduced the idea of 'development plans', which aimed at holistic redevelopment to celebrate the post-war age. Unfortunately, the first development plans were disappointingly dull, being based on the narrow concerns of road widening and other service considerations, rather than any more general vision for an improved way of life. As a result, many of the 'new environments' created in the 1950s and 1960s were a failure – the tower blocks of the period, for example, are now recognised to be unsuitable for everyday life in the UK, while the destruction of familiar town centres had a negative impact on quality of life. These failures gave rise to a growing popular interest in the wider historic environment, and there was a widespread reaction against the unwanted changes. Groups of enthusiasts saved rashly-closed railway branch lines, canals and the like, and in the late 1960s the growing concern for the country's historic environment was acknowledged by central government with the introduction of the 1967 Civic Amenities Act, which brought in the concept of 'Conservation Areas'. The first such areas were based on historic town centres and consisted of tight groups of historic buildings. However, the success of this new concept led to its being extended to cover wider areas after 1973 when the idea of 'the familiar and cherished local scene' – that is areas not just made up of historic buildings – was accepted as a basis for designation.[3] Just as the late 1940s ushered in a new optimism about a 'Brave New World' of town planning, the 1970s, despite being 'the decade that taste forgot', produced a raft of Conservation Areas which safeguarded many town centres against the rampant redevelopment that had decimated traditional places even more extensively than the Blitz.

This was in keeping with the general re-evaluation of many aspects of everyday life that took place in the 1970s. The popular television programme

---

3   Department of the Environment Planning Circular 46/73.

'The Good Life' represented a new-found appreciation for traditionally-grown food. The Arts and Crafts movement resurfaced with a revival of hand-made goods and the beginnings of what we would now call 'localism', something also apparent in the resurgence of markets, full of local and specialist produce. Disillusionment with bland, industrial products not only contributed to the emergence of interest in 'classic cars', but also led the Ford Motor Company to produce 'customisable' Cortinas which offered so many permutations that it was almost as if no two cars were the same – although they all rusted in the same way. It all seemed to represent the pursuit of stability and lasting values in a rapidly changing world.

In the 1980s, the increasingly widespread Conservation Areas became very fashionable, with estate agents in particular promoting them as desirable places to live. Local Conservation Area Advisory Committees were set up to give the local community a say in their management, although most members seem to have been primarily concerned with protecting their enhanced property values, rather than with championing aesthetic and historic considerations.

The decade also saw a revival of 'cultural tourism'. Package holidays in the Spanish sun were no longer enough for many, and instead travellers increasingly sought out destinations that were of historical interest. It is unclear whether tourists were particularly attracted to World Heritage Sites at this stage, but many Sites have certainly been branded as tourist destinations in recent years.

With such a swell of public concern and interest in heritage it was inevitable that some form of categorisation and stability would eventually become necessary. This process is illustrated by the case of the market for 'classic cars' (only defined as such in the 1970s), in which prices reached dizzy heights in the 1990s, before crashing. Cars with a historical association, such as those that had won the Le Mans race, had a special value, but given the probability that such a machine would have gone through several body and engine changes over the course of time, the meaning of this association was open to question, and court cases were even fought over the right to display a chassis plate with the 'historic' numbers of a revered car. It was time to rationalise the position, and this ushered in a more widespread concern for authenticity and integrity, as illustrated by the rise of the so-called 'oily-rag' approach to classic car maintenance.

With the rise of interest in classic cars from the 1970s, *concours d'elegance* meetings rapidly generated a breed of restoration that owed more to gloss than originality. Restoration became more 're-creation' at the expense of a vehicle's patina of age. The issues are fascinating. If a vehicle is to be made roadworthy it must have appropriate tyres, and inevitably these will be modern since tyres produced thirty years ago or more will have decayed (indeed, there have been tragic cases where fastidious owners suffered fatal accidents caused by blow-outs of their ancient rubber tyres). Brake systems have similar problems: whilst the risks of using an out-dated braking system may be acceptable in the case of a veteran car doing at best 30 miles per hour, they cannot be accepted in the case of an E-type Jaguar which can reach 150 miles per hour. Modern traffic is much faster and much busier than in the classic cars' heyday, and so it also makes sense to carry out upgrades on suspension, cooling systems and so-on, to create a vehicle happy with the modern environment. With all the underpinnings upgraded, why not make use of modern paints to improve the finish? A clean engine bay is nice, but why not chromium-plate the air filters to add a touch of sparkle? It is easy to see how the glossy look-a-likes at the Pebble Beach *concours* in California were conceived, but a backlash against this modernising approach was inevitable.

This backlash has taken the form of a strong drive in the last few years to recognise the qualities of unrestored cars which display a patina of time. As outlined above, there will always be compromises, including the use of modern fuels and oils, but the use of an oily rag to give cover to rusty metal and keep parts lubricated can keep a vehicle on the road with a minimum of 'restoration'. This 'oily-rag' treatment of classic cars is now increasingly popular, ensuring that the originality (admittedly still a difficult concept) of the machine is accepted and its completeness is such that a simple clean will enable it to function as it was designed to. After all, in some cases any intervention into the historic fabric of a vehicle would destroy not only its patina of age, but an essential connection to the car's history. The Austin-Healey that was involved in the tragic accident at the 1955 Le Mans race which killed more than eighty people was recently sold for an enormous sum, despite being in poor condition. (Although in this case the car had, in fact, been repaired immediately after the accident, so its 'historic' fabric associated with the race had already been modified.) A Frazer-Nash which had spent seventy years resting on the bottom of a Swiss lake also attracted an enormous bid, despite being little more than a rusty fragment.

These sales point to perhaps the most interesting aspect of the historic vehicle world – its active marketplace and the way considerations of originality and historical association affect a car's market value. Whilst a thorough restoration of a classic car including upgrades to achieve modern driving standards still attracts a premium, prices for unrestored vehicles capable of 'oily-rag' treatment are increasingly approaching such premiums. Evidently 'historical association' carries considerable importance in the valuation of classic cars, whereas this aspect appears to be much less significant in the evaluation of potential Sites in the World Heritage context.

3. Values in World Heritage Sites

This process of rationalisation and identification of values has also found its way into the arena of World Heritage. All proposals for new World Heritage Sites must now be accompanied by a 'Statement of Outstanding Universal Value' (SoOUV). Such statements are also being prepared for Sites already inscribed.

This recognition of 'outstanding universal value' means that Sites are seen as part of the world heritage of mankind as a whole, and as such deserve to be protected and transmitted to future generations. The concept of OUV now underpins the whole World Heritage Convention and all activities associated with inscribed properties. The 1998 Global Strategy meeting in Amsterdam proposed a definition of OUV as 'an outstanding response to issues of universal nature common to or addressed by all cultures'.[4] OUV means cultural and/or natural significance which is so exceptional as to transcend national boundaries and to be of common importance for present and future generations of all humanity. At the 2005 UNESCO Special Expert Meeting in Kazan on the concept of OUV it was put forward that 'definition and application of OUV are made by people and will be subject to evolution over time', thereby recognising that the process of nomination for World Heritage is taking place in the context of a continually broadening definition of cultural heritage. The idea of fixed reference points over time is not necessarily possible nor even desirable. A reshaping of cultural heritage is taking place in every country and is linked directly or indirectly to the application of the World Heritage Convention. This means that over the years since the first inscriptions, new types of cultural heritage have been recognised, nominated for inscription and

---

4 Report of the World Heritage Global Strategy Natural and Cultural Heritage Expert Meeting, 25-29 March 1998, Amsterdam, p. 18, http://whc.unesco.org/archive/amsterdam 98.pdf

in many cases inscribed on the list. What remains fixed are the criteria accepted by the World Heritage Committee as justification of OUV at the time of inscription. Retrospective preparation of a SoOUV must therefore be undertaken according to those past criteria, and so the work involves a certain element of 'going back in time'.

In sum, the SoOUV sets out not individual qualities, but the totality of qualities that together give a property OUV. The SoOUV thus overarches the whole management and conservation of a property, since management of each Site must be focused on sustaining the OUV for which it was inscribed. The SoOUV is also the essential reference point for:

> Monitoring
>
> Periodic reporting
>
> Potential reactive monitoring
>
> Possible danger listing (in 2012 Liverpool and the Tower of London were placed on the Danger List by UNESCO)
>
> Deletion (Dresden was removed from the World Heritage list by UNESCO in 2005)

The Statement of Outstanding Universal Value is therefore of great benefit to the relevant State Party and to all stakeholders involved in the management of a World Heritage property. It not only facilitates a clear understanding of what has been inscribed on the list and why it has OUV, but also gives direction to management of the Site by indicating which of the property's attributes need to be maintained in order to sustain its OUV.

4. The Content of the Statement of Outstanding Value

The SoOUV should contain the following:

A brief synthesis including a summary description and summary of values and attributes:

  (i) Criteria (the UNESCO criteria according to which the Site is inscribed, see above).

  (ii) The Authenticity of the Site.

  (iii) The Integrity of the Site.

  (iv) Management demanded to sustain the OUV through an overall framework and long-term expectations.

(i) Criteria

The criteria listed earlier in this paper are the current versions. The use of the criteria has only been mandatory since 2002, and in the case of some early Sites (43%), nominations were made by State Parties without reference to any criteria. Moreover, it is important to recognise that these criteria have changed and evolved over time and, as mentioned previously, retrospective statements of OUV must be made against those criteria in operation at the time of inscription.

UNESCO have subtly modified the cultural criteria several times since 1977.[5] For example, in 1977 criterion i was stated as 'represents a unique artistic or aesthetic achievement, a masterpiece of creative genius'. By 1983 the 'or aesthetic' had been removed. Maritime Greenwich is an example of inscription under criterion i (inscribed 1997).

The evolution of criterion ii was more significant. In 1977 it read 'have exerted considerable influence over a span of time or within a cultural area of the world on subsequent developments in architecture, monumental sculpture, garden design and landscape design, related arts or human settlements'. By 1996 this had been changed to 'exhibit an important interchange of human values over a span of time or within a cultural area of the world, on developments in architecture or technology, monumental arts, town planning or landscape design'. This effectively expanded the criterion and opened the door to World Heritage Sites based on technological advances. Examples of inscription under criterion ii include the Ruins of the Buddhist Vihara at Paharpur, Bangladesh (1985), and later the Humberstone and Santa Laura Saltpeter Works in Chile (2005) and the Blaenavon Industrial Landscape of south Wales (2003), both of which were inscribed under the revised version of the criterion.

Criterion iii was also expanded. In 1977 it referred to Sites being 'unique, extremely rare, or of great antiquity', but by 1996 this had become 'bear a unique or at least exceptional testimony to a cultural tradition or to a civilisation which is living or which has disappeared'. Messa Verde National Park was inscribed under the earlier criterion but the enlarged wording covering cultural landscapes, a testimony to evolving traditions, saw the Stone Circles of Senegambia and Senegal inscribed in 2006.

---

5   The criteria are listed in full in the UNESCO Operational Guidelines for the Implementation of the World Heritage Convention. For full details of the various versions of the guidelines cited in this section see http://whc.unesco.org/en/guidelines/

In 1977 criterion iv required that Sites 'be among the most characteristic examples of a type of structure, the type representing an important cultural, social, artistic, scientific, technological or industrial development'. This was tightened in 1996 to 'be an outstanding example of a type of building or architectural or technological ensemble or landscape which illustrates a significant stage in human history'. Examples of the changing Sites inscribed under criterion iv include the Silver Mines of Potosi, Bolivia (1987) and the Town Houses of Victor Horta, Belgium (2000).

Criterion v stated in 1977 that a Site should 'be a characteristic example of a significant traditional style of architecture, method of construction, or human settlement that is fragile by nature or has become vulnerable under the impact of irreversible socio-cultural or economic change'. By 2005 this had been limited to 'be an outstanding example of a traditional human settlement, land use, or sea-use which is representative of a culture or human interaction with the environment especially when it has become vulnerable under the impact of irreversible change'. The historic city of Kairouan in Tunisia (1988) was inscribed under the earlier criterion, while the Agave Landscape and Ancient Industrial Facilities of Tequila, Mexico (2006) were inscribed under the modified version.

Criterion vi stated in 1980 that Sites should 'be directly or tangibly associated with events or with ideas or beliefs of outstanding universal significance', altered in 2005 to 'be directly or tangibly associated with events or living traditions, with ideas, or with beliefs, with artistic and literary works of outstanding universal significance' – yet another opening up of a criterion.

(ii) Authenticity

There is sometimes confusion between the concepts of authenticity and integrity. Authenticity is the link between attributes and outstanding universal value. This link must be truthfully and credibly expressed on the basis of verifiable sources of information.

Before 2005 the test of authenticity referred to four attributes: design, material, workmanship and setting. That is, only *tangible* aspects of heritage were included. Since 2005, however, *intangible* heritage has been included in assessments of authenticity, so that the test now includes form and setting, materials and substance, use and function, traditions, techniques and management systems, location and setting, language, spirit and feeling. Thus a much broader range of attributes that might carry OUV can be identified. This is a very significant shift away from the tangible.

As an example, the OUV of an urban area might be carried by the following attributes: structures, spatial plans, traditions and living communities, a socio-economic whole working collaboratively. Authenticity relates to how well these attributes reflect OUV, and can be compromised if the attributes are weak – if communities cease to thrive, buildings collapse or traditions disappear. A statement of authenticity should therefore say whether the relevant attributes are thriving, and convey their message credibly and truthfully.

(iii) Integrity

The concept of integrity can be applied to both natural and cultural properties, although since 2005 it has only been applied to cultural properties. Integrity is the completeness/intactness of the attributes that carry OUV, a measure of the wholeness of the property. Are all the elements necessary to express the property's OUV included within its boundaries? Is the property of adequate size to ensure the complete representation of the features and processes which convey the property's significance? Does the property suffer adverse effects from development or neglect? A statement of integrity needs to answer these questions, stating whether the collection of attributes that carry OUV are all contained within the property's boundaries, that no parts have lost these attributes, and that the attributes are not under threat.

(iv) Protection and Management

The attributes that convey OUV need to be maintained, conserved, managed and protected in order to sustain a property's OUV. Statements need to be set out demonstrating how this is to be achieved in both the long and the short term.

5. The Practice of Managing a World Heritage Site

The evolution of definitions, along with the widening of the criteria, has produced a much more rational inscription process. However, while the concept of OUV may appear straightforward, in practice the definitions of concomitant values can prove difficult. For example, in the case of the Maritime Greenwich World Heritage Site, the historic tea clipper the Cutty Sark, located at the heart of the Site, would seem to be highly significant and deserving of Attribute of OUV status. This is especially the case given that the ship is cherished locally, is recognised at a national level with its Grade 1 listing, and is even known internationally as the last surviving clipper. However, despite the ship being an historic building on the statutory list, because it is movable, English Heritage, interpreting the UNESCO criteria, refuse to support it as an Attribute of OUV.

6. Management of World Heritage Sites

While UNESCO, an international agency, is responsible for inscribing World Heritage Sites, responsibility for their management and protection lies with the nation states of the participating countries. In the United Kingdom this role is undertaken by the central government's Department of Culture Media and Sport (DCMS). DCMS is advised by the UK branch of the International Council for Monuments and Sites (ICOMOS), English Heritage and its equivalents in Scotland, Wales, and Northern Ireland.

A prerequisite for inscription is the preparation and adoption of a World Heritage Site management plan. In most cases this is prepared locally by a steering group consisting of local organisations and interests, with the help of national advisory bodies. Management plans have to be approved by the UNESCO Conservation Committee but this body's infrequent meetings (once every 6 months) and its consequent bulky agendas mean that full discussion of the plans for each Site is rare. However, UNESCO has also put in place a system of 'Periodic Reporting' which demands that each Site be the subject of an assessment every 5 years. This assessment considers the state of the Site and the management of its attributes in order to identify issues of concern. Where problems become significant in advance of this process, UNESCO acts swiftly by sending a delegation of inspectors to assess the situation. This can lead to a Site being placed on the 'World Heritage Sites in Danger List', as is currently the case with Liverpool in the UK. In extreme cases, where threats have been identified and no remedial action has been taken, UNESCO will remove a property from the World Heritage List, as recently happened with Dresden in Germany.

The preparation of a World Heritage Site management plan is a costly and specialist exercise (assessed by DCMS at £20,000 in 2008). There is no funding available from either UNESCO or DCMS, so the task and its costs fall to the local steering group. Most UK Sites have a locally based, locally funded coordinator who prepares and updates the plan.

7. Political and Other Tensions

As a central government department, DCMS is subject to political oversight, and this can have a major impact upon the department's work in the heritage sector. During the 1980s the Tory administration under Margaret Thatcher severed relations with UNESCO, and the relationship was only reinstated in 1997 when a Labour administration came to power. At a more local level, meanwhile, World Heritage Site steering groups are often chaired by local government councillors, and where central and local government are represented by different parties this can introduce a fundamental political rift. The situation becomes even more complex in those cities where there is also an elected mayor: in London there are four World Heritage Sites within the city, and the Mayor of London includes concern for their wellbeing in the London Plan. Thus there can be three different levels of political influence, and these are perhaps most strongly felt where there are issues of funding involved. Heritage of international standing may be perceived locally as irrelevant, and even regarded with hostility. The use of scarce local resources for its safeguarding may therefore be considered unimportant or even immoral compared with meeting the needs of local public services. Fortunately there are sources of funding external to local budgets which recognise such heritage. English Heritage and the other national heritage organisations are in a position to offer grant aid, while the Heritage Lottery Fund has proved very supportive of the UK World Heritage Sites, giving grants for a number of restoration projects.

The position of World Heritage Site coordinator is also an important consideration. Within the twenty-eight UK Sites there are a variety of arrangements, depending on the nature of the Site in question. Blenheim Palace, for example, is privately owned and so its management is undertaken through its own organisation, while the management of Hadrian's Wall has been taken to a sophisticated level by the establishment of a trust, funded by the fourteen Local Authorities and others which lie along its length. In many cases, however, the coordinator is based within the Site's Local Authority, often as part of the town planning department. While this may provide some influence when dealing with planning applications, it also has the disadvantage of tying the role to a professional service, possibly to the detriment of a wider view.

8. Legislation and Administration

The only power UNESCO can exercise over World Heritage Sites is to remove them from the World Heritage List; their protection depends on legislation adopted by the nation state. In the UK there is no system of protection for World Heritage Sites operated at the central government level. Instead, most measures dealing with the wider historic environment have effectively been delegated to the local level.

The UK has an established and sophisticated town planning administration that controls development through the granting of planning permission. Historic buildings are protected by their inclusion on a 'list' of buildings of special architectural or historic merit. 'Listed Building Consent' must be obtained for changes that affect the fabric of such buildings. Some buildings and structures can also be scheduled as 'ancient monuments' which require additional consent for any changes. In the case of historic areas, meanwhile, Conservation Areas can be designated within which consent must be sought for any demolition work. Further protection is afforded on some individual issues such as the control of advertisements, and highways issues, which can be of particular importance, are also mainly a responsibility of the Local Authority.

Recently there were moves in the UK to introduce the concept of a 'historic asset' throughout building and conservation legislation, in order to identify the key elements of a building or environment that might come under threat from, for example, a development proposal. However, the Bill that would have established this was abandoned in 2009, and instead the status quo remains. This means that the location of a development proposal within a World Heritage Site can be regarded as a 'material consideration' when a planning application is being decided. To assist in the protection of the UK's World Heritage Sites, Local Development Frameworks (previously Local Plans) prepared by the Local Planning Authority can contain policies specifically directed at their protection and enhancement.

9. Some Conclusions

'Heritage' as a concept has become mainstream since the Second World War, representing many values ranging from nostalgia to reminders of the darker side of human nature. It can be a romantic notion and a blueprint for regeneration. 'Heritage' has evolved over the last 40 years to cover the most prized works of human genius as well as the most beautiful natural places. It has also come to mean an appreciation of the lowly places that represent a familiar and cherished local scene. 'Heritage' is now seen as going beyond the tangible to include places of intangible heritage where significant living traditions survive.

A hierarchy of assessments of heritage has evolved from the international through national to local levels. Each level has its own values, with some values being shared and some not. Systems to define and then protect those values vary in strength. International values have to be protected by the application of national systems of law. Thanks to the Town Planning Acts, national and local systems for the protection of heritage are well developed in the United Kingdom, although an all-encompassing piece of legislation to define heritage assets and rank them for protection has yet to make the statute books.

At the top of the 'heritage hierarchy', World Heritage Sites are inscribed by UNESCO and respected by those nation states supporting the organisation. National legislation, however, makes scant reference to the concept of World Heritage and this causes confusion at the local level, where politicians who 'know what they like' may not grasp the significance of an international attribute.

Generally speaking, the rise of information technology has enhanced appreciation of both special places and the values of the people who cherish them. The rise of 'cultural tourism' has also helped, and the blurring of the line between 'holiday makers' and 'learners' points the way to a better-shared future. Where once a summer holiday meant a beach in Spain, it may now mean a trip to Auschwitz or Hiroshima where international values have to be absorbed in order to achieve any kind of understanding.

The recent destruction of World Heritage Sites in the Middle East and elsewhere as a result of political and religious conflict has emphasised the need to safeguard such international treasures through awareness, education and physical protection. An appreciation of local values through the consumption of local goods, including food, could be built upon to further this understanding of others' values. In spite of the rise of religious extremism and the threats of climate change and global conflict, I remain optimistic that heritage values at all levels will endure and consolidate.

13. Safeguarding Heritage:
From Legal Rights over Objects to Legal Rights for Individuals and Communities?

Marie Cornu[1]

Heritage protection for the twenty-first century is clearly an issue that raises a number of questions – regarding the very concept of cultural heritage, and how the law embraces that concept and sets its boundaries; regarding the fundamental purpose – to preserve and pass on – implied by the word 'heritage'; regarding the multiple legal environments at the regional, national and international levels in which heritage law stands. Legally, there are many different ways to organise the connection between memory, history and heritage and, in this respect, diversity rules.

Cultural heritage law is a large body of legislation which was developed relatively recently. National legislation was generally introduced during the nineteenth century, while international law on cultural heritage was developed at the end of the nineteenth century and in the second part of the twentieth century. The first important convention was enacted in 1954;[2]

---

1   This chapter is based on a presentation given at the Oxford University colloquium on 'The Future of the Past: Memory, History and Cultural Heritage in the Twenty-First Century', organised by the Faculty of Classics of the University of Oxford in cooperation with the Maison Française d'Oxford (CNRS). This contribution has been translated by Marie Trape (CECOJI-CNRS) and revised by Catherine Heygate.

2   The 1954 Hague Convention for the Protection of Cultural Property in the Event of Armed Conflict, http://portal.unesco.org/en/ev.php-URL_ID=13637&URL_DO=DO_TOPIC& URL_SECTION=201.html

          http://dx.doi.org/10.11647/OBP.0047.13

a protection plan designed for war-time, it was the starting point in the construction of international law relating to the conservation of cultural heritage. Other major legal instruments would follow, such as the 1970 UNESCO Convention on illicit trafficking of cultural property[3] and the 1972 Convention concerning the protection of world cultural heritage.[4] While I do not intend to explore this complex legal architecture in detail in this brief essay, I will highlight a few particular aspects of it that, in my view, reflect a change in our thinking about the protection of cultural heritage over the past two decades. These aspects concern the issue of defining heritage, and the process by which heritage is legally identified.

Regarding the concept of cultural heritage in its relation to memory and history, I will start with the example of French law, bearing in mind that other countries have a similar history, particularly in Europe where legal models evidently circulated across borders. Initially, when heritage protection was in its early days, the founding concept was that of the historic monument and not, in fact, the more inclusive term 'heritage', which came later (in the 1970s in France). This notion of a historic monument referred equally to buildings (such as castles or cathedrals) and to objects, the primary concern being for artistic and historic interest, concepts which can be found in most legislation on heritage.

Building upon this concern for artistic and historic interest, the first legislative texts – especially France's law of 31 December 1913 – developed an elitist approach. In France, this founding legislation introduced a public easement, a technique never previously used in the heritage field, whereby the owner of any building classified as a historical monument was placed under supervision and was forbidden from making any changes that might alter the physical integrity of the property without the permission of the ministry of culture. This approach to protection was founded on the exceptionality of the historical monuments in terms of their artistic or historic value. The buildings identified as historical monuments were artistic masterpieces. They were, according to Théodore Reinach, one of the architects of the 1913 law, stone books in which the memory of the nation had settled, and as such they could contribute to the construction of that

---

3   The 1970 UNESCO Convention on the Means of Prohibiting and Preventing the Illicit Import, Export and Transfer of Ownership of Cultural Property, http://portal.unesco.org/en/ev.php-URL_ID=13039&URL_DO=DO_TOPIC&URL_SECTION=201.html

4   The 1972 UNESCO Convention Concerning the Protection of the World Cultural and Natural Heritage, http://portal.unesco.org/en/ev.php-URL_ID=13055&URL_DO=DO_TOPIC&URL_SECTION=201.html

memory.[5] This protection scheme, a venture of national interest, thus only took into consideration exceptional things.

In the course of the twentieth century, however, the heritage field underwent a double extension, at once typological and chronological, according to Françoise Choay's analysis in *L'allégorie du patrimoine*.[6] The extension was typological in that new items, which had not previously fallen within the purview of the legislation, began to be protected. This extension arose from the development of a more inclusive concept of heritage, which not only designates exceptional or rare items, but can also be applied to a trace or a memory. On this basis, modest, ordinary objects can become heritage because they carry the memory of various human activities, such as farming, industry, and technology. As a result, tools, habitats, workplaces and machines are now being protected. This ethnological approach began to be adopted in the field of heritage in the 1970s, at precisely the moment when the concept of cultural heritage was coming to the fore. The term 'cultural heritage' was not chosen by chance, and is indicative of the more global and inclusive vision that was then emerging.

The extension of the heritage field was also chronological. As Choay has pointed out, in the 1960s the chronological framework of heritage protection hardly went beyond the early nineteenth century, even though no such temporal limit was imposed by the legislation.[7] Since the 1960s, however, ever more recent elements have been brought within the heritage framework, to the extent that twentieth-century heritage has now made its way into the categories of public policies on cultural heritage.

Thus the boundary of what constitutes heritage has evolved. Indeed, the concept of heritage turns out to be a highly malleable framework which is constantly changing and developing. By contrast, the legal formulation of heritage, and hence the legal instruments of heritage protection, are still quite close to the earliest formulations of the concept. Heritage law defines the status of physical things; it identifies material wealth. Of course, the intangible dimension is not entirely absent, indeed it is at the heart of the idea of artistic and historic interest. However, when legislators develop a protection scheme, they design it to protect physical items, regardless of whether those items have an intrinsic value arising from their exceptionality or rareness, or whether they function as traces or memories. Inevitably,

---

5   A. Auduc, *Quand les monuments historiques construisaient la nation* (Paris: La documentation française: Comité d'histoire du ministère de la culture, 2008).

6   F. Choay, *L'Allégorie du patrimoine*, coll. La couleur des idées (Paris: Seuil, 1992).

7   *Ibid.*

this physically-oriented approach to heritage shapes decision-making in relation to protection schemes and, therefore, their legal formulation.

France's 1913 law established a procedure for classifying properties whose conservation 'presents a public interest from an artistic or a historical point of view'. As a result, the ensuing easement focused upon conservation, and the idea of conservation remains paramount in legislative texts, whether in terms of physical conservation (i.e. respect for a property's physical integrity) or legal conservation, expressed in such provisions as the rules of indefeasibility and inalienability, or measures to prevent heritage objects leaving the country. I refer specifically to French law here, but this approach is common to a number of states, including Italy, Spain, Germany, Greece and Egypt, and it prevails in important international conventions. The 1972 World Heritage Convention, for example, protects physical heritage in the form of sites and monuments, and the objective of conservation is still at the centre of its protection mechanism.[8]

This approach, whereby heritage protection law is organised on the basis of material realities, has changed dramatically in the past two decades. The new perspective, which is apparent in the way cultural heritage is legally identified and defined, has introduced a profound change in the very nature of heritage law. This evolution in the legal concept of heritage is reflected in two instruments, the 2003 UNESCO Convention for the Safeguarding of Intangible Cultural Heritage,[9] and the 2005 Council of Europe Framework Convention on the Value of Cultural Heritage for Society (the Faro Convention).[10]

The UNESCO Convention introduces the concept of intangible heritage into international law for the first time. Strictly speaking, the concept of intangible heritage used here was not an ex nihilo creation, since some states, notably Japan and Korea, had already established protection for their intangible heritage before 2003. However, the concept is completely new in the field of international law, and at present it is not recognised in the legislation of most states. What does this concept refer to? According to the UNESCO Convention, intangible cultural heritage means 'the practices, representations, expressions, knowledge, skills – as well as the

---

8   For the text of the 1972 Convention see http://portal.unesco.org/en/ev.php-URL_ID=13 055&URL_DO=DO_TOPIC&URL_SECTION=201.html

9   http://portal.unesco.org/en/ev.php-URL_ID=17716&URL_DO=DO_TOPIC&URL_ SECTION=201.html

10 http://conventions.coe.int/Treaty/EN/Treaties/Html/199.htm

instruments, objects, artefacts and cultural spaces associated therewith – that communities, groups and, in some cases, individuals recognise as part of their cultural heritage'.

The most obvious innovation lies in the object of the Convention's protection – it deals with intangible heritage, with practices and expressions of skills that were not previously in the legislator's field of vision. Beyond the intangible character of the elements to be protected, however, there is a more fundamental change in the way heritage is designated. Intangible heritage consists of elements that communities, groups and individuals recognise as part of their heritage. As a result, heritage is defined by its relationship with a group, whereas in the standard protection system, this relationship and the associated identification of rights holders is more distant and diffuse, even though the idea of community does exist. The change embodied in the UNESCO Convention does not, therefore, only affect the substance of heritage and the distinction between the physical and the intangible. After all, the Convention also protects the 'instruments, objects, artefacts and cultural spaces' associated with intangible cultural heritage. The more profound evolution lies in the identification of support communities and the recognition of their power to designate an element of cultural heritage. It is this sense of belonging which produces cultural heritage. With this understanding, we are moving away from the usual systems of protection.

A very similar approach was adopted with the Faro Convention, which was enacted shortly after, in 2005, and which states that 'for the purposes of this Convention, cultural heritage is a group of resources inherited from the past which people identify, independently of ownership, as a reflection and expression of their constantly evolving values, beliefs, knowledge and traditions. It includes all aspects of the environment resulting from the interaction between people and places through time' (Art. 2). The text also provides a definition of a heritage community, which has the capacity to define heritage as follows: 'a heritage community consists of people who value specific aspects of cultural heritage which they wish, within the framework of public action, to sustain and transmit to future generations' (Art. 2b).

The clear similarities in the processes by which cultural heritage is defined in these two conventions reveal a change in both the legal construction of heritage protection, and in the very nature of that law. With the evocation of communities and groups, with the idea that heritage reveals itself in a sense of belonging, it seems that we are moving away from a property law founded on a public interest in protection, and towards a law granting individuals a right on this property. Under this new approach, the individual or the group is at the centre of the definition of cultural heritage, and so they are also at the centre of the protection system more generally. It is clear that human rights law has influenced these legislative texts (as is the case in most fields of law): the safeguarding of heritage is articulated in terms of the protection of the fundamental rights of communities and groups. This is particularly apparent in the Faro Convention, which, in its preamble, recognises 'the need to put people and human values at the centre of an enlarged and cross-disciplinary concept of cultural heritage', and in its first article defining the aims of the Convention, states that:

> 'The Parties to this Convention agree to:
>
>> (a) Recognise that rights relating to cultural heritage are inherent in the right to participate in cultural life, as defined in the Universal Declaration of Human Rights;
>>
>> (b) Recognise individual and collective responsibility towards cultural heritage;
>>
>> (c) Emphasise that the conservation of cultural heritage and its sustainable use have human development and quality of life as their goal;
>>
>> (d) Take the necessary steps to apply the provisions of this Convention concerning:
>>
>>> – The role of cultural heritage in the construction of a peaceful and democratic society, and in the processes of sustainable development and the promotion of cultural diversity;
>>>
>>> – Greater synergy of competencies among all the public, institutional and private actors concerned'.
>
> 'Emphasising the value and potential of cultural heritage wisely used as a resource for sustainable development and quality of life in a constantly evolving society; Recognising that every person has a right to engage with the cultural heritage of their choice, while respecting the rights and freedoms of others, as an aspect of the right freely to participate in cultural life enshrined in the United Nations Universal Declaration of Human Rights (1948) and guaranteed by the International Covenant on Economic, Social and Cultural Rights (1966)'.

This concern for heritage had already been defined in these terms in various legal texts relating to the protection of fundamental rights, especially in those texts dealing with the rights of minorities or indigenous communities. With the UNESCO and Faro Conventions, however, the same concern was extended to the instruments for the protection of cultural property. Worldwide, this understanding of heritage in terms of fundamental human rights is now beginning to have some bearing on the issue of international restitutions, for example in relation to objects possessing considerable symbolic meaning, or to human remains held in museums.[11]

Another evolution in the field of heritage law, which is again apparent in the UNESCO and Faro Conventions, concerns the fact that heritage protection now includes the concepts of sustainable development and integration. The concept of sustainable development is particularly prominent, and is changing the very definition of heritage. Initially, heritage was defined as something to be preserved and passed on to future generations. Nowadays, it also has social, environmental and economic aims. In the light of this, heritage law, which had originally developed as an autonomous branch of law, is clearly being influenced by other legal disciplines such as environmental law and economic law. It is still too soon to say what will come from this. Certainly the outcome can be positive, but there is also a risk that the strength of heritage protection may decrease.

---

11 On this tendency, see: M. Cornu and M.-A. Renold, 'Le renouveau des restitutions de biens culturels: les modes alternatifs de règlement des litiges', *Journal du Droit International* (Clunet), 2, 2009, pp. 493-533. This article was also published in English: M. Cornu and M.-A. Renold, 'New Developments in the Restitution of Cultural Property: Alternative Means of Dispute Resolution', *International Journal of Cultural Property*, 17, 2010, pp. 1-31.

Appendix: Links to Selected International Charters and Conventions on Cultural Heritage

The 1954 Hague Convention for the Protection of Cultural Property in the Event of Armed Conflict
>   http://portal.unesco.org/en/ev.php-URL_ID=13637&URL_DO=DO_
>   TOPIC&URL_SECTION=201.html

The 1964 Venice International Charter for the Conservation and Restoration of Monuments and Sites
>   http://www.international.icomos.org/charters/venice_e.pdf

The 1970 UNESCO Convention on the Means of Prohibiting and Preventing the Illicit Import, Export and Transfer of Ownership of Cultural Property
>   http://portal.unesco.org/en/ev.php-URL_ID=13039&URL_DO=DO_
>   TOPIC&URL_SECTION=201.html

The 1972 UNESCO Convention Concerning the Protection of the World Cultural and Natural Heritage
>   http://portal.unesco.org/en/ev.php-URL_ID=13055&URL_DO=DO_
>   TOPIC&URL_SECTION=201.html

The 2003 UNESCO Convention for the Safeguarding of the Intangible Cultural Heritage
>   http://portal.unesco.org/en/ev.php-URL_ID=17716&URL_DO=DO_
>   TOPIC&URL_SECTION=201.html

The 2005 Council of Europe Framework Convention on the Value of Cultural Heritage for Society
>   http://conventions.coe.int/Treaty/EN/Treaties/Html/199.htm

The Operational Guidelines for the Implementation of the UNESCO World Heritage Convention
>   http://whc.unesco.org/en/guidelines/

List of UNESCO World Heritage Sites
>   http://whc.unesco.org/en/list/

This book need not end here...

At Open Book Publishers, we are changing the nature of the traditional academic book. The title you have just read will not be left on a library shelf, but will be accessed online by hundreds of readers each month across the globe. We make all our books free to read online so that students, researchers and members of the public who can't afford a printed edition can still have access to the same ideas as you.

Our digital publishing model also allows us to produce online supplementary material, including extra chapters, reviews, links and other digital resources. Find *Cultural Heritage Ethics* on our website to access its online extras. Please check this page regularly for ongoing updates, and join the conversation by leaving your own comments:

http://www.openbookpublishers.com/isbn/9781783740673

If you enjoyed this book, and feel that research like this should be available to all readers, regardless of their income, please think about donating to us. Our company is run entirely by academics, and our publishing decisions are based on intellectual merit and public value rather than on commercial viability. We do not operate for profit and all donations, as with all other revenue we generate, will be used to finance new Open Access publications.

For further information about what we do, how to donate to OBP, additional digital material related to our titles or to order our books, please visit our website: www.openbookpublishers.com

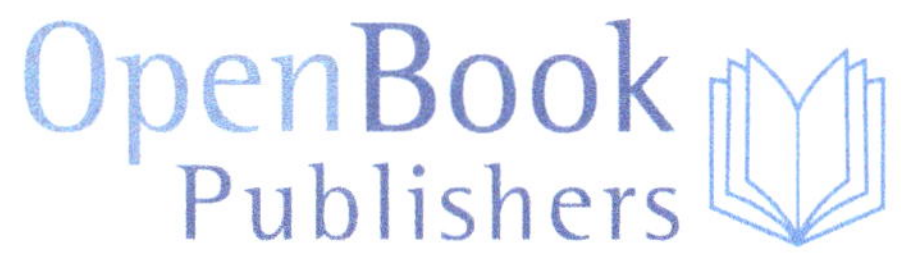